Planning Cash Flow:
A Problem-Solving Approach

Planning Cash Flow:
A Problem-Solving Approach

Joseph E. Finnerty

American Management Association

This book is available at a special
discount when ordered in bulk quantities.
For information, contact Special Sales Department,
AMACOM, a division of American Management Association,
135 West 50th Street, New York, NY 10020.

Library of Congress Cataloging-in-Publication Data

Finnerty, Joseph E.
  Planning cash flow.

  Bibliography: p.
  1. Cash flow. 2. Cash management. I. Title.
HG4028.C45F55 1986   658.1'5244   85-48221
ISBN 0-8144-7652-X

Printing number

10 9 8 7 6 5 4 3 2 1

Contents

About the Author

Joseph E. Finnerty is Professor of Finance at the University of Illinois, Champaign. He was previously Associate Professor of General Business and Finance at the University of Massachusetts, Amherst.

Professor Finnerty has M.B.A. and Ph.D. degrees in finance from the University of Michigan and has written numerous books and articles on financial topics. He is a member of the Financial Management Association and the American Finance Association.

Introduction

The management of cash flow is essential to the success of every enterprise, whether it be public or private. In fact, cash management is probably more critical to the success of an enterprise than making an individual sale or providing a service for a period of time. A business can lose a single customer or can suspend services for a short period without irreparable damage. However, let an imbalance in cash flow occur that forces a cash manager to miss a payroll, a debt payment, or a tax deadline and, quite possibly, the company is entirely out of business. This is a rather harsh penalty for one mistake or oversight on the part of the cash manager.

During the 1960s and 1970s, when we were experiencing high rates of inflation and the attendant high interest rates, the idea of cash management became well accepted and integrated into the financial function of the firm. With the recession and the attendant drop in inflation and interest rates that we've been experiencing during the 1980s, the management of cash has retained its importance, perhaps for different reasons. Nevertheless, whatever the underlying reasons (inflation and high interest rates or recessions and scarcity of credit), the objective of managing a company's cash position in an effective and efficient manner is still critical to the success and well-being of the firm.

Each section of this volume begins with a management overview of the topic under discussion. This is followed by brief summaries of important concepts, with statistical charts and worksheets providing illustrations and opportunities for readers to apply the principles described. A three-part case study is included for readers who wish to develop a sample cash flow management program from problem analysis through the preparation of an action plan.

Section 1 introduces the concept of working capital and shows how it interrelates with various company objectives as well as with functional areas of the firm—accounting, marketing, production, and the like.

Section 2 presents an overview of the cash management function in light of changing environmental and market conditions that are currently taking place. Emphasis is placed on the sound relationship that must be established and maintained between the cash manager and the banking community. Particular emphasis is placed on the elements that must be considered to ensure a strong relationship between a company and its banker. The various services and fees that can be expected from the banking community are then discussed.

The basic tools of analysis for cash management are developed in Section 3. The interrelation between the forecasting and budgeting processes are emphasized. The various planning options are then developed in light of the overall indication of the firm's cash position, which is uncovered in the pro forma budgeting process. Since every situation is unique, common problems are identified. Each cash manager must learn to adapt these general principles to his or her specific circumstances. The initial part of the case study allows the reader the opportunity to follow the entire forecasting, budgeting, and planning process in detail.

Section 4 discusses the various techniques that can be considered when a cash manager must speed up the inflow of cash or slow down the outflow. The costs as well as the benefits to be derived from each technique are presented to allow the reader to get a feel for the applicability of each technique in a given circumstance. The second part of the case allows the reader to select various options for solving the problems uncovered in the first part of the case.

The sources of short-term financing to meet expected shortfalls in the firm's cash flow are covered in Section 5. If, on the other hand, the firm has an excess of cash, a range of possible investment opportunities are presented in Section 6. The final part of the case gives the reader a chance to formulate a plan of action to meet the problems uncovered in the first two parts of the case analysis. The cash manager will have to either devise a way of financing the firm's cash shortfall or devise an investment strategy for any idle funds. To make the case as realistic as possible, both courses of action will be considered over the firm's planning horizon.

The final section of this book contains readings and a bibliography. Each of the readings has been selected for its clarity, conciseness, and ability to communicate the practicality and usefulness of a specific topic in cash management. The selected readings were chosen for two purposes—first, to give the reader a perspective of the current thinking of managers who are working with cash flow problems on a day-to-day basis; and second, to present a wide range of ideas and techniques that are being discussed as possible ways to improve the management of a company's cash flow.

Definitions

Every profession or functional area of business has its own jargon. The following terms are those more commonly used in connection with working capital. **WORKING CAPITAL**

Working capital is the dollar amount or total of a firm's current assets. Current assets include cash, marketable securities, investments, accounts receivable, and inventories. These assets are considered liquid because they can be converted into cash within one year. The dollar amount of these assets varies from time to time because of seasonal variations in sales and cyclical variations in general business conditions. Hence the level of working capital held by a company is not constant.

Working capital can be thought of as consisting of two parts—permanent and temporary. Permanent working capital is the dollar amount of working capital that remains fairly constant over time, regardless of fluctuations in sales. Temporary working capital is the additional assets required to meet the seasonal or cyclical variations in sales above the permanent level.

Working capital management is a much broader concept than working capital because it involves the management of current assets, current liabilities, and the interrelationship between them. In practice we tend to make no distinction between the investment decisions regarding current assets and the financing decisions regarding current liabilities. In fact, quite often these two are so closely related that we talk about spontaneous financing of assets—for example, when a firm buys some inventory on credit. In such a situation, both assets and liabilities are increased simultaneously thereby providing, at least in the short run, the financing for the investment. **WORKING CAPITAL MANAGEMENT**

Net working capital is the difference between current assets and current liabilities. It is a financial indicator that can be used in conjunction with ratios to gauge the liquidity of a company. In general, an abundance of net working capital is considered desirable because it suggests that the firm has ample liquidity to meet its short-term obligations. As we shall see, this may not always be the case. In fact, one of the objectives of cash management is to reduce excess or redundant net working capital to a minimum and thereby reduce the cost of holding idle assets. **NET WORKING CAPITAL**

1.

Corporate Working Capital

An Overview of Corporate Working Capital

The subject of this book is cash flow, or in other words, how money moves through a business enterprise. Everyone has a general understanding of what money is and how it can be used. A simple definition of money, one used by the Federal Reserve, is: Money is made up of the currency in circulation and checking account balances. The characteristics that must be present for something to serve as money are, first, a store of value; second, ready acceptance; and third, easy transferability.

MONEY

Throughout history, we've seen various things serve as money—for example, the giant stones of the Yap Islanders, the tobacco currency of early American colonists, gold, silver, shells, and even paper. The key feature that these diverse things have in common is that the participants in the economy were willing to use them for transaction purposes or to represent the accumulation of wealth. From this understanding of the function that money serves, we can move to a much more sophisticated concept—that of the flow of funds.

When financial managers talk of the flow of funds or working capital, they are referring to the fact that money as we know it—corporate cash and checking accounts—is actually increasing or decreasing as a result of management actions or decisions. However, they are also referring to factors or accounts that are not really money but serve as close substitutes. Such things as inventory, accounts receivable, financial instruments, and other types of marketable securities are all affected by economic or corporate activity. As these accounts change, the ultimate effect is a change in the level of corporate cash. But before these so-called near monies are actually turned into money, we can keep track of them by observing the corporate flow of funds.

Maximum cash generation is usually the primary objective of the financial manager. This objective is based on the assumption that any business is only as sound as the management of its cash flow. However, cash flow management is not an isolated task in the normal operation of a business. Instead, managing cash flow means being deeply involved with every aspect of business operations. Consequently, any and all management effort must be directed to at least satisfying cash flow requirements while managers try to achieve the other objectives of the company. To be more specific, cash flow must be considered to achieve survival, profitability, growth, and finally, the efficient use of corporate resources.

CASH MANAGEMENT

No one objective or goal predominates at all times. The goals are interrelated to such a degree that it is in the best interest of management to work toward attaining all the goals simultaneously. At any given time, priorities may vary as to which objective is most crucial, but all of them must ultimately be achieved to run a successful enterprise.

Keynes' famous statement ''In the long run, we're all dead'' does not necessarily apply to the corporate form of business. Survival becomes one of the primary objectives for any business. Temporary illiquidity or lack of financial resources may lead to suspending payments of corporate obligations. As long as creditors accept deferred or rescheduled payments, the short-run problems may be worked out and the business may survive. The ultimate threat of creditors is to drive a business into bankruptcy, which is in effect the admission by management that the cash value from dissolving the business is worth more than trying to keep the business going.

From the cash flow manager's perspective, the desire for survival demands that the firm be managed in such a way as to guarantee the maximum cash flow possible. Thus, management seeks to convert the company's investment in inventories and receivables into cash as quickly as possible. Remember that this desire to speed up cash inflow must be balanced against growing revenues and increasing profits. In the extreme case, a company could make every product on an order basis and demand cash payment. This would eliminate inventories and receivables. No doubt the competitive structure of the industry would reduce this strategy to a very unprofitable one in short order.

Other things being equal, the higher the profits a company generates, the more successful it is in achieving its other goals. However, as a business seeks to maximize profits, it must take greater risks. As the risk increases, the need for careful cash management becomes much more important. As a business strives to become more profitable by becoming more competitive, there is a cost in terms of higher inventories, more efficient production equipment, and more liberal credit policies to encourage sales. Competitive strategies increase the firm's need for cash flow by slowing down the rate at which working capital is converted into cash and by increasing the amount of resources tied up in each of the working capital components. Indeed, the cash manager will constantly be forced to balance profitability, growth, and survival as he or she tries to ensure that the company not only has sufficient funds but also is using those funds in an efficient fashion.

Rapid expansion in revenue and increase in market share are the things that make marketing management an exciting profession. Marketing-oriented individuals measure their success not by increased profits but by the increase in this year's revenues over last year's or by the percentage of market share a given product line has achieved. In striving for these objectives, quite often the risks of rapid growth are overlooked. The major problems begin to surface when the cash management system has not kept up with the rapid growth and its attendant increase in risk.

The efficient use of leverage is of primary importance to sustaining rapid growth. The owners of a company do not have the liquid resources to provide all of the cash necessary to finance the growth, and so external funding must be sought. Usually this external funding is in the form of debt, which increases the overall risk for the company. In and of itself, leverage is neither good nor bad. However, the misuse of leverage can place severe drains on the cash flow of a firm at a time when the company can least afford these drains.

An effective financial manager must balance the multiple objectives of the firm and keep in mind that there are many ways to achieve these objectives and use the firm's resources efficiently. Too much emphasis on any one of these goals can lead to very severe cash flow problems. The effective management of cash flow is necessary to achieve the multiple objectives simultaneously.

The components of working capital are the current assets listed on a firm's balance sheet—cash, marketable securities, accounts receivable, and inventory. We can envision the flow of funds through a company as the process of continuously converting one asset into another. Cash is used to buy the necessary raw material that will be used in the production of goods and services. These goods are sold to customers. This increases accounts receivable. As customers pay their bills, accounts receivable are once again turned into cash. If there is a temporary surplus of cash, it may be used to purchase marketable securities. By holding marketable securities, a firm can earn interest on surplus funds but can quickly convert these funds back into cash when needed. The company then repeats the cycle. The amount of funds and the speed at which the funds move from one account to another are the essential elements of cash flow management.

Cash is listed first on the balance sheet because it is the shortest-term, most liquid asset. A company may keep a small amount of actual currency on hand as petty cash, but this quantity of cash is usually very small compared to the company's demand deposits or checking account balances. These demand deposits are the principal way in which a corporation pays its bills.

Cash

The main problem that financial managers face is maintaining the cash account at an appropriate level. If they hold too little cash, they run the risk of not being able to pay the bills or take advantage of opportunities that arise. On the other hand, holding too much cash is not good, because the interest that would have been earned if the funds had been properly invested is lost. The process of balancing too little versus too much cash demands most of a cash manager's attention.

Marketable securities are closely related to cash. In fact, they are often called cash equivalents and may be combined with cash on the company's balance sheet. Investing in marketable securities involves purchasing money market instruments. These include treasury bills, commercial paper, certificates of deposit, and other short-term investments. A ready secondary market exists for such securities because most companies regularly buy and sell them before they mature. Because such a large market exists, any company can easily sell these instruments at a price close to their true value. This is why they are called marketable securities.

Marketable Securities

Most firms invest excess cash balances in marketable securities because they earn an annual interest rate that, in recent years, has been as high as 20 percent but is usually in the 5 to 10 percent range on a pretax basis.

As a financial manager, you are faced with two problems when managing the marketable securities account. First, how much money are you going to invest? And second, what maturity are you going to look for? When making this decision, remember that, other things being equal, the longer the maturity, the higher the yield on the investment.

The criteria that should be considered by the cash manager when evaluating marketable securities, as well as the reasons for investing in marketable securities, are discussed later in this section.

Accounts receivable consist of the money owed to the company by customers. Accounts receivable exist because most firms sell on credit. Customers buy now and pay later.

Accounts Receivable

Accounts receivable usually constitute a very large component of a company's working capital. Thousands, even millions, of dollars can be tied up in a firm's accounts receivable. Why do companies make such a large commitment? The answer is, of course, that most companies extend credit to customers. This is primarily for marketing reasons. Customers are more willing to buy on credit, and very often competitors are willing to offer credit. In order to make a sale, the firm must offer credit, too. In most businesses, credit terms are determined by traditional industry practice and competitive conditions.

Many financial managers work very closely with the marketing department to determine credit terms. This is because financial managers are responsible for obtaining the funds needed to finance accounts receivable. However, financial managers do have some control over the level of accounts receivable by ensuring prompt billing and collection. As a financial manager, your responsibility concerning accounts receivable includes maintaining receivables at an affordable level and collecting them as quickly as possible.

Inventories

Inventories are the physical materials that a company uses to make its products or to sell directly to its customers. Companies maintain inventories for two main reasons: first, it is more efficient and less expensive to buy from suppliers in large quantities; and second, many customers demand a wide selection of products and fast delivery. If a company is not able to offer its customers wide choice and fast delivery, it will lose sales to competitors.

We have discussed the four components of working capital—cash, marketable securities, accounts receivable, and inventory. Associated with each of these components are problems that arise if the amount of funds tied up in any one component is too small or too large.

Too much cash has an opportunity cost of forgone interest, which will hurt profitability. Too little cash may lead to a situation in which the company is unable to meet its commitments and is forced into bankruptcy despite profitable operations. An excess of funds tied up in marketable securities can lead to slower company growth because the funds have not been efficiently used for expansion. Insufficient funds in marketable securities may lead to an inadequate safety margin in the cash account.

Too little cash tied up in accounts receivable may indicate a noncompetitive credit policy, a business downturn, or a dwindling market for the company's products. Too large an amount in accounts receivable may indicate an overgenerous credit policy, which, in turn, could lead to collection and bad debt problems and insufficient use of the firm's resources.

Finally, too much inventory incurs the risk of obsolescence as well as additional costs of storage, insurance, and handling. On the other hand, too little inventory may place the firm in a noncompetitive position.

THE ACCOUNTING PERSPECTIVE VERSUS THE FINANCIAL PERSPECTIVE

A manufacturer or wholesaler seldom generates a sale directly in exchange for cash. Instead, the firm exchanges a product for the IOU of the customer according to predetermined selling terms. When a company purchases inventory, the cash payment typically follows the actual receipt of the inventory by 30 days.

From the accounting perspective, no distinction is made between an actual transaction and a cash transaction. Thus, on the seller's side, a transaction requires a record of the sale on the day it occurs, even though no cash actually changes hands. The buyer's side also records the purchase and, at the same time, records an increase in inventory and accounts payable. But the actual transaction has no immediate effect on the cash account of either company. This is known as accrual accounting. We can define accrual basis accounting as the recognition of revenue when it is earned and the recognition of expense in the period in which it is incurred, without regard to the time of receipt or payment of cash.

Financial accounting enables a manager to measure the financial performance of a firm by properly matching the firm's revenues and expenses as they occur. At the same time, however, accrual accounting does not provide the proper picture of the cash flow through the company. Although it is well known that corporate managers seek to maximize profit and maintain corporate liquidity, accounting theory focuses almost exclusively on measuring and reporting profitability. Any use of an accrual accounting system to measure cash flow is just as foolhardy as the use of a cash budget to measure profitability. These diverse systems were designed to measure different types of activity.

All of the future discussion in this book will focus on cash flow. Therefore, any accrual accounting information that is used will have to be adjusted before it can be used in a meaningful fashion. Under strict cash basis accounting, revenue is recorded only when cash is received, and expenses are recorded only when cash is paid out. The determination of income on a cash basis is based on the collection of revenue and the payment of expenses. The principle of matching revenues and expenses is ignored. Consequently, cash basis financial statements are not in conformity with generally accepted accounting principles.

In recent years, many users of accounting statements prepared in accordance with generally accepted accounting principles have been concerned that these statements do not reflect the economic reality of the company's financial condition. Through the use of alternative methods of recognizing inventory, depreciation, lease arrangements, pension liabilities, investment in affiliated companies, investment tax credits, and so forth, managers have considerable latitude in deciding just what the bottom-line figure will be.

This profusion of acceptable accounting alternatives has come about because accountants believe that financial statements based on accrual accounting are more meaningful for evaluating economic performance than are statements prepared on a cash basis. As a result, some companies can show healthy net income figures and, at the same time, lack the cash flow necessary to ensure survival. A good example of this phenomenon was the W. T. Grant Company. It showed positive net income from 1966 to 1974, while it had a negative cash flow from 1971 to 1974. As we all know, bankruptcy proceedings began in 1975.

One of the main objectives of this section is to clearly define the differences between the accounting perspective and the financial perspective. Each serves an important function and uses different forms of analysis. The important point is that, if we are interested in the company's cash flow, we must be prepared to modify or alter a strict accounting viewpoint that focuses on net income.

THE REASONS FOR HOLDING CASH

As we have already said, cash is listed first on a company's balance sheet and is considered a component of working capital. Cash is made up of demand deposits and currency. Now let's examine the reasons for holding cash.

There are three principal reasons for holding cash. First, a company needs cash for transactions. This cash is used to pay bills, wages, taxes, and meet other company obligations. We have already seen that having a positive net income does not guarantee that a company has enough cash on hand to meet all of its obligations.

The second reason for keeping a supply of cash is to have it available as a reserve. The old rule of saving for a rainy day is just as applicable for corporations as it is for individuals. Financial managers cannot predict exactly what future cash needs will be. Therefore, managers must have some cash in reserve to meet unexpected needs. The exact amount of cash held in reserve depends on the degree of uncertainty about these needs. If there is a great deal of uncertainty about day-to-day cash needs, the company will have to maintain a large cash reserve. The necessity for maintaining a large cash reserve is lessened if the company has fast, dependable, and easy access to short-term credit. For example, if a bank extends a line of credit that can be used during times of cash shortages, lower cash reserves can be maintained.

Finally, holding cash is essential to meet bank requirements. When banks make loans or extend lines of credit, they usually require compensating balances. A compensating balance is a specified amount of cash (typically 10 percent of the loan or the line of credit) that the company must maintain in its demand deposit account at all times. Today, the banking industry is becoming more competitive, and banks are beginning to unbundle their services. In other words, banks are beginning to charge a fee for each service rather than asking for a deposit in lieu of the fee. As a result, this third reason for holding cash is becoming less important. (The discussion of bank charges in Section 2 includes further information on bank fees and compensating balances.)

INVESTING IN MARKETABLE SECURITIES

Most cash held in demand deposits earns no interest. Therefore, once the basic corporate needs for cash are satisfied, the financial manager should invest extra cash in the most productive manner possible. Many cash managers invest at least a part of this surplus money in marketable securities. As mentioned earlier, marketable securities earn a reasonable rate of return and offer the advantage of being quickly convertible into cash.

There are four criteria that should be considered when evaluating marketable securities: safety, marketability or liquidity, yield, and taxability. Safety refers to the probability that the full principal will be returned without any loss. Financial managers require a very high degree of safety in marketable securities. Marketability refers to how quickly and easily a security can be converted into cash. This factor is especially important if the security is being held as a reserve for the cash account, because it may have to be sold on very short notice. Yield is the interest or the price appreciation received from holding the security. Some securities pay interest; other securities sell at a discount and pay full face value at maturity. The effect is the same as paying interest. Some securities may have tax-free interest; discount securities may be taxed at a different rate than interest paying securities; and so on. Therefore, a cash manager must be aware of the corporation's tax situation in order to select the best type of marketable security.

There are three main reasons for investing in marketable securities. One is that they act as a reserve for the cash account. In other words, marketable securities are held to meet unexpected cash needs. Therefore, as noted earlier, their marketability is very important because they may have to be sold quickly.

Securities can also be used to meet known cash outflows. Frequently, the need for certain cash outflows can be predicted. One example is taxes. Every company regularly withholds taxes from employees' pay checks. This money is paid to the government on a monthly or quarterly basis. The cash manager knows the exact amount and the due dates of these payments in advance and can purchase securities that mature at the correct time.

A third reason for investing in marketable securities is that company profits benefit. Cash managers describe funds not needed for cash reserves or taxes as "free" because such funds are not constrained by specific liquidity requirements. Therefore, cash managers can invest free cash for a higher yield after considering taxes, even though such investments are less liquid and may be a bit more risky.

The various options for investing excess cash in marketable securities will be discussed in greater detail in Section 6.

LIQUIDITY AND CASH MANAGEMENT

Liquidity is required in any organization so that the firm is able to meet its obligations as they come due in order to take advantage of unforeseen opportunities. This aspect of working capital is one of the major concerns of the cash manager. The cash manager must try to balance all of the goals of the firm simultaneously, while, at the same time, coordinating the various functional areas of marketing, production, purchasing, and the like.

During the Great Depression of the late 1920s and early 1930s, financial managers first began to be concerned with liquidity and cash management. Prior to this time, most of a financial manager's time and effort was spent choosing the appropriate financing instruments and deciding what the impact of those instruments would be on capital structure. With the dramatic increase in the number of business failures during the Depression, the need for liquidity management became clear.

In fulfilling wartime requirements resulting from the onset of World War II, cash management was not considered important. Rather, managers were faced with the crucial question of efficient production, given severe shortages. After the war, the amount of corporate liquidity was so large and interest rates were so low that little attention was paid to cash management.

Key developments in cash management began during the early 1950s as companies began to draw down corporate liquidity. The basic question cash managers asked was: How do we provide adequate cash to meet bill and debt obligations at a minimum cost? This problem was put into focus as managers started dealing with the uncertainty of matching cash receipts and cash disbursements. The major tenet of cash management emerged as "conserve cash at all costs." The major areas of cash management emerged as cash balances, cash collections, cost disbursements, and cash planning and budgeting.

As inflation accelerated during the 1960s and 1970s, two major aims of cash management developed. These were, first, to speed up inflows of cash and, second, to slow down cash outflows. As we have seen, the cash management function must be integrated into overall company planning in order to achieve the firm's multiple goals.

CREATING AN INTEGRATED CASH MANAGEMENT SYSTEM

There are two main benefits to be derived from a cash management program—first, incremental profits that will augment net income and, second, freed-up resources (namely, cash) that can be used for other corporate purposes. Both of these benefits are worthwhile, but the most important benefit is probably an effective cash management system. Such a system will not only pay for itself but should also have a positive effect on net income.

Reviewing the cash management cycle from beginning to end is the best approach to integrating cash management with overall company planning. The objective of the review is to find all the ways (that are consistent with the firm's other objectives) to speed up inflows and slow down outflows. The emphasis should be on evaluating all corporate functions that, from a financial executive's standpoint, can potentially affect cash flow.

An integrated cash management analysis, as we shall see, involves reviewing the firm's billing and collection procedures in light of industry practice and competition. The purpose of the review is to shorten the time it takes for payments to be put to some useful purpose.

The other side of the process involves reviewing the firm's disbursement practices with the idea of slowing down the outflow without hurting credit standing or profitability. Many techniques are available for ensuring payment in a timely fashion and, at the same time, trying to conserve cash.

The relationship the company has with its bank and the form and amount of bank compensation must be reviewed carefully. In addition, an in-depth review of forecasting and planning procedures must be done to ensure that management has a good understanding of the company's cash flow cycle. Both the timing and the amounts of flows must be taken into consideration so that the firm's short-term investment performance will produce an acceptable rate of return.

A total review of a cash management system should also look beyond cash mobilization to information mobilization. This ensures that the decision maker receives information quickly so excess funds can be invested or short-term liabilities reduced. Clearly, it makes no sense to mobilize a company's cash if productive uses for the additional funds are not exploited.

The next step in a cash management system is to integrate it with the financial management information system. This means setting up a planning and budgeting system that identifies projected financial needs, forecasts surpluses or deficits of funds, and then makes coordinated decisions to use those funds most effectively. Systematically coordinating short- and long-term activity allows a financial executive to know at all times what is happening at the bank, in the firm's marketable security portfolio, to the firm's capital budget plans, and to overall corporate liquidity needs.

The benefits of using cash more efficiently are readily apparent. But if all of the financial functions are combined, the overall cost of managing such a system is reduced. Thus, from both income generating and cost reduction perspectives, a cash management system can be self-sustaining.

To develop and implement broader, integrated systems, cash managers must take more responsibility for coordinating and working with executives in the other functional areas of the firm. It is also important to review corporate policies and procedures to determine whether there is full interaction in the cash management function.

As a result of the wide-ranging impact of cash management on the entire firm, financial executives have a more complex job than ever before. Such executives must broaden their interests and interactions while at the same time performing the traditional financial functions. For example, they have to interact with the purchasing department and with the materials management staff. They also must play a much larger role in contract negotiations. Too often, contracts are left to the legal department, and some important financial considerations may be overlooked, especially as these considerations relate to the firm's cash management policies. Costs, payments, disbursement schedules, progress payments, and other financial considerations are of concern to financial executives. They should be involved in negotiations before contracts are finalized.

The idea of taking a companywide view rather than looking specifically at individual operations make eminent sense. The cash manager should broaden his or her perspective and think of cash management as an activity that is affected by all components of the company's operations. All decisions that are made and actions that are taken throughout the company affect cash flow and, hence, cash management. This includes everything from production scheduling and inventory control to marketing and credit policy—from tax policy, negotiation, accounting, and control to personnel and payroll. The effects of cash management have an impact on all areas of a company.

The simple statement that cash management speeds up inflows and slows down outflows must be put into perspective for it to be effective and useful. Emphasis should be placed on evaluating how well the organization performs in all cash management areas and how effectively the concepts of cash management are communicated throughout the corporation as a whole.

The way a company organizes to manage cash depends primarily on its size. In a small firm, officers may hold dual titles, such as president and treasurer. There may be a very small staff or one person who has the sole responsibility for cash management. In a medium-sized company, specialization begins to occur. Several people are responsible for cash management. Large companies find it necessary to have a department devoted exclusively to cash management and often have cash managers in the firm's regional offices.

Flow of Funds

The flow of funds through an organization encompasses all segments of the corporation and is related to all decisions within the firm. This flow of cash, or flow of funds, is one of the main concerns of the cash manager. The flow of funds diagram below illustrates how funds flow through a company. Because the flow is circular and continuous, it is possible to start anywhere in the chain.

Flow of Funds

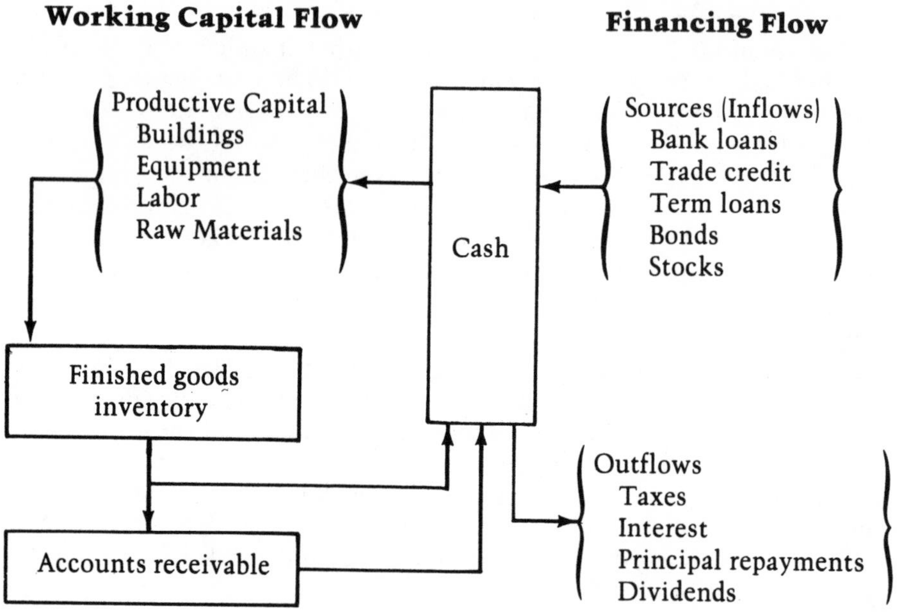

Working Capital Flow   **Financing Flow**

Productive Capital
Buildings
Equipment
Labor
Raw Materials

Cash

Sources (Inflows)
Bank loans
Trade credit
Term loans
Bonds
Stocks

Finished goods
inventory

Accounts receivable

Outflows
Taxes
Interest
Principal repayments
Dividends

The flow of funds or cash flow refers to the movement of money through the business. The time it takes for these funds to complete a full cycle reflects the average duration that a firm's cash is invested in inventory and accounts receivable, both of which are nonearning assets. Therefore, it is in a company's best interest to keep the cash cycle as short as possible.

To see the relationship between the various accounts and the cash cycle refer to the cash cycle chart below.

Cash Cycle

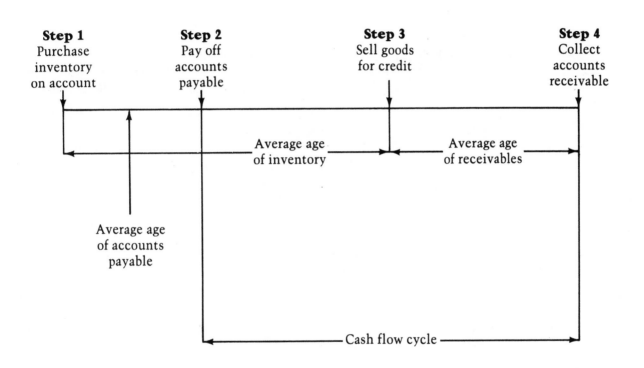

The table below shows how cash, accounts receivable, inventory, and accounts payable will be affected by each of the four steps in the cash cycle.

	Changes in Accounts			
Account	Step 1	Step 2	Step 3	Step 4
Cash	0	–	0	+
Accounts receivable	0	0	+	–
Inventory	+	0	–	0
Accounts payable	+	–	0	0

Calculating the Cash Flow Cycle

The cash flow cycle is defined as the average age of inventory plus the average age of accounts receivable less the average age of accounts payable. Or as the cash cycle chart indicates, the cash flow cycle is the average time it takes for a company to pay out cash and receive a cash inflow that completes the transaction.

The cash flow cycle can be calculated using the following equation:

$$\text{Cash flow cycle} = \text{Average age of inventory} + \text{Average age of accounts receivable} - \text{Average age of accounts payable}$$

$$= \frac{360 \text{ days}}{\text{Cost of goods sold} \div \text{Inventory}} + \frac{\text{Accounts receivable}}{\text{Net credit sales}} \times 360 \text{ days}$$

$$- \frac{\text{Accounts payable}}{\text{Credit purchases}} \times 360 \text{ days}$$

To illustrate how this equation can be put to use, let us look at ABC Company where:

Cost of goods sold   = $470,570
Inventory   = $345,420
Accounts receivable   = $ 70,820
Net credit sales   = $575,460
Accounts payable   = $ 26,890
Credit purchases   = $352,927

Substituting these figures in our equation, we calculate the cash flow cycle of ABC Company as:

$$\text{Cash flow cycle} = \frac{360}{\$470,570 \div \$345,420} + \frac{\$70,820}{\$575,460} \times 360 - \frac{\$26,890}{\$352,927} \times 360$$

$$= 265 + 44 - 27$$

$$= 282$$

In the above example, ABC's cash cycle is 282 days. It is not possible to decide at this point if this amount of time is too long or too short because it represents a lot of factors that we will consider in the remainder of this book. Calculating your company's cash flow cycle is the starting point of any analysis that you will have to perform to answer the question: Is cash being effectively managed in my company? Use the space on page 16 to calculate the cash flow cycle for your company.

The Cash Flow Cycle for Your Company

Instructions: Using the equation for determining the number of days in the cash flow cycle, substitute the pertinent figures and calculate the length of the cycle for your company.

Cost of goods sold   = $_____

Inventory   = $_____

Accounts receivable   = $_____

Net credit sales   = $_____

Accounts payable   = $_____

Credit purchases   = $_____

$$\begin{matrix} \text{Cash flow} \\ \text{cycle} \end{matrix} = \begin{matrix} \text{Average age} \\ \text{of inventory} \end{matrix} + \begin{matrix} \text{Average age of} \\ \text{accounts receivable} \end{matrix} - \begin{matrix} \text{Average age of} \\ \text{accounts payable} \end{matrix}$$

The Matching Principle

One of the fundamental principles of finance is matching the cash inflows from assets with the cash outflows from their respective sources of financing. The technique of hedging can be used when trying to accomplish this objective.

Financing temporary current assets with short-term sources of funds and financing fixed assets and permanent current assets with long-term sources of funds illustrates how the matching principle is put to work. The basic strategy of the perfect hedge is to match the expected inflows and outflows of funds. This is fundamentally sound financing because the inflows of funds from the sale of assets are being used to repay the loans that financed these acquisitions. When the cash inflow is in excess of the required cash outflow, the situation is considered to be more conservative than the opposite case in which the cash outflow is greater than the cash inflow. This imbalance must be met by rolling over short-term financing or seeking other sources of funds. This is considered to be an aggressive approach.

The DEF Company (page 18) demonstrates the trade-off that exists between risk and return when using different approaches to the matching principle. The trade off should be kept in mind when a company is considering a change in its sources of funds in response to changing conditions. The aggressive approach should be used when firms are expanding their working capital during the recovery and prosperity phases of the business cycle. Alternatively, during the recessionary phase, a more conservative approach may be more appropriate.

A Conservative Versus an Aggressive Approach to the Matching Concept

The figures below illustrate the results DEF Company would achieve by employing an aggressive approach or a conservative approach to matching its cash inflows with its cash outflows.

DEF Company
(Dollars in Millions)

Assets

Current assets	$100
Fixed assets	100
Total assets	$200

Liabilities

	Conservative	Aggressive
Short-term liabilities (at 7%)	$ 25	$100
Long-term debt (at 12%)	125	50
Equity	50	50
Total liabilities plus equity	$200	$200

Income Statement

	Conservative	Aggressive
Earnings before interest and taxes	$50.00	$50.00
Less:		
Interest	(16.75)	(13.00)
Taxes (at 40%)	(13.30)	(14.80)
Net income	$19.95	$22.20
Current ratio $\left(\dfrac{\text{Current assets}}{\text{Current liabilities}}\right)$	4.0	1.0
Net working capital $\left(\dfrac{\text{Current assets} -}{\text{Current liabilities}}\right)$	$75.00	$0.00
Rate of return on equity $\left(\dfrac{\text{Net income}}{\text{Equity}}\right)$	39.9%	44.4%

Your Company's Approach to the Matching Principle

Instructions: Enter the figures for your company in the space provided below. Then determine whether your company uses the aggressive or conservative approach to the matching concept.

Your Company (Dollars in Millions)	
Assets	
Current assets	_____
Fixed assets	_____
Total assets	_____
Liabilities	
Short-term liabilities (at _____%)	_____
Long-term debt (at _____%)	_____
Equity	_____
Total liabilities plus equity	_____
Income Statement	
Earnings before interest and taxes	_____
Less:	
Interest	_____
Taxes (at _____%)	_____
Net income	_____
Current ratio	_____
Net working capital	_____
Rate of return on equity	_____

Summary

This section has put working capital into the proper perspective for managers concerned with managing the cash flow of their firms. They must realize that planning and managing cash flow are more than just managing account. Although the cash account is one of the major assets that affects cash flow, other current assets and current liabilities, and quite often long-term assets and financing, also have an impact on the cash cycle of the firm. It is this cash cycle and its duration that we will be most concerned with as we evaluate various strategies and techniques for cash flow planning.

The concept of working capital and management's philosophy of trying to maintain it at a particular level are also important. If management is aggressive, it may take one approach to the matching principle that will have direct impact on the cash flow planning process. If management tends to be more conservative, other options may be available. Above all, when we are dealing with the cash flow planning process, it must be remembered that we are involved with a very dynamic situation that is closely related to the character of the decision maker. Therefore, given the exact same situation, two different managers can reach satisfactory solutions that may be entirely different from one another.

2.

Corporate Cash Management

Corporate Relationships with Banks

In this section, we will discuss the relationship between the corporate cash manager and the banking industry. We'll also look at the development of the U.S. payments system and talk about banking services, charges, and relations.

RECENT CHANGES IN BANKING

The decade of the 1980s is bringing a dramatic change to banking in the United States. There is fierce competition, not only among depository financial institutions but also among such other organizations as retail store chains, insurance companies, securities brokerage firms, and the like. They are all beginning to offer various types of financial services utilizing the payment system.

In reviewing the reasons for changing from a paper-based check or credit card form to an electronic form, it is important to realize that over 80 percent of the value of all U.S. payment transactions, primarily those for corporations and financial institutions, is handled by some form of electronic funds transfer, known as EFT. However, in terms of the volume of transactions, paper checks and credit cards account for approximately 85 percent and 13 percent of the number of transactions, respectively.

The Financial Institutions Deregulation and Monetary Control Act of 1980 required that the Federal Reserve system end its implicit pricing policy of utilizing reserves of member banks to offer payment infrastructure services free to both members and nonmembers. Beginning in October 1981, the Fed was required to charge explicitly for the cost of payment services. Using paper checks has, in effect, been subsidized by the Fed because it offers a free check collection system that financially rewards those corporations and individuals sending payment checks to distant locations. An example of this is using a checking account on the East Coast to pay suppliers on the West Coast. This incentive to use the check collection system to slow down cash outflows will be restricted somewhat by the Monetary Control Act, but opportunities will still exist for exploitation by the cash manager.

During the 1980s, banks have begun to expand across state lines because of changes in the bank holding company legislation. Such expansion is expected to continue during the next several years. This has occurred first in regional markets in neighboring states serving the same metropolitan areas and will gradually spread to a true nationwide system. In addition to the competition among banks, there is competition from organizations that are not regulated as are banks and thrift institutions. Cash management accounts offered by brokerage firms and money market mutual funds will enable individual consumers to enjoy the benefits of cash management. Retailers, travel and entertainment card organizations, and data processing organizations are all competing to provide services to the individual. This increase in competition should raise the expectations as well as the sophistication of the individuals with whom the cash manager will deal in the marketplace.

Large money transfers, used by corporations and financial institutions to mobilize funds nationally and internationally, have changed from generally telegraphic-type messages with high handling costs to standard data formats that are automatically handled from start to finish. These transactions, which are in excess of $2 million, are often called high-value, low-volume transactions. During the 1970s, the Fed Wire Network, referred to as the Fed Wire, was used to transfer cash funds on a national basis. Now, the network known as the New York Clearing House Interbank Payments System (called CHIPS) can transfer funds on a same-day basis. On the international scene, the Society for Worldwide Interbank Financial Telecommunications (called SWIFT) enables its members to move funds on a worldwide basis. The large major money market banks interface with these systems, thereby giving them the capability for the global movement of funds.

These corporate and institutional electronic services functions are good for large-value transactions in which the assurance of proper handling is far more important than the cost per transaction. The cost of the services would generally be prohibitive if used for lower-value transactions.

ESTABLISHING A SOUND BANKING RELATIONSHIP

A sound banking relationship is essential for the long-term success of any business. Indeed, that relationship can ensure that the business has a source of external financing to fill any gaps that may develop in its cash flow cycle. Moreover, an experienced banker can provide valuable counsel.

A sound banking relationship doesn't happen in the first meeting with a banker. Nor does a working relationship result from merely borrowing funds. A business builds a banking relationship over a long period of time and in a fashion that is mutually beneficial for both the company and the bank.

The groundwork for a sound banking relationship includes, first, open lines of communication in both directions; second, timely financial information; and third, a fair return for the amount of risk the bank takes.

The communication process between client and banker is most effective when it begins with personal rapport and personal contact. The better your personal relationship with the bank officer, the better your company's banking relationship will be. To enhance the personal relationship, you should provide the bank with historic financial as well as pro forma statements for your company. In addition, references, although not always required, seem to help in most cases. Indeed, the more the banker knows about the company's financial circumstances, the better able the bank is to structure a package that will meet the firm's needs.

The idea of only giving positive information to a banker couldn't be further from the way to handle the situation. You should communicate any actual or potential problems to the banker at the beginning. From the banker's perspective, the bank won't feel very comfortable with an account that continually surprises it with negative information 30 days after the event has occurred. This reflects badly on management's ability to forecast the trends of the business. A rule of thumb is that, as long as you maintain open lines of communication, whether the news is good or bad, the bank will be able to help solve most of the company's financial problems.

Finally, you should expect to pay a fair price for the services rendered by the bank. When a bank feels that your company's business is worth having, you are well on the way to establishing a sound banking relationship.

Banks play an important part in any cash management program. For a cash manager to make the most effective use of banks, he or she should understand the many services they offer and the costs of these services. Banks are both helped and hurt by the increasing number of corporate cash management programs. Banks are hurt because an effective cash management program reduces the levels of cash in the company's demand deposit accounts. At the same time, however, banks are helped because they can sell a wide variety of new services to companies with corporate cash management programs.

Once a company has selected one or more banks, continuing communication is important. So we'll emphasize the principles involved in maintaining close contact with the bank officers.

The growing trend in the use of cash management affects banks in several ways. When a company collects its receivables faster and pays its bills more slowly, its bank gains because the company's cash balances are larger. If a company uses automatic wire transfers, the banks that receive the cash are helped and those that lose deposits are hurt. When a company begins to monitor its cash balances and invest excess funds in attractive, short-term outside (nonbank) opportunities—such as treasury bills or commercial paper—the average balance in the company's demand account is reduced. As a result, the bank's lendable supply of interest-free money is decreased.

The net effect of a cash management program is usually to reduce the average balance a company maintains in its demand account. At first, many banks felt threatened by this reduction in deposits because banks lend these deposits. Therefore, a reduction in deposits leaves them with less money to lend. Then some banks realized that the scarcity of cash and the variety of attractive investment opportunities make corporate cash management programs inevitable. Rather than fight cash management programs, some banks developed new services to help cash managers. Other banks followed suit for competitive reasons. Today, many banks work actively with their customers to help design more efficient cash gathering and disbursing systems. In this way, banks have strengthened relationships with their customers and have been able to sell a variety of new cash management services, such as lockboxes and management of accounts payable.

Many large banks offer negotiable certificates of deposit, known as CDs. These are interest bearing obligations of the bank. Because CDs are negotiable and because some banks and many government securities dealers maintain an active secondary market for them, the CDs of major banks are quite liquid. Interest rates are generally competitive with those of other short-term investments. (The use of CDs as an investment instrument for managing a firm's surplus cash will be discussed in Section 6.)

Banks today offer short-term (often 90-day) as well as long-term (one- to 20-year) loans for real estate, buildings, and equipment. In addition, many banks lease equipment to large customers. A lease is a form of loan and is usually considered an intermediate-term (3- to 5-year) form of financing.

Cash managers typically use short-term loans from banks to cover seasonal needs for money. For example, a company may have to build up its inventory just before the peak selling season. This increase in inventory ties up the company's cash. A short-term bank loan gives the company the cash it needs during this peak season. Similarly, if a company's customers tradi-

BANK SERVICES

Certificates of Deposit

Loans

tionally stretch out the time they take to pay bills during a certain season of the year, a short-term bank loan will help the firm finance these extra receivables and still maintain an adequate cash level.

Lines of Credit

In addition to making loans, banks also offer lines of credit. A line of credit is an agreement by the bank to lend up to a certain amount of money, if needed, for a certain period of time. For example, a company may foresee that it could need as much as $500,000 next summer. Rather than wait until the last minute to arrange for a loan, the company may negotiate a line of credit. In other words, the bank agrees to lend up to $500,000 on an as-needed basis. This assures the company that money will be available when needed but does not obligate the company to borrow the money. By extending a line of credit, the bank benefits in two ways. First, the agreement strengthens the bank's relationship with the customer and practically guarantees that the company will come to that bank when it needs money. Second, the bank charges the company for this service.

Bank loans and lines of credit as options for obtaining short-term cash will be discussed in greater depth in Section 5.

Financial Advice and Information

Today, banks offer an increasing variety of financial advice and information. These services include analyzing collection systems, funds concentration methods, and disbursement systems. A bank may also recommend programs to reduce mail float and check collection float and give investment advice. Banks also provide information to corporate customers. Such information includes collection reports, often by wire, from geographically scattered lockboxes and account reconciliations, often including float analysis. A bank may monitor and report on a demand account. This service includes a daily report of account activity and the company's exact cash balance. A bank often provides information on foreign exchange rates and quotes on selected money market instruments—for example, certificates of deposit, government and federal agency securities, commercial paper, and the Dow Jones Industrial Average.

Computer Services

Many banks today offer computer services to prepare payrolls, monitor accounts receivable, and prepare checks for suppliers. Banks offer these services primarily to smaller companies and to branch offices of larger firms that do not have their own computers.

Some banks offer time-shared computer services. With this service, a cash manager has a computer terminal in his or her own office with direct access to the bank's computer. The cash manager can then immediately obtain such information as exact account balances, float reports, foreign exchange rates, and money market quotes. In addition, most bank time-sharing services offer programs to calculate cash flow, return on investment, and yields to maturity on bonds. Some banks also offer computer models for determining the best cities for a lockbox network.

Lockbox Services

Many banks now offer lockbox services to customers. With such a service, the company continues to bill customers, but customers send payments to a post office box. The bank opens the post office box as often as every hour and deposits all the received checks. Because lockboxes are usually located near customers, this system speeds up cash flow by reducing both mail float and check collection float. Calculating the cost of utilizing a lockbox system is discussed later in this section, and the lockbox as a basic cash management device is explored in Section 6.

Banks also provide regional concentration accounts. A company may establish several of these accounts around the country and then instruct each of its local branch offices to send the day's receipts to the nearest regional concentration account. This is usually done by depository transfer check or by wire. At the end of each day, the regional concentration bank wires all funds above a certain minimum to the company's main head-quarters account. Thus, funds move quickly from a customer to a local branch office bank to a regional concentration bank to the company's bank.

Banks may use several different compensation methods to charge a customer for the services they provide. A cash manager should study these different forms of compensation and work with the bank to figure out which method or combination of methods will work best for his or her company.

Banks charge for their services in two basic ways—fees and minimum balances. Using the fee method, a bank sets a specific price for each of its services. Using the minimum-balance approach, a bank provides many services free but requires that the company maintain a specified minimum balance. For example, one bank may charge 10 cents for each check the company writes, 15 cents for each deposit, 3 cents for each deposit item, and so on. Another bank may not charge for these services but may require the company to keep at least $200,000 in its checking account at all times.

In general, cash managers prefer the fee approach because such fees are tax-deductible. Every month, the bank itemizes the services it has provided and indicates the price of each service. The company pays this bill and deducts the expense from its taxable income. Minimum balance re-quirements cost the company money because the company loses the in-come it could earn elsewhere on these funds. The lost income, however, is not tax deductible.

Banks generally prefer a minimum-balance form of compensation for two reasons: first, balances provide money for the bank to lend; and second, a bank's growth is commonly measured by growth in deposits rather than sales (interest on loans, service fees, and so forth). Despite bank preferences, the use of service fees has increased significantly in recent years. The reason is that banks have underpriced their services (when they price them at all) and have offered a correspondingly low earnings allowance on deposits. Therefore, cash managers simply buy services from banks that are offering bargain prices. Then, rather than leave money in the bank, the managers place cash in more attractive outside investments. When some banks in an area offer services on a fee basis, many other banks in the same area must do so as well for competitive reasons.

Now, many banks offer companies a payment option on deposit account activity. In other words, companies can either maintain balances or pay fees for checks written, deposits made, and special services—such as stop-payment orders. At the same time, many banks accept only fees (not balances) for specific services, such as handling trust accounts, data process-ing, and investment services. Because cash management services are deposit-related, many banks offer companies the option of paying by fee or by maintaining a specified balance.

From a bank's point of view, float is the time between when a check is deposited and when it is actually collected from the issuer's account. For smaller customers, banks often offer immediate availability of deposits. For larger customers, they calculate either an average float or the actual number of days of float.

Banks calculate an average float by determining the average number of days checks take to clear. For example, half the checks a particular bank handles may clear in a day, 30 percent in 2 days, and so on. The bank then applies the average float time to all accounts. For example, if a bank calculates its average float as 1½ days and a customer deposits a $10,000 check, $5,000 will be available one day after deposit, and the remaining $5,000 will be available on the second day. In other words, half in one day and half in 2 days equals 1½ days average float.

Although the average-days method is simpler for banks, it is not fair to all customers. For instance, a company depositing mostly cash and local checks (a supermarket, for example) does not have the full use of its cash as quickly as it should. On the other hand, a company depositing mostly out-of-town checks that require three or four days to collect makes out better with the average-days method.

To solve this problem, some banks compute actual-days float by deferring the availability of deposited funds on an item-by-item basis. To do this, the bank examines each deposited check individually and determines the exact number of days it will take for the check to clear. The bank does this using a predetermined collection table, generally based on the Federal Reserve availability schedule.

Because of the work involved, few banks compute actual-days float by hand. Instead, they use a fully automated demand deposit accounting system. In such a system, the collection time in days for each bank in the country is computer-programmed. Float calculation then becomes automatic.

As a compromise measure, banks without sophisticated computer systems calculate the average-days float, not for the bank as a whole but for specific large customers. This approach is relatively easy to carry out and is fairer to customers who deposit primarily cash and local checks.

You can calculate float's cost to your firm using the formula presented later in this section (see "Objectives and Techniques of Cash Management"). Section 4 then discusses playing the float as a technique to conserve cash.

Every company must make monthly or quarterly tax deposits for Social Security and income tax payments. The corporation can pay these taxes directly to the U.S. Treasury Department or to any authorized bank. When a corporation pays an authorized bank, the funds usually remain in the bank a few days before they are withdrawn ("called") by the Treasury. Therefore, banks that receive these tax deposits benefit from the free use of the money.

Cash managers have recognized the value of tax payments and now request earnings credit on these deposits. Banks argue against giving an earnings credit on tax deposits for two reasons. First, the law requires companies to pay their taxes by specified dates. The money then no longer belongs to the company, and the company has no right to earnings on this money. Second, when the Treasury leaves money for a few extra days in a bank's tax accounts, the Treasury is actually compensating the bank for performing services such as tax collection bookkeeping. Again, the company has no right to these earnings.

Even though these reasons for opposing earnings credit on tax deposits may be valid, it is still true that companies have control over the bank to which they make their payments. When some banks in an area offer earnings credit on tax deposits, other banks in that area must do the same or run the risk of losing a company's tax deposits.

Quite often, banks do not specify the exact minimum balance they expect from a customer; they simply ask that it be reasonable. In such cases, some cash managers determine the balance they will maintain in the following way. They first establish a general level for the balance through discussion with bank officers. Then, over a period of months, they gradually reduce the average balance until the bank complains. This approach does not strengthen the company-bank relationship, but as long as banks allow it, this approach usually results in the lowest possible balance requirements.

CRITERIA FOR SELECTING A BANK

A large nationwide company requires three types of banks to handle all its needs. For example, local banks are needed to handle the receipts, and possibly the disbursements, of local branch offices. A large company with many branches throughout the country also has to select regional concentration banks to collect funds from the local branch office banks in each area and sometimes to channel disbursement funds to branch offices. And finally, such a company needs the services of one or more main corporate banks, usually in the city where corporate headquarters is located.

A company uses several criteria to select any of the banks just described. However, the importance of these criteria varies considerably depending on which type of bank is being evaluated. The six most important criteria are (1) location; (2) size—the bank's resources, operating record, and financial standing; (3) type of bank—wholesale, retail, or a combination; (4) services offered and staff expertise; (5) costs of services; and (6) management. We will now consider each of these criteria in turn.

Location

For disbursing cash, the more remote the bank, the better, because checks will clear slowly and provide both the company and the bank with extra cash. However, the right location is essential for efficient cash gathering.

If the bank receives deposits by mail (through either a lockbox system or the receipt of depository transfer checks from branch offices), it must be close to the main post office in its district. This allows frequent, often hourly, trips to the post office during the day so incoming mail can be processed promptly. If a bank must wait for the mail to be delivered to a branch post office, many hours of processing time will be lost every day.

It also makes a difference if a bank is located in the same city as a Federal Reserve bank. To understand the importance of location to check collection, it is useful to understand how banks collect checks using the Federal Reserve system. The Federal Reserve system is made up of 12 districts throughout the country, 12 reserve banks (one in the principal city of each district), and 24 branch banks. There are from zero to 4 branches in each district. These 36 banks form a national network so that any bank in the country can collect checks it receives.

In practice, each bank sorts the checks it receives and physically moves the checks to the nearest Federal Reserve bank. The Federal Reserve banks (including branches) transfer checks among themselves by plane and then distribute the checks to the original issuing banks in each area.

You can see now why a bank's location can be so important. If a bank misses a Federal Reserve deadline, all funds are tied up an extra day, but proximity to a Federal Reserve bank allows extra processing time. For example, a bank in downtown Atlanta can process checks up to half an hour before the Federal Reserve deadline and still make delivery to the Federal Reserve bank on time. A suburban Atlanta bank might have to stop processing checks two hours before the deadline, and a bank 100 miles from Atlanta might require a cutoff time of four hours before the deadline.

Transportation facilities such as a major airport also make a difference. Although the Federal Reserve network clears most of the checks in the banking system, many banks clear some checks directly between themselves. For instance, if a Boston bank regularly clears a large dollar volume of checks through a specific New York bank, these two banks may make arrangements to clear checks directly. The two banks thereby gain an entire night of extra processing time. In this case, the Boston Federal Reserve deadline for next-day availability of funds on checks from New York City is 10:30 P.M. By making direct arrangements with the New York City bank, the Boston bank can put its checks on the first Boston–to–New York flight the following morning at 7:00 A.M. and achieve the same availability. Because the airlines carry checks between banks with direct clearing arrangements, access to a major airport is essential for any bank trying to speed up its check collection ability.

In conclusion, therefore, banks near a major post office, near a Federal Reserve bank or branch, and near a major airport are the most efficient for collecting checks. Nearly all banks meeting these three criteria are located in the 36 Federal Reserve cities. A company's regional concentration banks and its main bank will almost always be located in one of these cities. Local banks must be near the company's local branch offices and near local customers for fast check collection.

Size

The size of a bank's assets is one measure of its ability to provide services. A small bank, even in an ideal location, simply cannot collect checks as quickly as a large bank. A small bank cannot provide 24 hourly pickups a day at the post office, nor can it justify a three-shift check collection operation.

What determines adequate size? One rule of thumb is that a bank's assets exceed $100 million. Only 5 percent of the country's banks fall into this group, yet they process over 60 percent of all deposited checks. Because of the high volume of checks per bank, most of these banks are organized to collect checks quickly. Smaller banks either deposit checks with correspondent banks for collection or rely heavily on Federal Reserve facilities. Both these methods slow down the availability of collected funds.

The rule of thumb of $100 million in assets is only a guideline. Each bank's capabilities should be judged on an individual basis. Local banks need not pass such a stringent test. A local bank of much smaller size, but with a solid operating record and healthy finances, is completely satisfactory.

One method of classifying banks is by the type of customers they seek. **Type of Bank**
Retail or personal banks seek individual consumers as customers, whereas
the customers of wholesale banks are business firms. The third classification is a combination bank that serves the needs of both individuals and
businesses. Personal (retail) banks usually have small assets and primarily
service personal checking and savings accounts. Business (wholesale) banks
have larger assets and primarily service industrial, commercial,
agricultural, and export-import accounts.

Almost all the largest banks in the country are combination banks. They
solicit both business and personal accounts. Combination banks usually
have a large office in the downtown business district and branch offices in
outlying districts and suburbs. These branches often specialize in personal
accounts, while most of the bank's business experts work in the main
downtown office.

Companies must recognize the difference between personal and business
activities in order to establish a satisfactory banking relationship. Very
often, smaller companies mistakenly open accounts with consumer banks
or with the consumer-oriented branches of combination banks. They consequently find lending officers who are more oriented toward home mortgages
and car loans than toward business loans. In such cases, the company relationship suffers. Larger companies always have the correct type of bank for
their main corporate account, but their local branch offices around the
country sometimes choose the wrong type of bank because they do not
realize that different types of banks exist.

As we have seen, banks today offer a wide variety of services. In selecting a **Services and Staff**
bank, a company must be certain that the bank offers all the services the
firm requires—lockbox, wire transfer, and so forth. The bank should also offer a reasonable range of the services that the company may require in the
future. The cash manager should verify the expertise of the bank's staff by
reviewing staff credentials and checking with some of the bank's other service customers.

The fifth criterion is the cost of bank services. As we have already seen, **Cost of Services**
bank costs vary widely. Banks often charge different rates for similar services, and they may prefer payment in different ways (fees or balances). In
order to obtain the greatest value, a company must carefully compare the
services offered by each bank in the market with the costs for these services.

In selecting a corporate headquarters bank or an important regional concen- **Management**
tration bank, a company should also evaluate the bank's management.
Bank management includes both the contact officer and the bank's overall
management. Management factors to be considered include management
philosophy and quality, knowledge of the industry, concern for the company, and personal relationships between the bank and company personnel.
These factors are considerably more subjective than the other selection
criteria.

Just as banks evaluate companies, companies must regularly evaluate their **EVALUATING**
banks. A company treasurer should formally judge a bank at least once a **THE BANK**

year on the basis of three criteria: first, the bank's performance of contracted services; second, the quality of the bank's advice and new ideas; and third, the costs relative to other banks.

The way in which a bank performs contracted services can be evaluated objectively. First, were lockboxes, wire transfers, deposits, and reports all functioning at the agreed-upon pace? Second, was the bank consistently fast and reliable? And third, was the bank accurate? Were bank errors minimal?

A bank's advice and attitude are subjective factors but may be judged with respect to the quality of consulting and investment advice, if required. A banker should offer fast, accurate, and thoughtful advice on banking matters. A bank may or may not offer investment advice, depending on its agreements with the company. Rapport is also important. A banker should have a strong interest in the firm and its managers as well as reasonable knowledge about its business.

After rating the bank on these factors, the bank's performance should be compared with its costs. The company should also compare the prices of its bank with the prices of competing banks to make sure that the company is obtaining the best value.

Evaluation of Management Goals

The goal of cash management is to maintain the minimum cash balance that provides the company with sufficient liquidity to meet its financial obligations and to enhance the firm's profitability without exposing it to undue risk.

In order to put your judgment about the importance of various cash management goals into perspective, rate each of the five characteristics of cash management objectives listed below on a scale of 1 to 5, according to how important each goal is in your company (1 being very unimportant; 2, unimportant; 3, neutral; 4, important; and 5, very important).

1. Your firm has the ability to meet creditor obligations with existing assets.   1 2 3 4 5

2. Your firm has the ability to meet creditor obligations with unused bank credit lines.   1 2 3 4 5

3. Your firm has the ability to meet temporary financial problems as they arise.   1 2 3 4 5

4. Your firm has the ability to generate long-term debt or equity financing when needed.   1 2 3 4 5

5. Your firm has the ability to convert assets into cash in a reasonable time.   1 2 3 4 5

In a survey of the companies listed in the *Fortune 1,000* of 1978 conducted by Professors Johnson, Campbell, and Wittenbach, the following average responses were received. By comparing your responses to each of the characteristics with the averages from the survey given below, you will be able to put your judgment in perspective vis-a-vis that of the Fortune 1,000 managers.[1]

Comparing Your Responses with the Survey

Characteristics	Your response	Average response
1. Existing assets	_____	3.8
2. Bank credit lines	_____	3.7
3. Temporary problems	_____	4.4
4. Long-term financing	_____	3.9
5. Asset conversion	_____	3.6

[1] James M. Johnson, David R. Campbell, and James L. Wittenbach, "Problems in Corporate Liquidity," *Financial Executive*, March 1980, pp. 44-53.

Important Factors in Cash Management

The next comparison deals with the importance of various factors and their relationship to cash management. This set of opinions can be viewed as an inventory of your own understanding or philosophy of cash management. In the preference test below, you are asked to rate the relative importance of 35 factors that might affect liquidity planning or management on the same 1 to 5 scale as before. The 35 factors are divided into five groups.

1. Forecasting:

Cash flow projections for 1 year or less	1	2	3	4	5
Cash flow projections for 1 to 3 years	1	2	3	4	5
Cash flow projections for more than 3 years	1	2	3	4	5
Projected earnings of the firm	1	2	3	4	5
Planning models	1	2	3	4	5

2. Ratio analysis:

In general	1	2	3	4	5
Current ratio	1	2	3	4	5
Quick ratio	1	2	3	4	5
Inventory turnover	1	2	3	4	5
Receivables turnover	1	2	3	4	5
Payables turnover	1	2	3	4	5
Total asset turnover	1	2	3	4	5
Return on total assets	1	2	3	4	5
Return on owners' equity	1	2	3	4	5
Profit margin ratio	1	2	3	4	5
Times interest earned	1	2	3	4	5
Debt-to-equity ratio	1	2	3	4	5

Importance of ratio analysis when business is:

Highly liquid	1	2	3	4	5
Moderately liquid	1	2	3	4	5
Barely liquid	1	2	3	4	5
Illiquid	1	2	3	4	5

3. Asset management:

Management of cash surplus	1	2	3	4	5
Receivables management	1	2	3	4	5
Inventory management	1	2	3	4	5
Budgeting for capital expenditures	1	2	3	4	5

4. Liability management:

Good relations with bankers	1	2	3	4	5
Aggregate lines of credit	1	2	3	4	5
Bond ratings	1	2	3	4	5
Short-term interest rates	1	2	3	4	5
Longer-term interest rates	1	2	3	4	5

5. Other factors:

Current operating earnings	1	2	3	4	5
Timely, accurate management reporting system	1	2	3	4	5
Operating management's awareness of the impact of its decisions on liquidity	1	2	3	4	5
Macroeconomic factors	1	2	3	4	5
Firm's accounting and/or tax policies	1	2	3	4	5
Financial strength of customers	1	2	3	4	5

The results of the survey conducted by Professors Johnson, Campbell, and Wittenbach are given below for comparison. The article by Johnson, Campbell, and Wittenbach entitled "Problems in Corporate Liquidity" is reproduced in the selected readings section of this book. At this time, it may be very beneficial for you to read this article to see how the authors interpreted their findings.

Survey Results of Importance of Various Factors on Liquidity Management

Factors	Your Response	Average Response
1. Forecasting:		
Cash flow projections for 1 year or less	_____	4.7
Cash flow projections for 1 to 3 years	_____	4.0
Cash flow projections for more than 3 years	_____	3.2
Projected earnings of the firm	_____	4.3
Planning models	_____	3.2
2. Ratio analysis:		
In general	_____	3.4
Current ratio	_____	3.3
Quick ratio	_____	3.0
Inventory turnover	_____	3.9
Receivables turnover	_____	3.9
Payables turnover	_____	3.2
Total asset turnover	_____	3.2
Return on total assets	_____	4.0
Return on owners' equity	_____	4.1
Profit margin ratio	_____	4.3
Times interest earned	_____	3.3
Debt-to-equity ratio	_____	4.2
Importance of ratio analysis when business is:		
Highly liquid	_____	3.0
Moderately liquid	_____	3.6
Barely liquid	_____	4.3
Illiquid	_____	4.2
3. Asset management:		
Management of cash surplus	_____	3.8
Receivables management	_____	4.3
Inventory management	_____	4.4
Budgeting for capital expenditures	_____	4.3
4. Liability management:		
Good relations with bankers	_____	4.4
Aggregate lines of credit	_____	4.2
Bond ratings	_____	3.9
Short-term interest rates	_____	3.4
Longer-term interest rates	_____	3.7
5. Other factors:		
Current operating earnings	_____	4.3
Timely, accurate management reporting system	_____	4.3
Operating management's awareness of the impact of its decisions on liquidity	_____	4.0
Macroeconomic factors	_____	3.5
Firm's accounting and/or tax policies	_____	3.9
Financial strength of customers	_____	3.5

The Costs of Holding Cash

Holding cash is a use of funds, not only in accounting convention but also in fact. By maintaining a cash balance, a company ties up potential purchasing power. If the cash is in the form of demand deposits, it normally earns nothing and thus is wholly unproductive. (The exception is the NOW, or negotiated order of withdrawal, account, which is available only to individuals. This account pays interest while allowing checks to be drawn.) If cash is invested in marketable securities, it earns interest. For example, short-term corporate certificates of deposit (CDs) produced a yield ranging between 7 and 8 percent during 1985. But even this is probably considerably lower than the before-tax rate of return that a company earns on its operating assets. Thus, cash balances carry an opportunity cost. If cash is being held unnecessarily, the financial manager is not acting in the best interests of the stockholders.

Note also that, even if the company has exhausted the investment opportunities open to it, there is still no justification for holding large amounts of funds in the form of unproductive cash balances. The cash can be used to retire long-term debt, thereby reducing corporate interest expense. Or it can be used to increase the wealth of the common stockholders, either by repurchasing some of the company's common stock to increase earnings per share on the rest, or simply by issuing a cash dividend to stockholders. (Using the latter option, however, may expose stockholders to an incremental income tax, which could substantially consume the dividend.)

There is another cost of holding cash. During the 1970s, inflation became one of the major problems in the United States. It reached an annual rate of almost 20 percent. In this environment, funds tied up in idle cash balances are more than just unproductive—they are rapidly losing purchasing power. That is, there is a real cost, as well as an opportunity cost, to holding cash. In an inflationary environment, every effort must be made to keep idle cash balances at a minimum. The situation is analogous to running on a treadmill. As the speed of the treadmill increases, the jogger must run harder just to stay in place; so it is with high rates of inflation. Cash and marketable securities accounts must be managed more aggressively just to keep them from losing value.

The Costs of Cash Inadequacy

Unfortunately, there are also costs associated with having insufficient cash. The ultimate cost of serious cash inadequacy is obviously illiquidity, which could lead to insolvency, followed by reorganization or liquidation. But even a less serious cash shortage has a cost. A less serious cash shortage is one that is not a crisis but that makes the company slow in paying its bills.

The most obvious cost of a cash shortage is the cost of not being able to take advantage of suppliers' discounts by paying bills promptly. The terms on which a company buys materials and supplies are typically "2 percent, within 10 days; net within 30 days." This means that the company can deduct 2 percent from its bills if it pays them within 10 days of receiving them and that payment in full is due within 30 days. Now, 2 percent may not sound like very much. But the company is giving up 2 percent just for the privilege of paying its bills 20 days later (the difference between 10 days and 30 days). To realize what this privilege costs, we have to convert 2 percent to an annual rate. The annual rate is calculated as follows: 20 days is one-eighteenth of a year, so the true rate is 2 percent times 18, or 36 percent. In other words, by paying its bills 20 days later than the discount date, the company is in effect borrowing money at an annual interest rate of 36 percent.

The annualized cost of not taking a discount can be found by using the following formula:

$$\text{Annual cost of not taking a discount} = \frac{\%\,\text{Cash discount}}{100\% - \%\,\text{Cash discount}} \times \frac{365\,\text{Days}}{\text{Date for net payment} - \text{Date for discount payment}}$$

The following table shows the theoretical costs of slow payment as a function of postponing payment. The figures are calculated using terms of 2/10, net 30, and the number of days the funds are used is the net payment date minus the discount payment date. The theoretical cost is determined using the above formula.

Payment Date	Number of Days Funds Used	Theoretical Cost
30th day	20	36.7%
40th	30	24.5
50th	40	18.4
60th	50	14.7
70th	60	12.2
80th	70	10.5
90th	80	9.2

It may be argued that if a company is short of cash and is paying its bills late to stretch out its funds, then it will very probably not pay at the end of 30 days. The company will, in fact, pay as late as possible. If we assume that it pays suppliers' bills 60 days after receipt rather than 30, then by sacrificing the 2 percent discount, the company has gained 50 days of additional credit. This reduces the cost of forgoing discounts from 36 percent to about 15 percent. However, such a policy cannot be maintained indefinitely. It greatly harms the company's relations with its suppliers and possibly with the financial community as well. It should certainly be reserved for real emergencies.

This brings us to the other major cost of operating on inadequate cash balances: the danger of damaging the company's external relations with its suppliers, its commercial bank or banks, other lenders, and credit rating agencies. A company that consistently pays its bills late will eventually find that suppliers will allow only cash purchases, so an important source of short-term funds will have been lost. Similarly, a company that maintains very small balances in its demand deposits will be a very unprofitable customer for the banks, which may then be unwilling to help if a real emergency arises. In addition, a chronic shortage of cash will lower the company's credit rating, as determined by Dun & Bradstreet and other rating agencies. Many financial intermediaries, such as insurance companies, base their lending decisions on these credit ratings, and thus, yet another source of funds will have been lost.

Objectives and Techniques of Cash Management

Given that cash balances have a cost, anything that can be done to decrease these balances without increasing the risk of cash inadequacy will contribute to the profitability of the business and the wealth of its shareholders. In general, the objective of cash management is to speed up the inflows of cash and slow down the outflows. A number of techniques for using cash were discussed earlier in this section. The following discussion will highlight these techniques.

Float is the time delay between the moment when funds are disbursed by a buyer and the moment when the funds can be used by the seller. This delay between disbursement and receipt is caused by mail, processing, and clearing time. In other words, it is the amount of money that is tied up in the system, without any owner.

The expression that "time is money" applies particularly well to float. The cost of float can be calculated by the following formula:

$$\text{Cost of float} = \text{Amount of dollars in system} \times \text{Opportunity cost of funds} \times \text{Processing time (days)} \div 360$$

In this equation, the amount of dollars in the system can be determined by finding the difference between the firm's actual bank balance and the firm's cash book balance. The opportunity cost of funds can be approximated by the interest rates available in the money markets, and the processing time is the number of days from when the payment is first made until the firm's bank balance is actually reduced.

GNI, Inc., illustrates how a company can set up a system to reduce the cost of float. The company has three offices—headquarters in Atlanta and branch offices in New York and Los Angeles. GNI's daily sales volume is $2 million, and all sales are for credit. The average collection time (float) is anywhere from two to five days, depending on many external factors. If GNI uses a lockbox system to reduce the float, the collection of funds will be speeded up. The table below illustrates the reduction in float when a lockbox system is used.

Location	Daily sales volume	Average float to Atlanta	Total float*
Without lockbox			
Atlanta	$ 500,000	2	$1,000,000
New York	1,000,000	4	4,000,000
Los Angeles	500,000	5	2,500,000
	$2,000,000		$7,500,000
With lockboxes			
Atlanta	$ 500,000	1	$ 500,000
New York	1,000,000	2	2,000,000
Los Angeles	500,000	2	1,000,000
	$2,000,000		$3,500,000
		Reduction in float	$4,000,000

* Daily sales volume × average float

The reduction in float multiplied by the opportunity cost (GNI uses 10 percent) gives the potential savings of GNI's using lockboxes in New York and Los Angeles.

$$\$4,000,000 \times .10 = \$400,000$$

In general, any time the float can be reduced on funds coming into a company, the following formula can be used to evaluate the benefit of using a particular technique.

$$\text{Net benefit of technique} = \text{Reduction in float} \times \text{Opportunity cost} - \text{Cost of implementing the technique}$$

Determining the Cost of a Lockbox

The decision of whether or not to use a lockbox system depends on several key variables. These are:

1. Total annual dollar volume through the lockbox system (represented in the formula below as V).
2. The time in days saved on the average check—that is, the number of days currently required to collect a check less the number of days expected with the lockbox system (shown as T in the formula).
3. The interest rate on freed funds, usually the expected rate for marketable securities (i).
4. The number of items to be processed annually (N).
5. The handling cost per item charged by the bank (h).
6. The cost of a wire transfer from the lockbox bank to the company's main bank (W). This is usually sent each business day (or 260 times in a year).
7. The minimum balance, if any, required by the lockbox bank (M).
8. The fee for the lockbox system (f).

Using these variables, we can develop a formula for the savings or earnings from a lockbox system and another formula for the cost of such a system. The formula for the savings or earnings from a lockbox system, if compensating balances are used, is:

$$\text{Earnings} = \frac{V}{365} \times T \times i$$

If we use the following as an example,

V = annual volume = $30 million
T = time saved = 6 days
i = interest rate = 6%

these figures produce a total annual savings of $29,589.
  The formula for the cost of a lockbox system is:

$$\text{Cost} = N \times h + 260 \times W + M \times i$$

In our example, the corresponding figures for costs are:

N = number of items annually = 20,000
h = handling cost per item = $0.07
W = cost of wire transfer to central bank = $3.00
M = minimum balance required by lockbox bank = $300,000
i = interest rate = 6%

Using these figures, we can calculate that the total cost of the lockbox system in this example is $20,180. If a straight fee is charged for the lockbox system, we compare this fee to the cost under the compensating balance method and elect the lowest cost option. In our example, the flat fee for the system is $17,500 per year. Therefore, the manager would elect to pay the flat fee for the lockbox system. Therefore, since the lowest cost of the system is $17,500 per year and the benefits are $29,589 per year—that is, the benefits exceed the cost—it would be profitable to use a lockbox system in this case.

Zero Balance Accounts

Many firms with multiple divisions maintain numerous bank accounts so that each division can make disbursements to cover operating and other expenses. One technique that has been developed to minimize the cash balances held in numerous banks is the zero balance accounts. The term *zero balance* stems from the fact that the accounts are managed so that they have a zero balance most of the time.

A zero balance account system consists of various divisional checking accounts and a corporate checking account, all located in different banks. When deposits are made in a divisional account, funds are transferred periodically into the central corporate account, and the balance in the divisional account is reduced to zero. Conversely, when a division makes disbursements, the corporation instructs the bank to transfer a sufficient amount of funds from the corporate account into the divisional account in time to cover the checks when they are presented for payment.

The major advantage of a zero balance system is that the corporation maintains control over cash outflows while the divisions still have autonomy in making disbursements. This technique reduces the amount of cash the company has tied up in its checking account.

Negotiating Fees and Regional Balances with the Bank

Cash managers often use an account analysis to estimate the worth and cost of the cash management services the company receives from its bankers. In other words, an account analysis done by a cash manager estimates how profitable the company's account is to the bank. (Banks should do this, too, but many do not.) An account analysis shows the costs of all services rendered by the bank, the compensation received by the bank, and the net profit or loss to the bank. A typical account analysis that a bank uses is shown on page 46. You can use the same form to see if your company is a profitable customer of the bank. To do this, first estimate the amount the bank earned on the account during the month. Begin with the bank's average daily balance shown on its ledger and subtract the float (checks deposited but not yet cleared) using a two-day average float time and then subtract the reserve requirements (16.25 percent). This leaves the investable funds available to the bank. Then multiply the amount of investable funds by the bank's annual earning rate, which you can estimate as the prime rate. Divide the earnings by 12 to get the bank's total earnings for the month from the account.

Next, you must estimate the cost to the bank of the services it provided during the month. Estimate the cost of each check and deposit by examining how much the bank charges individuals with checking accounts. Find out the number of checks written and number of deposits made by looking at the company's monthly account statement. Estimate the cost of special services (such as credit reference checks or newsletters) at approximately the price charged by similar outside services.

Finally, income minus cost of services gives the profit (or loss) to the bank. If the account appears too profitable to the bank, you can safely reduce your company's average balance.

Cash managers find that many banks are willing to prepare this account analysis for company review. By understanding the source of each item in the account analysis, the cash manager can successfully negotiate a realistic minimum average cash balance for the company.

Account Analysis for ABC Corporation, August 1982

I. Demand deposit daily average: Ledger $87,840.00		Collected	$87,840.00
Less: Fed. Res. Bd. reserves @ 16.25%			14,274.00
Average daily funds available:			73,566.00
Earnings for month (73,566 X 12)			6,130.50
Credit @ 11.0% per annum			674.36

II. Banking Services Performed	Unit Price	Volume	Amount
A. Standard services:			
Deposits processed	$0.56	36	$ 20.16
Items deposited	0.05	3000	150.00
Checks paid	0.15	3	0.45
Drafts paid			
Wire transfers	5.00	10	50.00
Collection items			
Coupon envelopes entered for collection			
Bonds entered for collection			
Security drafts entered for collection			
Returned items			
Stop payments	4.00	3	12.00
Treasurer's checks			
Certified checks	1.50	2	3.00
Coin rolling			
Payroll preparation			
Statements rendered	4.00	1	4.00
Other			
Subtotal			
B. Individualized services:			
Lockbox			
Data transmission			
Account reconcilement			
Safekeeping			
Computer			
Commercial paper—agent			
Other			
Subtotal			
C. Investment and/or advisory services:			
Credit information			
Investment advice			
International			
Proxy			
Computer			
Other			
Subtotal			
Total services that have been priced			239.61
Account position as a result			$434.75

Summary

Most businesspeople have a preference for liquid assets, such as cash and short-term marketable securities, to meet their day-to-day disbursements. The form of this cash, be it in a demand deposit, a reduction in float, or an unused line of credit, has a cost. It is the job of the cash manager to select the source and form of cash for liquidity purposes that have the lowest cost. We've looked at some techniques for evaluating the cost of liquidity. The actual evaluation of costs is closely related to the individual situation and so it is hard to generalize a specific method. However, the account analysis is usually a very good starting point.

The evaluation of the objectives of cash management and the factors that affect cash management allowed us to gain a perspective of how our beliefs coincide with the cash managers of the Fortune 1,000 companies. It also served as an introduction to the various factors that are related to cash management and cash flow planning, which is the topic of the next section.

3.

Forecasting, Budgeting, and Planning

The Forecasting, Budgeting, and Planning Process

In this section, we will see how companies develop cash forecasts, then use them to prepare the cash budget. The budget allows the cash manager to identify specific problem areas and evaluate alternative solutions. Then the manager can formulate a cash plan that will meet any shortfalls.

Cash forecasting plays a critical role in the development of a firm's short-run financial plans. In times of stress, cash forecasts alert a manager to pending financial problems before they become serious. In normal periods, a cash forecast helps a manager determine the size and maturity of the working capital portfolio. It also helps minimize the amount of cash that must be held in balances.

Because the forecasting goals of companies differ significantly, a great variety of forecasting methods has been developed. Many firms feel most comfortable with methods that rely on the structure provided by a company's financial statements. These statements, such as the cash budget and pro forma income statement and balance sheets, are based on a sales forecast together with assumptions about inventory policy and accounts receivable policy. Other types of forecasting models rely on statistical relationships that are evaluated using regression methodology. A third approach to cash forecasting is the payments pattern method. This approach relates components of the cash flow to their sources. It then estimates the time it takes from when the funds originate at a source until they are available for corporate use. The cash budget is a good example of this approach. It can be done on a monthly, weekly, or even daily basis.

The cash flow budget provides the early warning signals that allow management to react and prepare for any shortfalls of cash or to make plans for investing any excess cash that may become available. Indeed, it is the focal point of the entire cash management effort.

The next step in our cash management sequence is planning; this is the way a company figures out how to adjust its cash balance to an optimum level. The two steps in cash planning are, first, determining an appropriate cash level and, second, deciding how to bring the company's cash balance to this level.

We will discuss each of these three integral steps of cash management in sequence: forecasting, budgeting, and planning.

FORECASTING

For a financial executive, the ability to forecast the future consistently is the keystone to success. Whether the forecaster uses informal gut feelings about what will happen in certain situations or sophisticated computer-based forecasting models, the bottom line is determined by whether future outcomes are consistently identified. In spite of the fact that perfect or even very high accuracy may not be possible when trying to forecast even short-term future events, a financial executive must still try for the most accurate forecasts possible. However, forecasting is, above all else, a matter of judgment. Therefore, even though models and techniques give seemingly concrete numbers, we must superimpose managerial expertise on these quantitative predictions to make them useful.

Once forecasts are generated, they must be used. Primarily, they are used as input to the planning process. The basic planning process consists of evaluating alternatives in light of the forecasts and selecting courses of action. Then subsequent performance must be evaluated in the context of the goals set forth in the plans. The control aspect of planning is very important—it serves as feedback to the forecaster and planner on how well they did. For our purposes, we will view the process as a three-step procedure—that is, forecasting leads to budget preparation, which, in turn, leads to planning. Each step in the process has a feedback loop that allows the user a chance to react to any new information.

Annual cash forecasts are an important part of a company's business plans. Companies occasionally carry out their planning without carefully considering cash needs. For example, a company planning a new product may fully analyze potential income and expenses but may neglect to allow for the increased cash needed for inventory, accounts receivable, and wages. A cash forecast will alert the company to the danger of a shortfall before it becomes a reality.

In addition to preventing the company's cash balance from falling below an acceptable minimum and predicting the availability of surplus cash for investment, cash forecasts serve several other purposes. First, a cash forecast helps the manager use cash efficiently. A cash manager who accurately forecasts cash balances can often use available cash to better advantage and avoid borrowing heavily one week and then having a surplus the following week. Second, an accurate cash forecast helps a manager predict seasonal needs for cash. Third, by knowing cash needs in advance, a cash manager can select the best combination of short-term and long-term loans that will minimize overall interest costs. Fourth, a cash forecast includes the schedule of large repayments, such as those for bank loans and bonds, so a cash manager can plan for maturing obligations.

An accurate cash forecast also helps a cash manager arrange loans and sales of stock to provide capital for expansion well in advance of need. The forecast helps to avoid borrowing money earlier than necessary.

Many suppliers offer cash discounts on bills paid promptly. A company that knows it will have surplus cash available can safely take advantage of these discounts. A company with surplus cash may also save money by buying materials and supplies on sale or in larger-than-normal quantities.

A cash forecast shows a company's ability to pay interest and therefore pinpoints the amount of debt the company can safely incur. And finally, cash forecasts help ensure that adequate cash will be available to pay dividends to stockholders.

Most companies prepare an annual cash forecast showing inflows and outflows for each month. Many cash managers also prepare shorter-range (one- to three-month) forecasts showing expectations for each week of the period. If cash balances are low or profit margins are narrow, a company may generate a cash forecast covering each day of the coming few weeks.

In general, the accuracy of cash forecasts decreases for either very long- or very short-term forecasts. The accuracy of long-term forecasts suffers because it is difficult to predict cash flows several months in the future. At the other extreme, the accuracy of daily cash forecasts suffers because random events cause the forecast to differ from actual events. For example, bad weather or a mail delay could slow down cash receipts for a day or two. Such problems would upset a daily cash forecast but would not affect a weekly or monthly forecast.

In spite of the reduced accuracy of short-term cash forecasts, they do offer additional information. For example, a forecast covering one month may show an adequate opening and closing cash balance on hand, but during the month, cash may drop to a dangerously low level.

If the company's cash flow is analyzed on a weekly basis, the timing of cash inflows and outflows during the month may cause trouble. Because cash must be disbursed near the beginning of the month and cash is not received until the end of the month, this company may run out of cash sometime during the beginning of the month. This firm clearly cannot use a cash forecasting interval longer than a week.

In determining the time period to be covered by a cash forecast, two factors should be considered: first, the purpose of the forecast and, second, the company's general business characteristics. For example, if the forecast is to be used to decide whether the company has adequate short-term credit lines from banks, a 12-month forecast divided into months would be the best choice. This is because bank loans are typically made for a few months at a time. If cash inflows and outflows are not closely coordinated, this forecast should be subdivided into weeks or should at least estimate midmonth cash needs. Another consideration in determining the time period to be covered by a cash forecast is planning how to invest surplus cash most efficiently. Because cash can be profitably invested for a few days at a time, a three-month forecast divided into weeks or even days might be chosen.

The characteristics of a company's business affect the time horizon of its cash forecast. For example, if a company's sales fluctuate widely and unpredictably, the company will be unable to forecast cash flow accurately for long time periods. This is also true for companies using raw materials that fluctuate a great deal in price. On the other hand, a firm with stable and predictable sales and costs can develop accurate cash forecasts for a year or more at a time. In practice, many companies develop cash forecasts that cover several time periods, depending on the ultimate use of the forecasts.

Later in this section, we will see in greater detail how significantly the choice of planning intervals can affect the usefulness of the cash flow plan as a tool for predicting fluctuations in a firm's cash balance.

Methods of Preparing Short-Term Forecasts

Cash managers use two basic methods in preparing short-term forecasts—first, the receipts and disbursements method and, second, the adjusted net income method. Many companies use both methods because each has particular advantages.

Using the receipts and disbursements method, a cash manager simply predicts how much cash the company will receive and how much it will pay out. For the time period being forecast, the cash manager estimates all cash inflows, such as collections of receivables, interest income, and sale of assets. The manager then estimates all cash outflows, such as payroll, supplier invoices, tax payments, and dividend payments. Companies use this method primarily for day-to-day control of cash for time horizons up to three months.

The exact items that appear under cash inflows and cash outflows, as well as the number of such items, vary considerably from one firm to the next. In general, a company lists its most important sources and uses of cash. If greater accuracy is required, the items are subdivided to provide more detail.

Having selected the items under cash inflow and cash outflow, the cash manager must then carefully forecast each item for the coming days, weeks, or months. In general, cash outflows are easier to estimate and control than cash inflows. A cash manager can usually estimate very accurately when and how much money will be required for payrolls, insurance, taxes, and dividends. On the other hand, cash inflows usually depend on another person's decision (to pay a bill, for example) and are therefore more difficult to estimate. This is especially true of estimating the timing of accounts receivable collections.

How does a cash manager estimate the sources of cash? Companies use several methods, depending on the accuracy required, the number of customer accounts, and the regularity of sales and collections. The simplest method is to look at the dollar amount of recent collections and adjust it for any known change in sales. For example, if you see that collections have been about $100,000 a month recently and you also know that sales were up 20 percent last month, you could roughly estimate this month's collection at $120,000.

Companies that keep track of the average number of days that their customers take to pay bills can use a more accurate approach. First, tabulate the percentage of customers paying within 30, 60, and 90 days. Suppose you find that 60 percent of your customers pay within 30 days, 30 percent pay within 60 days, and the remaining 10 percent pay within 90 days. With this information, you can estimate that collections for the current month will equal 60 percent of the last month's sales plus 30 percent of the previous month's sales and 10 percent of the sales in the month before that.

Companies with a small number of large customers cannot depend on the statistical method just described. In this case, the cash manager must examine the payment history of each individual account separately. For example, if a company has five very large customers and one of those customers begins to delay payments an additional 30 days, this will seriously impede the company's cash flow. On the other hand, if a company has thousands of customers and one begins to delay its payments, there is relatively little effect.

Cash managers in companies with large, decentralized operations usually depend on the local credit managers for forecasts of collections. Local credit managers have the best understanding of expected collections from the customers in their area. For example, John Smith, the local credit manager in Area A, may know that a strike of truck drivers has temporarily hurt business in his area and that customers will be slow in paying for a month or two. He may also know that one large customer, which normally pays in 30 days, stretches payments to 60 days during the winter season.

If a company has a very large number of customers, it is impossible to consider each customer on an individual basis. In such cases, companies divide receivables into categories such as regular large customer, regular small customer, new customer, government, and so on. Then for each major category, they develop collection estimates based on historical patterns. This simplifies the task of projecting receipts from many customers but still maintains reasonable accuracy.

When companies want to control cash flow very tightly, the cash manager may have to forecast collections on a daily basis. This is difficult but may be worth the effort if large amounts of money are involved. To project daily cash receipts, the cash manager must fully understand the company's daily billing pattern as well as the payment patterns of all important customers. For example, the cash manager would have to know that a certain large customer pays its bills on the fifteenth and thirtieth of every month and that these payments take two days to arrive by mail. Accurate forecasting of daily cash receipts is detailed and time-consuming work.

As mentioned earlier, a company has greater control over cash payments than cash receipts; therefore, forecasting payments is easier. The exact date and amount of cash payments for payroll, interest, taxes, and dividends can be predicted accurately. Cash payments to suppliers can be estimated by working from the sales forecast. The sales forecast implies a specific production schedule, which in turn, indicates needs for raw materials and supplies. You can then estimate when materials will be needed, when supplier invoices will be received, and when these invoices will have to be paid. If the company has a standard payment schedule, such as every Thursday or the fifteenth and thirtieth of every month, cash outflows for supplier invoices can be estimated accurately.

The next step is preparing a receipts and disbursements forecast. Many different formats can be used for preparing this forecast. All formats include the cash balance at the start of the period, estimated receipts, estimated disbursements, and finally, the balance at the end of the period.

The receipts and disbursements method of forecasting shows a company's expected cash transactions in detail, which helps the firm control cash inflows and outflows. The approach is flexible and can be used for daily, weekly, or monthly forecasts. Although this method is very accurate and complete for short time periods, it is subject to error when used for time periods longer than a few months. This is because the method focuses on cash transactions and not on longer-term changes in balance sheet items such as receivables.

In the receipts and disbursements method, cash transactions are usually projected on the basis of historical figures, and a slowly growing level of receivables and inventory may be overlooked. Therefore, for longer time periods, many cash managers prefer the adjusted net income method because this method concentrates on long-term changes in the level and composition of working capital.

The adjusted net income approach concentrates on changes in the company's balance sheet. Because it focuses on changes in the levels of company assets rather than on day-to-day cash transactions, this method automatically has a broader viewpoint than the receipts and disbursements method. A broader viewpoint makes the approach more useful for estimating general long-term cash needs but much less useful for companies facing day-to-day cash problems.

As with all cash forecasts, the adjusted net income approach has four main elements—the opening cash balance, sources of funds, applications of funds, and finally, the ending cash balance. The difference between the adjusted net income approach and other approaches is in the method used to calculate sources and applications of funds. There are three principal sources of funds.

First, net income after taxes or profit from operations is clearly a source of funds.

Second, depreciation is a noncash tax-deductible expense. In other words, it reduces taxable income but does not cause any change in cash flow itself. The fact that taxable income is reduced causes the amount of tax liability to be reduced. This, in turn, lessens the cash outflow associated with tax payments. The fact that the firm pays less in taxes is, in effect, a cash inflow because the firm has more cash available.

Third, any increase in a liability is a source of funds, but understanding this requires careful thought. For example, if a supplier ships raw materials to a company, the cost of these materials is deducted from sales and therefore lowers reported earnings. However, if the supplier's invoice is not paid (that is, if accounts payable rise), then the money that is owed the supplier is still available to the company. Thus, an increase in a liability increases the company's cash. Similarly, if tax liabilities rise, the company has continued use of the cash that it owes the government. Again, an increase in liabilities indicates more cash in the company. Finally, if another liability, short-term borrowings, increases, the company also gains cash. This explains the term *adjusted net income*. The source of cash is the company's net income adjusted for depreciation and increases in liabilities.

There are two principal applications of funds—dividends and increases in assets. Dividends are a cash distribution of profits to the owners of the corporation. Increases in assets include: (1) capital expenditures—cash spent for equipment, building, or real estate; (2) increases in accounts receivable—if customers pay slowly, additional cash is tied up; (3) increases in inventory—as inventory grows, the company loses cash; and (4) increases in other assets. If, for example, a company loans money to a subsidiary or makes a deposit on a future purchase, these increases in assets require cash.

The difficulty of forecasting each of these items varies considerably. Companies can usually estimate very accurately the cash needs for dividends, debt repayment, and most short-term to intermediate-term capital expenditures. Similarly, companies can closely forecast depreciation. By studying budgeted sales and costs, companies can fairly accurately estimate profits and the resulting tax liabilities. The level of accounts payable is closely related to company sales, and the company has some control over the rate at which it pays suppliers. The most difficult estimates concern changes in working capital accounts, primarily accounts receivable and inventory.

Companies use two basic methods for forecasting changes in working capital accounts. The first method is to calculate the ratio of the balance sheet item to sales. This method is usually adequate for companies with steady, nonseasonal sales patterns and no significant annual growth. A typical ratio, for example, might indicate that receivables at the end of each month are equal to 1.5 times sales for that month. The cash manager simply uses the company's sales budget to estimate changes in working capital requirements.

The second method of forecasting changes in balance sheet items is the direct estimate. Cash managers using this approach often begin with a ratio calculation, as just described, but then consider seasonal and historical patterns. For example, the cash manager may know that the ratio of receivables to monthly sales is usually 1.5, but he or she expects it to rise near Christmas. Frequently, the cash manager will also draw on knowledge of other departments (including production, purchasing, and credit) when making these estimates.

Cash managers often use another method to forecast cash. It is called the predetermined balance sheet method. Companies that prepare comprehensive budgets also prepare forecasts of balance sheets. Some firms may have an estimated balance sheet for the end of each month in the planning period. By comparing predicted balance sheets for successive months, the cash manager can determine the change in each element of working capital as well as in other items on the balance sheet. This approach is much simpler than the receipts and disbursements method for companies that prepare projected balance sheets, because most of the work is already done.

However, as in the case of the adjusted net income approach, this method does not forecast future cash receipts and expenditures individually. Therefore, it is not as useful for short-term cash forecasting and may not help a company having a very small cash balance that must monitor the cash position weekly or daily. Furthermore, if actual results differ from those projected on future balance sheets, new cash forecasts cannot be prepared until the balance sheet forecasts are revised.

A company with a strong cash management system uses a combination of these forecasting methods. For example, the financial manager might use the receipts and disbursements approach for three-month forecasts that are divided into weeks and perhaps days for the very near term. This enables the manager to control cash balances accurately and to invest any temporary cash surpluses profitably. For time horizons of 3 to 12 months, this manager would probably use the adjusted net income approach, subdivided into months. This forecast will help guarantee that credit lines are adequate.

Company treasurers are traditionally responsible for preparing cash forecasts. In strongly centralized companies, the treasurer's staff prepares the entire forecast. In decentralized or multi-industry companies, each division usually prepares its own forecast as part of the budgeting process. Then the treasurer combines the individual forecasts into a companywide forecast.

Just like budgets, cash forecasts must be tested. Short-term receipts and disbursements forecasts should be compared with actual cash records. Similarly, forecasts based on the adjusted net income approach should be compared with the company's balance sheets. Any significant differences should be reported back to the individuals who prepared the forecasts so the reasons for the differences can be determined.

Companies with strong cash management systems plan in advance by preparing a cash forecasting calendar each year. Such a calendar includes the milestones for the forecasting process—timing, instructions and responsibilities for each forecast, forecast review, and forecast revision.

A sample six-month cash flow forecast will be presented later in this sections, followed by a worksheet that can be used by the financial manager to forecast the cash flow of his or her own company.

BUDGETING

Now let's turn our attention to the cash budgeting part of the process. A cash budget shows the cash flow that is anticipated in the coming year if business is normal. However, this budget goes beyond the simple summation of the cash receipts and disbursements. It tries to indicate the actual timing of cash going into and out of the business. The precision of the budget depends on the characteristics of the company, coupled with the accuracy of the forecast that is used as a starting point.

Any cash budget begins with making a detailed list of assumptions concerning the forecasts on which the budget is based, as will be discussed further later in this section.

The financial manager then develops a forecast of receipts and disbursements. The sales forecast can be derived using any of the methods discussed. The cash budget recognizes the fact that the primary source of cash inflow for a company comes not from sales but from the collection of accounts receivable. In addition, a company may raise cash from external sources through short- and long-term financing or the sale of assets.

The collection experience of a company's accounts receivable is the starting point in estimating the cash flow from sales. If the business has made any changes in its credit terms or policy or if its customer base has changed, the cash manager must incorporate the impact of these changes when estimating cash receipts. Any variations from normal experience should be looked at very closely to get an appreciation for the impact that the change will have on the firm's cash flow.

Most cash outflows, or disbursements, can be classified into one of four types—payment for purchases of raw materials; payment for wages, rent, maintenance, and other operating expenses; payments to provide capital in the form of interest, principal repayment, and dividends; and finally, payments for taxes. Usually, a company has enough historical experience to forecast these cash outflows with a high degree of accuracy.

Of course, payments to provide capital are the most certain, because interest and debt repayment are contractual obligations, which must be met to avoid bankruptcy. Operating expenses may be related to the forecast level of sales and may vary somewhat with changes in expected revenues. However, remember that a certain portion of the operating cash outflow is fixed and is not related to revenues, so that if sales fall or do not reach expected levels, the change in disbursements usually will be less than the change in revenues. Note that depreciation and other noncash operating expenses do not appear in the cash budget, since they represent accrued expenses for which there is no cash outflow during the period.

PLANNING

The last step in preparing a cash budget is calculating the end-of-the-month cash balance—that is, interrelating the starting level of cash, the cash inflows, and the cash outflows to determine the amount of excess cash available or the cash deficit, which must be made up by borrowing. This surplus or deficit determines what sort of cash management plans will have to be formulated for the coming year.

This final step in the budgeting process is the most creative because cash managers try various strategies to meet cash shortfalls or invest cash surpluses. Of course, there is little concern from the cash managers' perspective if cash receipts exceed cash disbursements, resulting in excess funds that can be invested. However, if any monthly flow drops the ending cash level below some predetermined minimum, cash managers must act. They can meet the need by raising funds externally to make up the cash shortfall. Or they can change the amount of investment in inventory or the credit policy to reduce accounts receivable to meet the cash shortfall.

Experimenting with various alternatives allows the cash manager to present a convincing argument to the providers of short-term credit or to other company managers for a certain course of action. By anticipating problems before they become serious, a cash manager acts in a proactive fashion. As a result, he or she is in a much stronger position to manage the company effectively. Failure to foresee the possibility of deficits and reacting in a hasty fashion after they've actually occurred puts cash managers in a very defensive position and leaves them very little room for bargaining.

Most of the time, the cheapest and easiest solution to meeting a cash shortage will be to arrange a line of credit of sufficient size to meet the shortfall. The credit can be paid off from excess cash when it is available. However, the cash flow budget initiates other positive actions that can also eliminate a cash shortage without external financing. For example, a cash manager may convince the marketing department that reducing the level of accounts receivable through a more restrictive credit policy or a tighter collection policy may eliminate the need for external financing. In fact, this may well be the cheapest means of meeting a cash shortfall.

Similar logic applies to inventory level if marketing or production people can be convinced that sales volume can be sustained by a lower level of inventory. Lowering investment in inventories frees up cash. This cash can be used to meet a shortfall without external financing.

In certain cases, a company may find it cost-effective to finance a shortfall by extending or delaying payment of its disbursements. This strategy must be evaluated in light of the impact that slower payment will have on the firm's overall credit rating.

Another strategy is to reevaluate revenue targets and revise them downward. In other words, a company may find that it can avoid the need for external financing by lowering its sales targets. In some cases, reducing revenue growth becomes the best course of action to meet a cash flow problem.

In any case, whichever strategy a cash manager finally chooses, close coordination within the company and with short-term suppliers of funds must be maintained. The major contribution of a cash flow analysis is that a cash manager knows the extent, severity, and duration of the problem that must be solved.

To complete the transition from cash forecasts and cash budgets to cash plans, a manager must show how the daily, weekly, or monthly cash balance will be adjusted. Because marketable securities can be converted into cash quickly, it is customary to show cash and marketable securities together and then calculate the cash overage or shortfall.

Dividing a company's need for cash into cash needed for day-to-day transactions, reserve cash, and cash for a compensating balance simplifies the difficult problem of determining an appropriate cash level. For example, the required level of transaction cash obviously depends on the number and amount of anticipated transactions. The only definite requirement for this segment of a company's cash balance is that it be sufficient to cover the checks presented against it. Therefore, cash managers typically adopt a rule, such as maintaining a certain number of days of payables, for this segment.

To estimate the reserve of safety cash requirements, a cash manager may tabulate the daily change in the cash account. Daily changes range from large increases in cash to large decreases in cash, but most such changes will be small. Because the major problem is running out of cash, a cash manager is interested only in large decreases in cash. He or she might therefore select a reserve cash balance that would allow for all but the very largest cash decreases. Finally, the company needs to maintain any compensating balances required by the bank. The amount of a compensating balance is always specific. To determine the appropriate daily opening balance, a cash manager simply adds together the three types of cash needs. If the daily opening balance is significantly above this amount, then the excess cash can be used to purchase marketable securities. On the other hand, if the opening balance is substantially below the desired level, the company should sell marketable securities to bring the balance up to the desired level.

A cash manager can carry out the same type of analysis to determine a safe monthly opening balance. In this case, the manager will probably want to allow for larger cash reserves because, as we have seen, cash levels may vary significantly during a month. A level that is safe at the beginning of the month may not be safe in the middle of the month.

This final step in the cash management process involves not only creativity on the part of cash managers but also salesmanship. They must evaluate all the possible alternatives and reach a conclusion on the best course of action. Given that they have done an effective job in generating alternative courses of action and selecting the best one, they then must convince other company managers of the reasonableness and acceptability of their decisions. Or if they have decided to meet the problem by external borrowing, they must convince the bank that the company deserves the additional funding. Quite often this last step is the most difficult one in the entire process. The most accurate forecast coupled with the most carefully determined cash budget and plan will not be effective unless a cash manager can put these tools into action and achieve his or her objective.

Later in this section, we will see a sample "Cash Flow Plan," which provides a concrete illustration of how one financial manager dealt with cash shortfalls and excesses over a half-year period.

The Three Steps in Planning

Forecasting, budgeting, and planning are the basic parts of what has come to be called the corporate planning process. As a general rule, planning as broadly defined contributes to higher profits, improved decision making, and a reduction in the number of critical mistakes. The three-step process of planning involves making decisions and taking actions today that will affect the future of the firm. Because no one can predict the future with any consistent degree of accuracy, the planning process must be continuous and ongoing. The three steps of forecasting, budgeting, and planning must be constantly revised to fit each new situation based on the continual inflow of new information. Hence, this constantly changing environment makes for an unending task of constantly revising and reworking the plan.

Because the future changes so frequently, plans made at any one point in time should not be expected to work precisely as initially formulated. Plans should be amended to reflect new information about the firm's environment that will alter decisions. The key lesson to be learned by any planner is that there is grave danger in adhering to plans made in the past that are not consistent with a new environment. An environment can change yearly, quarterly, monthly, or even daily. Plans were never meant to be carved in granite; rather, they are flexible tools that allow management to evaluate and analyze a fluid situation.

The three-step procedure of forecasting, budgeting, and planning can be viewed as a set of building blocks that are mutually supporting. These three steps can be diagramed as below to illustrate the interrelated nature of the planning process.

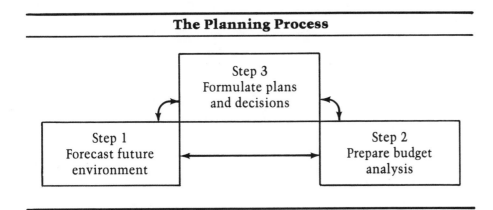

The Planning Process

Step 3
Formulate plans
and decisions

Step 1
Forecast future
environment

Step 2
Prepare budget
analysis

Given a forecast, usually a demand forecast of sales and a supply forecast of the factor costs, financial managers first perform a budget analysis and then prepare a plan of action reflecting their decisions. The preceding discussion and the remainder of this section concentrate on the preparation of the budget analysis and the budgeting process. Section 4 will present various cash management techniques that may be considered as alternative courses of action that can be formulated into the cash management plan. Even though we have artificially presented planning as a three-step process, it must be remembered that each step is being constantly revised in light of new information. This suggests that, rather than planning being a sequential process, the three steps are dealt with simultaneously.

Planning Periods

Cash flow planning is essentially short term. All of the assets that make up working capital are short term in that they will normally turn over several times a year. The purpose of cash flow planning is to identify temporary cash shortages or surpluses and to deal with them. Permanent or long-term funds are properly the subject of long-term financing or decisions about capital investment.

Few companies undertake cash flow planning for more than a year in advance. Sometimes it is advisable to plan for more than a year—for example, in the case of a construction company where projects require eighteen months or two years to complete. But for most manufacturing, trading, and service companies, one year is a long enough planning horizon, and six months or less may well be adequate for some companies.

Since cash flow planning is concerned with fluctuations in cash balances, the interval of time used for planning is a more important consideration than the length of the overall planning period. The most common interval is one month. That is to say, a financial manager forecasts cash inflows and outflows over one month and then calculates beginning and end-of-month balances. This procedure is repeated for each of the other eleven months of the year if the overall planning horizon is one year. Using one month as the time period has the advantage of coinciding with the accounting period of most companies and probably also with their official period for collecting receivables.

But many companies use a shorter interval of time, and some large companies forecast by the day. Why is such a short interval necessary? If the company forecasts by the month and shows adequate balances at the end of each month, isn't it a waste of time to use a shorter interval? That this is not true can be shown in a dramatic example. Suppose a company uses a planning interval of one month. Its cash flow plan for one month might look like the one below.

It would appear from the monthly cash flow plan that all is well. The company's cash balance will stay steady at $30,000. But will it? Suppose we break down this forecast into a weekly cash flow plan as is done on page 64.

Cash Flow Plan for One Month

Cash at start of month	$30,000
Cash Inflows	
Accounts receivable collections	$55,000
Royalty payment	25,000
Proceeds of sale of surplus fixed assets	15,000
Total cash inflows	$95,000
Cash Outflows	
Salaries and wages (net)	$24,000
Raw material purchases	19,500
Supplies	5,000
Miscellaneous expenses	10,000
Rent	4,000
Income tax payment	25,000
Payroll taxes	7,500
Total cash outflows	$95,000
Cash at end of month	$30,000

The Same Cash Flow Plan by the Week

	Week 1	Week 2	Week 3	Week 4
Cash at start of week	$30,000	($ 2,250)	($ 9,500)	($ 2,250)
Cash Inflows				
Accounts receivable collections	$12,000	$15,000	$11,000	$17,000
Royalty payment				25,000
Proceeds of sale of surplus fixed assets			10,000	5,000
Total cash inflows	$12,000	$15,000	$21,000	$47,000
Cash Outflows				
Salaries and wages (net)	$ 6,000	$ 6,000	$ 6,000	$ 6,000
Raw material purchases	5,500	5,000	4,000	5,000
Supplies	1,250	1,250	1,250	1,250
Miscellaneous expenses	2,500	2,500	2,500	2,500
Rent	4,000			
Income tax payment	25,000			
Payroll taxes		7,500		
Total cash outflows	$44,250	$22,250	$13,750	$14,750
Cash at end of week	($ 2,250)	($ 9,500)	($ 2,250)	$30,000

As you can see, although the monthly cash flow forecast looks fine, the weekly forecast shows that the company will be in considerable trouble before the first week is over. This company would do well to choose a planning period no longer than one week and possibly shorter.

Other Factors That Affect the Planning Interval

There are several additional factors that should be taken into consideration when deciding on the length of the planning interval. These are:

- Inflation rates and opportunity costs.
- Size of cash flows.
- Executive time available for cash flow planning and cash management.
- Predictability of the size of cash flows.
- Predictability of the timing of inflows and outflows.
- Size of cash balances.

INFLATION RATES AND OPPORTUNITY COSTS

When inflation rates are at record high levels, the necessity for actively managing the company's cash position is obvious. When inflation rates decline, the need for active cash management is still there, although the costs and returns aren't as dramatic. Not only is it very expensive to borrow short-term funds, but there also may be periods when no funds are available at any price. A corporation that has not secured a commitment in advance will be unable to meet its cash requirements. Excess cash must be invested as soon as it becomes available, so as to avoid the erosion in purchasing power. Preparing a cash budget also allows the financial manager to see the impact of various decisions on speeding up or slowing down cash flows.

SIZE OF CASH FLOWS

Companies that plan their cash by the day usually have very large cash flows over short intervals. For example, $1 million invested at 12 percent for one day yields $328.75—a sum that makes it well worth one person's time to plan and invest cash daily. In contrast, $10,000 at 12 percent for one day yields less than $3.28. Thus, a company whose day-to-day cash balances do not fluctuate much more than this could hardly justify the management time required for daily cash planning.

EXECUTIVE TIME

Executive time is one of the scarcest resources of most companies. Thus, it may be that even if the time spent on daily cash flow planning would earn a return greater than the salary of the person who does it, that person's time might still be spent more productively in doing other work. Such a situation dictates a longer planning interval.

PREDICTABILITY OF THE SIZE OF CASH FLOWS

Usually, the size of cash inflows and outflows is much more predictable than their timing. But when it is not, unexpectedly small inflows combined with unexpectedly large outflows could create a serious cash shortage over a short time. This possibility must be avoided, either by carrying large balances to provide a safety margin or by maintaining a very short planning interval and a continuous watch on how actual events are conforming to plan. Which alternative is adopted will depend on the size of the balances needed and the management time available for short-interval cash planning.

It is often impossible to predict with accuracy the timing of cash flows, particularly cash inflows. For example, if cash inflows are received through the mail, they may arrive a day earlier or a day later than expected. Usually, because it is impossible to know exactly when a creditor will mail a check, the timing is much more uncertain than this. It may vary by several days or even by several weeks. Under these circumstances, daily cash flow plans are subject to error and may be no more useful than weekly or monthly forecasts.

PREDICTABILITY OF THE TIMING OF CASH FLOWS

From the point of view of avoiding insolvency, the size of cash balances in relation to cash flow has a bearing on the planning interval. If cash balances are large, temporary variations within a long planning interval such as a month are unlikely to place a company in jeopardy. But if a company is operating on inadequate balances, a strong net cash outflow over only a few days may bring balances down to dangerously low levels. In such circumstances, a short planning interval is necessary for survival, even if it could not be economically justified on any other grounds. For this reason, a company that normally uses a planning interval of one month may switch to weekly planning when its cash balances are dangerously low.

SIZE OF CASH BALANCES

Forecasting

Once the planning horizon and planning interval have been determined, the forecasting can begin. The first step is to forecast expected cash receipts during each planning interval. Sales receipts are normally based on the sales forecast and experience of the pattern of receivables collections. Other receipts, such as those from the sale of fixed assets, royalty incomes, and investment income, can also be predicted with a fair degree of accuracy. Later in this section we will discuss a technique that can be used when receipts are more uncertain. Meanwhile, it is sufficient to note that where there is doubt as to the size of the timing of receipts, the planner should forecast conservatively. Receipts higher than the forecasts may result in cash that might otherwise have been invested profitably; but receipts lower than expected may expose the company to illiquidity, which is far more serious.

In the following example of a six-month cash flow forecast done by the month (see page 69), the upper part, "Cash Inflows," illustrates the first step of planning cash flow.

Six-Month Cash Flow Forecast

	January	February	March	April	May	June
Cash first of month	$19,680	($10,020)	($ 1,820)	$13,180	$22,230	$13,670
Cash Inflows						
Sales receipts	$55,000	$57,000	$69,000	$61,000	$64,000	$65,000
Insurance claim					7,000	
Royalties on patent	4,000			3,500		
Total cash inflows	$59,000	$57,000	$69,000	$64,500	$71,000	$65,000
Cash Outflows						
Labor payroll	$23,000	$23,500	$24,000	$24,500	$31,000	$25,200
Salaries	4,800	4,800	4,800	5,600	5,600	5,600
Raw materials payments	31,000	15,500	18,250	11,650	28,760	15,625
Payments for supplies	2,400	1,800	2,000	2,000	2,000	2,000
Insurance			750			
Lease payments	1,000	1,000	1,500	1,000	1,000	1,500
Marketing expenses	500	500	1,500	500	500	500
Miscellaneous expenses	1,000	1,200	1,200	1,200	1,200	1,200
Dividends	18,000					
Income taxes	7,000			9,000		
Professional fees		500			4,000	
New production equipment					5,500	
Total cash outflows	$88,700	$48,800	$54,000	$55,450	$79,560	$51,625
Cash end of month	($10,020)	($ 1,820)	$13,180	$22,230	$13,670	$27,045

The next step is to forecast cash disbursements. Here planners again lean on past experience—what cash outlays are normally needed to maintain a given level of sales and so on? But they also need the help of their fellow executives. For example, if the purchasing department believes that commodity prices may soon be going up and plans to pick up several months' supply of raw material in the near future, the planner must know about it. If the marketing department is planning a major, expensive advertising campaign, the financial manager must be aware of the estimated cost and timing. Normally the financial manager will find most of this information in the profit budget or in later modifications of the budget, but this will not always be true. Every executive with the authority to commit large sums of money must be fully aware of his or her responsibility to keep the financial manager informed of future plans. The sample monthly cash flow forecast shows estimated cash outflows that should be included.

Once cash inflows and disbursements have been forecast, the planner can forecast cash balances at the end of each planning period. The results appear as the top and bottom lines of the six-month cash flow forecast.

The worksheet on page 71 may be useful in gathering the required information and estimated figures necessary to accomplish the first stage of the planning process, forecasting. Beside each entry the department or executive is noted from whom the appropriate information may be obtained. As you prepare a worksheet for your own firm, these suggestions will serve as starting points for gathering the information you will need.

Forecasting Worksheet for Cash Flow

Months Covered by Forecast		
Cash first of month	(Treasurer)	_____
Cash Inflows		
Sales receipts	(Billing & Collection)	_____
Income from investments	(Treasurer)	_____
Insurance claim	(Treasurer or legal staff)	_____
Royalties on patent	(Treasurer)	_____
Total cash inflows		_____
Cash Outflows		
Labor payroll	(Payroll department)	_____
Salaries	(Payroll department)	_____
Raw materials payments	(Disbursements or Inventory Control)	_____
Payments for supplies	(Disbursements)	_____
Insurance	(Treasurer or Controller)	_____
Loan payments	(Treasurer or Controller)	_____
Marketing Expenses	(Disbursements or Marketing)	_____
Miscellaneous expenses	(Disbursements)	_____
Dividends	(Treasurer or Controller)	_____
Income taxes	(Treasurer or Accounting)	_____
Professional fees	(Disbursements)	_____
New production equipment	(Treasurer or Controller)	_____
Total cash outflows		_____
Cash end of month		_____

As you begin to gather this information, you may get the impression that there is no one person who knows exactly what's going to happen. This is not surprising since we've already indicated that forecasting the future is a very difficult proposition. To overcome individuals' resistance to being pinned down to a single number forecast, it is a good idea to seek the information in terms of ranges of expected outcomes. The types of questions below can be very helpful when gathering information for a cash forecast. These questions are based on expected ranges, comparisons with the recent past, and personal experience.

1. What is your best guess about the level of _____ if we were to have a really bad quarter?
2. What is your best guess about the level of _____ if everything were to go as expected?
3. What is your most likely estimate of _____?
4. Given our normal growth, what would you expect to happen to the level of _____?
5. Given our current growth experience, what would you expect to happen to the level of _____?
6. Given top management's target growth, what would you expect to happen to the level of _____?
7. What do you think will happen to _____? Why do you think this will occur?

Once the information has been gathered, it must then be sorted into categories. For the sake of simplicity, we normally use three classifications—best case, most likely case, and worst case. By selecting a range of outcomes, three budgets, one for each category, can be prepared and the range of cash needs can be determined. In order to be useful, the extent of the range may have to be narrowed, as it is not very useful to talk about cash needs ranging from $1 to $10 million. This part of the planning process is usually the most difficult, but it also is the most informative and most important in terms of the final decision. Before moving to the more mechanical aspects of the process, you must be convinced that you have reasonable estimates upon which you can base your budget and plan.

Budgeting

The first step in preparing a cash budget is to make a detailed list of assumptions concerning the forecasts of inflows and outflows for the budget period. For example, some of the more common assumptions are:

1. Sales for the first six months will be 5 percent over similar months last year.
2. Credit sales are 90 percent of sales volume.
3. Of the credit sales, 90 percent are collected within 30 days; the remaining 10 percent are collected in the next month.
4. A pending insurance claim will be settled, and the funds will be received in May.
5. Quarterly royalty payments will occur during the first month of each quarter.
6. The labor payroll will be 5 percent higher than last year, reflecting the new union contract.
7. Salaries will be the same as last year for the individual months.
8. A large buildup of raw materials will be paid for in January; the remaining months will reflect expected sales levels.
9. Supplies will be the same as last year.
10. Insurance premiums in the first quarter will be paid in March.
11. Lease payments will reflect the new leases signed in December.
12. Marketing expenses will be 15 percent over last year.
13. Miscellaneous expenses will decrease by 3 percent over last year.
14. A dividend payable in January has been declared by the board of directors.
15. Estimated quarterly income tax is based on last quarter's results.
16. Professional fees will be as per memo No. 17 from treasurer's office.
17. Capital budget for this year indicates expenditure for May.
18. Maintain a minimum cash balance of $7,500.

The second step in the preparation of a budget is to develop the schedule of receipts and disbursements for at least the three scenarios of best, most likely, and worst cases. The figures are then put on the schedule. The magnitude of the numbers is very sensitive to the assumptions, and any figures that are out of line or don't seem right should be reevaluated to ensure that the forecasted figures and assumptions make sense.

The final step in the preparation of a cash budget is to calculate the end-of-the-month cash balance. This figure, which shows cash surpluses or deficits, is the main reason for going through the budget preparation process. The figure is used primarily to assist management in planning financial needs for the period. The cash budget serves a number of different purposes. It can be used as a starting point of the cash planning process. It can act as a standard of behavior against which the performance of company managers can be evaluated. It can serve as a control mechanism in that any deviations from the standard can be isolated and corrective action can be taken if needed. The final purpose of the cash budget is that it can be used as the starting point in "what if" or sensitivity analysis. For example, if revenues grow at a rate different than assumed, how will this affect the amount of funds required?

Planning

At this point, we have a cash flow budget, not a plan. Planning is the mental process of visualizing a set of events that the financial planner is determined to make happen in the future. It is not just a summary of what the planner expects to happen. But at this stage, planning can begin. Some of the cash balances at the end of each planning interval may be higher than needed; others may be too low or even negative. Financial planners first determine how to invest any excess cash in order to earn the maximum return on it. This decision, of course, depends on the amount and the length of time for which the excess will be available. Next, planners decide how to cover temporary shortages of cash exposed by the forecast. We will discuss various means of doing this in detail in the next section, but it should be pointed out here that the methods are not limited to short-term borrowing. Delaying purchases or payments until a later period, deciding to reduce or eliminate certain expenditures, selling marketable securities or other assets, accelerating collections, and so on are all possibilities to be considered.

The results of this kind of planning are shown in "The Cash Flow Plan." This plan is based on the "Six-Month Cash Flow Forecast" on page 69. The financial executive has decided to finance the cash shortage forecast in January by a $20,000 short-term bank loan with a yearly interest rate of 18 percent, which will be paid off in two equal installments in February and March. (The $19,400 actually received from the bank represents the loan less interest deducted in advance. This is known as a discounted loan). By March, the company has spare cash, which it can invest in short-term, interest-yielding securities—$5,000 in each of three months, March, April, and June.

However, this will cause cash to drop to a low in May—$8,070 by the end of the month. Instead of investing less in April or borrowing again from the bank, the planner has decided that paying some May bills can be deferred until June—$3,000 in professional fees and $2,000 for raw materials.

Cash Flow Plan

	January	February	March	April	May	June
Cash first of month	$19,680	$ 9,380	$ 7,580	$ 7,580	$11,630	$ 8,070
Cash Inflows						
Sales receipts	$55,000	$57,000	$69,000	$61,000	$64,000	$65,000
Insurance claim					7,000	
Royalties on patent	4,000			3,500		
Short-term bank loan	19,400					
Total cash inflows	$78,400	$57,000	$69,000	$64,500	$71,000	$65,000
Cash Outflows						
Labor payroll	$23,000	$23,500	$24,000	$24,500	$31,000	$25,200
Salaries	4,800	4,800	4,800	5,600	5,600	5,600
Raw materials payments	31,000	15,500	18,250	11,650	26,760	17,625
Payments for supplies	2,400	1,800	2,000	2,000	2,000	2,000
Insurance			750			
Lease payments	1,000	1,000	1,500	1,000	1,000	1,500
Marketing expenses	500	500	1,500	500	500	500
Miscellaneous expenses	1,000	1,200	1,200	1,200	1,200	1,200
Dividends	18,000					
Income taxes	7,000			9,000		
Professional fees		500			1,000	3,000
New production equipment					5,500	
Bank loan repayments		10,000	10,000			
Purchase of marketable securities			5,000	5,000		5,000
Total cash outflows	$88,700	$58,800	$69,000	$60,450	$74,560	$61,625
Cash end of month	$ 9,380	$ 7,580	$ 7,580	$11,630	$ 8,070	$11,445

Thus, once the financial manager has determined how to invest excess cash and how to cover cash shortages, he or she incorporates the results of these decisions into the cash flow forecast, which now becomes a plan. The planner's remaining responsibility is to ensure, insofar as is possible, that this plan is put into effect and is mirrored by actual results.

The accuracy of the forecasts that are used in preparing the cash flow plan is of critical importance if the plan is to be a useful tool. The less reliable the forecasts or the more uncertain the financial manager is about the unexpected events that may affect the cash flows, the larger the cash balances, lines of credit, or a combination of both that are required. GIGO (garbage in, garbage out) is an appropriate acronym in this case. If the planner does not have much confidence in the forecasts, the resulting plan will be of little value to the organization.

Summary

We use the three-step approach to financial planning because we are unable to consistently forecast future events. Although most financial mangers have excellent hindsight and it is worthwhile to learn from past mistakes, very few individuals know what is going to happen in the future. For this reason, the initial step of the planning process is concerned with making educated guesses about the future cash flows. The budgeting and planning steps are then performed with the idea in mind: Does this plan make sense in light of my own experience or does this plan make sense relative to what I expect will happen during the next year?

All during the planning process, there is a feedback situation present that enables the analyst to update the forecast in light of new information or a new view of the situation, which may be gained from actually preparing the budget. The analyst must understand that the planning process itself is the most important aspect of the entire exercise. The final plan is not definitive because it only serves as a guide to future behavior and is continually subject to revision.

The Case Study
Part One

The Case Study: Part One

Instructions: This case study consists of three parts. Each part has its own set of questions that you should answer as thoroughly as you can. Part Two of the case study continues on page 113, and Part Three continues on page 167.

SAN LARGO ORANGE BLOSSOM, INC.

ASSIGNMENT

The objective of this part of the case study is to allow the reader the opportunity to perform the first two steps of the planning process. After you have read this part of the case study, answer the following questions:

1. *List all of the relevant assumptions you would use in preparing the cash flow forecast. Indicate whether you think they are best case, pessimistic, or most likely.*
2. *Based on the forecast and the most likely assumptions, prepare a monthly cash budget for 1986. At this point in the case, you are not required to prepare a cash plan, however, you can start thinking about the various courses of action that you might consider.*

THE SETTING

San Largo Orange Blossom, Inc. processes and distributes frozen orange juice and other citrus products. The company owns a few groves, but most of the oranges it uses are supplied by independent growers under long-term contracts, often negotiated through local growers' co-ops.

The firm's main operations are located in Appalachalossa, Florida. The company has been in business since 1947 and is a highly profitable operation for its owners and founders, Fred and Bill Grant. Last year, both Fred and Bill decided to step down from the active operational management of the firm. This move promoted Jim Billingsley to the position of general manager of operations in both title and fact. For the last ten years, Jim has been the main force behind the smooth operation of the production and distribution segment of the business. Tim Michaels, who has been with the company for 25 years, was promoted to vice-president of personnel and administration and now handles all labor and raw material negotiations. He has done an excellent job in his new position.

Since Fred and Bill had formerly handled all of the accounting and financial aspects of the firm, there wasn't anyone groomed to step in and take over this aspect of the operation. Last year Pamela Pompallmousse, a recent MBA graduate, was hired and is doing a creditable job so far. When she was hired, Fred Grant made it clear to her that he expected the firm's finances to continue to be tightly controlled. Fred believes this is one of the main reasons for the company's success and durability. Over the years, he had handled all of the finances, and most of the procedures were well established in his head. This allowed for greater flexibility in responding to what Fred liked to call the annual cash crises.

In late December 1985, Pamela is in the process of establishing a formalized cash budgeting system. Although San Largo has consistently experienced good growth and profit making ability over the years, it always has been faced with a considerable number of cash flow problems as a result of its highly seasonal purchasing and sales pattern. During her first year, the cash flow problem had forced postponement of some bargain purchases of an unexpected bumper crop and also some badly needed new equipment, which impacted quite dramatically on the production process. Nothing like this had ever happened before and the Grants were quite upset because they had to pledge some personal assets in order to bail out the firm.

Pamela has collected reams of information, ranging from the actual cash flow for last year to estimates of next year's level of demand and operations. She has organized and assembled this information into two categories, outflows and inflows. The historical figures for 1985 and the estimated figures for 1986 are presented on the following pages. Pam is currently in the process of combining this information into a monthly cash budget for January through December 1986. She estimates that the sales figure for the current month will be $3M. As Pam mulls over all of this information, she decides to prepare a list of critical assumptions associated with the budget that will put the numbers in perspective. Then she will draw up the actual budget.

San Largo's Actual Figures—January-December 1985 (Dollars in Millions)

	Jan.	Feb.	Mar.	Apr.	May	June	July	Aug.	Sept.	Oct.	Nov.	Dec.
Cash Inflows												
Bank deposits	$3.0	$15.0	$17.0	$19.0	$2.0	$1.0	$0.5	$0.5	$0.5	$1.5	$1.0	$2.0
Bank loan from First Appalachalossa Bank (guaranteed by Fred and Bill Grant)	—	—	—	—	—	—	—	—	4.0	—	—	—
Sale of stock to Grants	—	—	—	—	—	—	—	—	—	1.5	—	—
Total cash inflows	$3.0	$15.0	$17.0	$19.0	$2.0	$1.0	$0.5	$0.5	$4.5	$3.0	$1.0	$2.0
Cash Outflows												
Salaries (first year of 3-yr. contract)	$1.5	$1.5	$1.5	$1.5	$1.5	$1.5	$1.5	$1.5	$1.5	$1.5	$1.5	$1.5
Raw materials purchases (third year of 10-yr. contract with Appalachalossa Co-op)	3.0	1.5	—	—	—	—	—	—	—	4.5	4.5	4.5
Raw materials purchases (open market)	—	—	—	—	—	—	—	—	—	—	5.0	—
Utilities	0.5	0.5	0.5	0.5	0.5	0.5	0.5	0.5	0.5	0.5	0.5	0.5
Marketing expenses	0.2	0.3	0.1	0.1	0.1	0.2	0.1	0.1	0.6	0.6	0.5	0.2
Miscellaneous	—	—	0.1	0.1	—	—	0.1	—	0.3	0.1	—	0.1
Interest payments	—	—	—	1.2	—	—	—	—	0.1	—	—	—
Loan repayment	1.5	—	—	1.5	—	—	1.5	—	—	1.5	—	—
Taxes	—	—	1.5	—	—	1.5	—	—	0.5	—	—	0.5
Dividends	—	—	—	—	—	—	—	—	—	—	—	—
Total cash outflows	$6.7	$3.8	$3.7	$4.8	$2.1	$3.7	$3.6	$2.1	$3.5	$8.7	$12.0	$7.3

San Largo's Estimated Figures—January-December 1986 (Dollars in Millions)

Estimated end-of-year cash balance (December 31, 1985)—$300,000

	Jan.	Feb.	Mar.	Apr.	May	June	July	Aug.	Sept.	Oct.	Nov.	Dec.
Sales (estimated 15% growth)	$18.0	$19.0	$22.0	$3.0	$1.0	$0.5	$0.5	$0.5	$2.0	$3.0	$3.0	$3.0
Salaries (second year of contract calls for 10% increase across the board)	1.65	1.65	1.65	1.65	1.65	1.65	1.65	1.65	1.65	1.65	1.65	1.65
Raw materials purchases (contract price 5% below current market in month of purchase)	3.3	1.65	—	—	—	—	—	—	—	6.0	6.0	6.0

Utilities: Billingsley expects a 10% increase to be on safe side.

Marketing expense: Mr. Grant wants to hold the line on marketing expenses in 1986.

Miscellaneous: Management agrees this should be about the same as 1985.

New equipment: New concentrator, costing $2M, must be paid for in July and August. Billingsley anticipates no problems with installation—therefore, pay half in July and half in August.

Interest payments: Mr. Grant insists that the personally guaranteed loan from First Appalachalossa be paid off in first quarter of 1986. It is to be used only for emergencies.

Taxes: Pam anticipates a profitable 1986 and estimates quarterly taxes at approximately $2M.

Dividends: The Grants want to return dividend payments to at least $1.5M per quarter and would not be adverse to raising them to $2M.

Minimum cash balance: Pam wants to allow a very conservative minimum cash balance to improve relations with First Appalachalossa—$500,000 minimum.

Materials to Complete the Case Study, Part One

Use the following forms to complete this part of the case study.

Assumptions You Would Make When Preparing the Cash Flow Forecast

---

Instructions: Next to each assumption, note whether it is the best case (B), a pessimistic case (P), or the most likely case (L).

_____

_____

_____

_____

_____

_____

_____

_____

_____

_____

_____

_____

_____

_____

San Largo's Most Likely Cash Flow Budget—January-December 1986 (Dollars in Millions)

	Jan.	Feb.	Mar.	Apr.	May	June	July	Aug.	Sept.	Oct.	Nov.	Dec.
Cash Inflows												
Sales												
Collections												
Total cash inflows												
Cash Outflows												
Salaries												
Purchases												
Utilities												
Marketing expenses												
Miscellaneous												
New equipment												
Interest												
Loan repayment												
Taxes												
Dividends												
Total cash outflows												
Beginning cash balance												
Net cash flow												
Ending cash balance												
Minimum cash balance												

4.

Cash Management Techniques

Maximizing Cash: Basic Management Techniques

In this section, we will discuss how companies maximize cash levels by speeding up cash gathering and slowing down cash disbursement. We will also see how companies maximize the use of funds by playing the float and temporarily investing committed funds. Finally, we will discuss some of the basic techniques companies use to control their cash.

TECHNIQUES FOR SPEEDING UP CASH GATHERING

Cash mobilization means freeing up unused or underused corporate cash. Cash gathering involves the complete sequence of steps taken in order to receive usable cash from customers. Usable cash refers to money the company can spend. Simply receiving a check from a customer does not create usable cash because this check must be deposited in the company's checking account and must usually be cleared by the customer's bank.

A cash manager has many opportunities to speed up cash gathering during the billing and receiving operation. Each of the steps in this operation should be examined individually to see if it can be eliminated or done more quickly and efficiently. The eight steps are: company prepares bill, company mails bill, customer receives bill, customer reviews bill and mails check, check arrives at company, company reviews check and deposits it, check clears through customer's bank account, and finally, cash is available for company use.

By reviewing this detailed list of collection steps, we can see where bottlenecks occur and decide what to do about them.

Get Bills to Customers Faster

Beginning with the first step, an obvious way to accelerate cash inflow is to get the bills to the customers faster. For example, if Company A bills monthly with 30-day credit terms, its customers will begin counting the 30 days upon receipt of the bill. Suppose Company A converts to twice-monthly billing. Now, customers who still comply with the 30-day credit terms will send checks sooner. Company A might also change to weekly billing or even to billing for each order. In this case, Company A could even include the invoice with the shipped materials, eliminating any delay between receipt of goods and receipt of bill by the customer.

Shorten the Billing Cycle

A shorter billing cycle is an attractive way to speed up cash inflow. But not all companies can reduce their billing cycles. There are several reasons for this. First, the faster cash inflow may not justify the paperwork involved in preparing bills more often. Second, customers who are used to monthly billing may ignore bills received in the middle of the month and therefore not pay any faster. Third, credit is a competitive marketing tool, and competition may not allow a shorter billing cycle (which effectively reduces credit). In addition, the small dollar value of each transaction may not justify more frequent billing. And finally, the nature of the business (particularly service businesses) may not logically lend itself to billing more often than once a month.

Speed Billing Information to the Accounting Department

Even companies that only bill monthly find it worthwhile to make sure that billing information flows quickly to the accounting department. For example, if billing information typically takes three days to travel to accounting, then when bills are prepared at the end of the month, the last three days of sales for the month will not be billed until the following month. By reducing the time for billing information to flow to accounting by two days, this company can add two extra days of billing to each month's invoices.

Encourage Quick Payment

Of all the steps in collecting money from customers, the company has least control over when the customer reviews the bill and mails the check. However, a company can take several actions to encourage customers to pay quickly. The first is to submit an accurate and easy-to-understand bill. Accuracy is important because if a customer finds an error, valuable time is lost while the error is corrected. Bills should be easy to understand so they can be processed quickly. Complicated bills cause misunderstandings, which take just as much time to correct as actual errors, or delays in processing.

The promptness of customer payments is also affected by the terms a company offers. A cash discount of 1 or 2 percent for payment within 10 days encourages many customers to pay quickly. Before a firm offers a cash discount, several things must be considered: first, the average time customers will take to pay with no discount (this is usually not 30 days but, more typically, 40 or 50 days); second, the speed with which customers will pay 10-day-discount invoices; third, the percentage of customers who will take advantage of a discount; and finally, the benefit of having extra cash compared to the cost of the discount.

Instead of offering a discount for prompt payment, some companies charge a penalty for late payment. This is typically 1.5 percent interest per month on the unpaid balance. This charge is most commonly used with consumer accounts and only occasionally with business accounts. Charging interest is subject to strict federal and state laws that vary widely from one state to another. When used with business accounts, late-payment penalties may cause ill will and can be difficult to collect.

Collections can also be speeded up by making it easier for customers to pay. A common technique is to enclose a preaddressed envelope or even a postage-paid envelope. Companies use this technique more often with consumer accounts, but in any case, it should be tested carefully to make sure that the faster collections more than pay the extra cost of envelopes and postage.

Use Local Collection

The simplest way of receiving payments is to instruct customers to send their check to company headquarters. The accounting office then compares the check with the original invoice and deposits it. But this procedure requires time for the check to arrive in the mail, for the accounting office to review and deposit the check, and for the check to clear the customer's bank.

If customers are scattered throughout the country, checks may take many days to arrive at company headquarters. During this time, the money is not available for company use. To speed up collections, companies decentralize their receivables collection procedures and collect customer checks at several places around the country. This significantly reduces the mailing time of customer checks.

The most commonly used collection centers are branch locations in various cities. The branch office deposits checks to a local bank. Because the bank is nearby, checks clear quickly and the money is then available for company use.

In many companies, local bank balances build up and are then forwarded to the disbursing account at headquarters. This system has several disadvantages. First, the local branch office may not be in the best location for fast funds transfers. The branch office may be close to customers, but it may not be in a Federal Reserve city. This slows down the transfer of funds to headquarters. Second, any delay in processing customer checks in the branch office will slow down the movement of funds to the home office.

Use an Area Concentration Banking System

Some of these problems can be overcome by using a banking service introduced in Section 2: the area concentration system. With this system, the customer mails the check directly to the local branch office. The branch office immediately deposits the check in a local bank. The local bank clears the deposited check in a day and transfers the funds to a regional concentration bank. The regional concentration bank automatically wires funds to the company's central bank account.

An area concentration bank network offers several advantages. First, it reduces the mail delivery time of the customer's check to one day. Second, it reduces the time for collecting a check to one day. And third, it prevents idle funds from building up in local banks. On the other hand, if the check is mailed to headquarters, mailing time could be three days, and check clearing adds two more days.

Use Cash Concentration

The essence of the cash allocation problem is moving money from a company's depository banks into a central cash pool in the company's concentration bank to fund disbursing accounts. Moving money from depository banks to the concentration bank is called cash concentration. Moving money into disbursing accounts is called disbursement funding.

There are three mechanisms for moving money between accounts at two different banks. The depository transfer check and wire transfers will be discussed later. The third mechanism, the electronic check, is the transfer of the check image between automated clearinghouses rather than through a wire network. In general, it is transmitted between two computers. The clearinghouses are normally controlled by the members who use the services. The electronic check takes one business day to clear rather than clearing the same day, as wire transfers do. It costs less than a depository transfer check or a wire transfer.

Most large companies transfer each day's reported receipts. Daily transfer of receipts is a very simple solution to the problem of cash allocation. But this simplicity is quite costly. Alternative methods—such as managing about a target, anticipation, and weekend timing—can substantially reduce the cost of the system.

Managing about a target means that the firm stipulates a target level for funds. When this level is achieved, the transfer takes place. No matter whether funds are transferred more than once a day or every few days, the cost per transfer is less than the cost incurred by transferring funds at the close of every business day.

Anticipation means initiating a transfer before formal notice of a deposit at the depository bank. Anticipation eliminates communication, processing, and clearing delays. Hence, it reduces the cost of moving funds. The process can accelerate transfers by one to three days when effectively employed. The most common use of anticipation is the adjusted field target technique. To illustrate this, assume a firm wants to maintain an average field balance of $8,000. But the bank statement shows that the combination of communication, processing, and clearing delays leaves an average of $7,000 that is in the process of being transferred. Therefore, the actual average balance is $15,000. To hit the $8,000 target, the cash manager makes a one-time transfer of $7,000 from the field bank and runs with an adjusted field target of $1,000. Because of the $7,000 average level of transfers in process, the actual average balance is the true target balance of $8,000. This procedure implicitly assumes a $7,000 average level of transfers in process. The ability to extract the entire $7,000 is dependent on the variability of the amount in process. This variability must be taken into consideration.

Use Lockboxes

Local collection, area collection, and cash concentration significantly reduce the time between when a customer mails a check and when that check is converted into usable funds. However, in many cases, a company's branch offices are not optimally located for efficient collections. In these cases, companies establish a network of regional lockboxes. The firm can select lockbox locations that are both close to customers and in Federal Reserve cities.

To set up a lockbox system, the company first rents a local post office box in each city selected. The company then gives its bank in each city permission to open the box. The company's invoices instruct customers to send payments directly to the post office box number. The bank picks up mail several times a day, microfilms the checks for record purposes, clears them for collection, and deposits them in the company's account. The bank then sends the company a detailed deposit slip.

There are two main advantages to lockboxes: first, the company does not have to handle and deposit checks from customers; second, deposits are made more quickly because customers mail checks directly to the city where they are deposited. A day or two later, the company knows what bills were paid and updates its records at leisure.

There are two important disadvantages of lockboxes. The first and most important is the cost. The bank requires payment for extra services—such as trips to the post office box several times a day, opening and processing mail, preparing deposits, and forwarding material to company headquarters. A bank is compensated in one of two ways—either in fees or in compensating balances. The cash manager must compare the fees for the lockbox system with the benefits of accelerated cash flow. (For a detailed discussion of how to calculate the cost of a lockbox system, refer to Section 2.) The manager must also weigh the opportunity cost of maintaining compensating balances against the fees and benefits of the lockbox system. The benefits of the accelerated cash flow may not exceed either the fee or the opportunity cost of the compensating balances. In such cases, a lockbox will not be worth the cost.

The second disadvantage of lockboxes is the effect on customers. Some customers are accustomed to having several days before their checks reach company headquarters. Such customers may resist a lockbox system that clears checks quickly and reduces their float. Dissatisfied customers react in two ways. Some look for a new supplier who offers longer credit terms. Others just continue mailing checks to headquarters in order to maintain the prior advantage of a long delay while their checks clear.

If you are trying to decide whether or not to establish a lockbox system, you should compare the cost of the most efficient system with the extra earnings from the released funds. If the earnings are greater than the costs, the system is profitable.

Determining the best locations for lockboxes is a very complex process. It involves documenting all the company's receipts by point of origin and then selecting trial cities for lockbox locations. For each trial city in a region, the cash manager must calculate the mail delivery time and the check clearing time for all receipts. Trial cities must then be tested to find the combination that offers the greatest net savings. Because of the number of variables involved and the number of combinations that must be tested, some banks offer a computer service to help solve this problem.

Even when a company uses an efficient system to deposit customer checks quickly, the deposited checks are not available for use at company headquarters. So next we'll discuss how money is transferred from regional banks to the main corporate bank using depository transfer checks.

Use Depository Transfer Checks

Depository transfer checks are a simple, low-cost, and reasonably fast way to move funds from one bank to another. These checks are nonnegotiable. They usually do not require a signature. And they are preprinted as payable only to a specific company account.

Depository transfer checks are used like this: Each day, a branch office deposits the checks it has received from customers in a local bank. The branch office also completes a depository transfer check and mails it to the company's regional concentration bank. In some cases, the concentration bank itself actually prepares the depository transfer check based on a call from the local branch manager. The concentration bank credits the depository transfer check to the company's account and puts the check into the regular collection system. By the time the depository transfer check comes back to the local bank for collection, funds from the checks deposited earlier are available for withdrawal. In effect, customer checks received at branch offices move directly to the concentration banks.

Because depository transfer checks are unsigned, anyone in a local office may issue one. But because they are nonnegotiable and payable only to a specific account at a specific bank, they are safe.

Wire transfers are the fastest way to move money between banks. The bank wire system is a privately operated national network connecting more than 200 banks in approximately 60 cities throughout the country. A wire transfer immediately transfers funds. On the same day that a regional depository bank receives collected funds for deposited checks, these funds can be moved to the company's central bank, and they are immediately available for use. Companies with established cash management programs usually issue standing instructions about the use of wire transfers rather than specific requests each time one is necessary. Typically, a company instructs its regional bank to wire-transfer any balances in excess of a specified amount.

Use Wire Transfers

In most cases, it is advantageous to use various combinations of concentration banking, lockboxes, depository transfer checks, and wire transfers. The selection depends on the size, type, and frequency of the funds involved and on customer location, as well as on the costs and availability of each service. These methods can be viewed as building blocks that can be combined to handle specific situations. The actual structure chosen is determined by comparing the benefits of various configurations to their costs and selecting the configuration that yields the greatest excess of benefits over costs in specific circumstances.

Establish a Captive Finance Subsidiary

During the last 40 years, a substantial number of firms in the United States have formed captive finance companies as subsidiaries. A captive finance company is a wholly owned subsidiary, the purpose of which is to provide wholesale financing for distributing the parent product and to purchase installment receivables for retail sales of the product. Company management believes that forming such a subsidiary enhances the firm's ability to raise outside funds.

A major justification for forming a captive finance subsidiary is the legal separation between operating decisions and financial decisions. Management believes legal separation leads to better credit decisions and to a cleaner situation for those who provide short-term funds.

Credit executives are often pressured to approve a sale even though evaluation indicates that credit should not be granted. Managers of captives are not immune to this pressure, but because the captive is a separate company, most of the pressure is removed. This is important from the credit executive's point of view.

Legal separation also makes the situation cleaner for lenders because receivables are not mixed in with the other assets of the firm. Lenders are able to clearly understand the firm's profit target, since the loan agreement usually stipulates that a certain earnings coverage standard must be maintained.

Forming a finance subsidiary in and of itself may not dramatically increase the amount of funds a firm may raise by short-term financing. However, if lenders are willing to give better terms, then in most cases, the cost of setting up the captive can be justified by the internal savings.

TECHNIQUES FOR SLOWING DOWN CASH DISBURSEMENT

We have discussed the techniques companies use to increase cash by speeding up cash inflows. Once a company has collected cash, it should try to conserve this cash as long as possible by using techniques to slow down cash outflows. Effective cash managers follow three important principles in cash disbursement: They pay bills as slowly as possible. They delay the actual transfer of funds even after bills are paid. And they minimize the amount of idle cash needed to meet obligations.

The first two principles are the opposite of the rules used to speed up cash inflow. To speed cash inflow, money must be collected as quickly as possible. To slow cash outflow, money must be paid out as slowly as possible. In cash gathering, it is important to transfer funds quickly to the company's disbursing accounts. In cash disbursement, however, the actual transfer of cash is delayed as long as possible.

Effective cash managers use several specific techniques, discussed below, to carry out these three principles of cash disbursement. (In addition to this overview of techniques for slowing cash disbursement, Section 6 will provide a further discussion of "Stretching Accounts Payable" from the perspective of obtaining short-term cash.)

Centralize the Accounts Payable Function

One of the first techniques a company uses to conserve cash is to centralize the accounts payable function. This serves several useful purposes. First, it reduces the amount of idle cash the company must hold. For example, if the company has 20 disbursing accounts scattered around the country at branch offices, each account must maintain a certain minimum balance. By eliminating these accounts and centralizing the payables function, the company can safely maintain a much lower minimum balance in a single account than it could in 20 separate accounts.

Second, a centralized payables account automatically decelerates a company's cash outflow. For example, a company with its payables department in New York may gain two or three days of float by paying a California supplier with a New York check rather than paying with a check drawn on a California bank. And third, centralizing accounts payable reduces or eliminates cash balances at branches. Thus, company cash can be more closely controlled and more aggressively managed.

Select a Distant Disbursing Bank

In addition to centralizing accounts payable, some companies select a disbursing bank far from most suppliers. This will add one more day of float. For example, a company may select a country bank in North Carolina for making payments to suppliers. By the time checks from New York, Chicago, or Los Angeles clear back through the North Carolina bank, the company has gained an extra day's use of its money.

Pay Bills at the Last Possible Moment

A company can also conserve cash by taking the maximum time allowed by law, agreement, or competitive conditions to pay bills. Paying bills too promptly is unnecessary, wasteful, and expensive. For example, paying a bill for $10,000 in 15 days when the terms are net 60 costs $74.00. This is calculated by multiplying the amount of the bill by the daily interest rate times the number of days early the bill was paid.

Paying a bill at the last possible moment is one technique of conserving cash, but as we saw in detail in Section 2 ("The Costs of Cash Inadequacy"), it may be expensive. If a supplier offers a cash discount for prompt payment, companies that can afford to pay promptly usually come out well ahead by doing so. And in taking a discount, companies should check state laws on mailing dates. In many states, checks mailed on the day the discount expires still qualify for the discount.

Use Drafts

A fourth technique of conserving cash is to use drafts, rather than checks, for payment. Drafts look like checks and can be used to pay local vendors. However, unlike checks, which are drawn on a bank, drafts are drawn on and payable by the issuer. Banks act only as the issuer's agent in the clearing process. Drafts flow through the bank to the issuer for examination and final payment. If the issuing company finds the drafts acceptable, it transfers money from a regular checking account to the draft account. These funds then flow to the receiver of the draft.

Drafts offer several advantages over checks. First, the company does not have to maintain a bank balance to cover the drafts it has written. Drafts are paid only after the receiver has deposited them and they have flowed through the clearing system to the issuer's bank. Second, because drafts are paid after they are received by the issuer, drafts circumvent the laws in many states against writing checks without sufficient funds on deposit. A third advantage is that the issuer can refuse payment of a draft. Fourth, a single reimbursement to the bank each day covers all drafts. Also, bank service charges for cashing drafts are often lower than for checks. And finally, branch offices can use drafts to pay local vendors without setting up a local checking account.

Drafts also have disadvantages. For example, suppliers may be reluctant to accept drafts because of the extra time required to collect the funds. Also, many small banks do not accept drafts. And finally, bankers object to drafts because the bank loses the money that would normally be kept in a demand checking account.

Many bankers oppose the use of drafts because of legal, operational, and financial problems. For example, if the company does not cover its drafts the day they are presented, the bank must carry them in a special account overnight. Bankers recognize certain uses of drafts as valid, however, particularly for payments requiring that the issuer examine and verify the endorsement before payment. For example, insurance companies may use drafts to settle claims because they must verify the payee's endorsement before approving final payment. In this case, the insurance company is using a draft as legal verification of signatures rather than as a cash management device. Although bankers object to drafts, many large companies insist on using them. The most common and acceptable use of drafts is by branch offices. Branch offices can write drafts without maintaining a local checking account. The accounting staff at headquarters maintains control by reviewing each presented draft. If the draft is for a legitimate and approved purpose, the central accounting staff honors it. Otherwise, the draft is refused.

If drafts are used, a company must make formal arrangements with its bank that clearly define the obligations and responsibilities of each party. Furthermore, even though a company can theoretically maintain a zero balance for drafts, few banks will accept this. In practice, banks may require that a company maintain a balance sufficient to cover one day's presentation of drafts.

Use Zero Balance Accounts

Zero balance accounts are another technique for conserving cash. To briefly review the Section 2 discussion of these accounts, they are special checking accounts that maintain either no cash balance or a very small cash balance. Checks presented to such an account for collection overdraw the account. Then the company must transfer funds from a master account to cover the overdraft. Usually, the master account is in the same bank as the zero balance account.

Zero balance accounts offer several advantages. First, the company does not have to maintain idle funds in many small branch accounts. Second, the company can closely monitor checks written by branch offices. Also, cash outflow is decelerated because local suppliers are paid from a distant central bank. Branch checks are coded, and the central bank's computer prints out a daily list showing the branch office code and the dollar amount of all checks that have cleared. And finally, the extra accounting costs of maintaining separate accounts are eliminated. Zero balance accounts offer a company most of the same control advantages as drafts and are much more acceptable to bankers.

A sixth technique used to conserve cash is to play the float. The float is the sum of a company's outstanding checks. Because there are always outstanding checks, a company's bank account usually has more cash in it than the books show; playing the float means investing this excess cash. Some cash managers carefully monitor their bank balances and then invest this already committed cash. By knowing exactly how long checks take to clear, an aggressive cash manager can invest this money for a few days at a time and still have adequate funds available to meet outstanding checks when they are presented. (The discussion in Section 2 of the objectives and techniques of cash management includes detailed information on how to calculate the cost of float—and hence, the potential gain available to the cash manager.)

Play the Float

Cash managers who play the float monitor balances as shown on the bank books, not on the company books. They make sure that the bank always shows sufficient cash to satisfy bank compensation requirements and daily transactions. Meanwhile, the company books may show a negative balance because checks have been written but have not yet cleared.

Let's use the Schwartz Company as an example of playing the float. On Friday, Schwartz has $200,000 on deposit at the First National Bank. On the following Monday, the company writes a check for $150,000. Knowing from past experience that this check will not clear for four days, Schwartz's treasurer calls the First National Bank and inquires about the availability of a money market investment for the next four days.

After advising the treasurer of the availability of CDs at 6.5 percent and federal funds at 5 percent, the bank officer then notes that the commercial paper market really fell off that morning, with the rates looking very good. In fact, paper maturing on Friday at 7 percent is available.

Schwartz's treasurer agrees to take $150,000 of top-grade paper, for which the bank will send out confirmations in that day's mail.

At this point, the Schwartz Company's books show a $300,000 debit for the day—reflecting the $150,000 check and the $150,000 purchase of commercial paper. In other words, Schwartz has a negative cash balance. At the same time, the First National Bank shows a $50,000 balance for the company—$200,000 from the previous week less the $150,000 used to purchase commercial paper. The bank has no knowledge of the $150,000 check that was written.

The following Friday the bank sells the maturing commercial paper for $150,233, which includes $233 in interest; credits this amount to the company account; and advises the Schwartz treasurer of the receipt of payment. The treasurer then tells the bank officer to expect presentation of the $150,000 check for payment that afternoon.

As expected, the $150,000 check is presented. This leaves a net balance in the Schwartz account of $50,233. The company's books show a credit of $150,233, which reflects the proceeds from the commercial paper, bringing its bank balance to $50,233. Before the end of the business day, Schwartz's treasurer checks with the bank officer and verifies that the check has in fact been presented for collection and that Schwartz's balance agrees with the bank's.

**Utilize
Computer-Generated
Data**

All companies should age their accounts receivable—that is, they should calculate the total dollar volume of receivables outstanding for 30 days, 60 days, and so on. If a company uses a computer to prepare invoices, simple programs make it possible to age accounts receivable automatically.

Computers can also help with accounts payable. Companies can enter a record of all bills into a computer when they arrive in the mail. The computer then produces payment checks on a daily, weekly, or monthly basis. The computer automatically takes advantage of all desired supplier discounts and writes checks for other bills at the latest acceptable date. Furthermore, because the computer contains a record of all bills and their planned payment dates, it can generate a printout of the company's cash needs for the coming one to two months. This helps short-term cash forecasting.

**Maintain Multiple
Accounts**

Companies often keep separate accounts for different purposes in order to maintain cash control. For example, a company may maintain separate accounts for receipts, accounts payable, payroll, dividends, and investments. Companies usually keep all these accounts at the same bank. The firm writes all its payroll checks on the payroll account. When these checks are distributed to employees, enough money from the main disbursing account is transferred to the payroll account to cover the checks. Separate accounts help a company see more clearly where its cash is going.

But maintaining multiple accounts presents two problems. First, if the company must maintain a balance in each account, the sum of these balances may be greater than the balance that would be required in a single account. Second, the company must carefully monitor interaccount transfers in order to keep track of the exact cash balance in each account. Otherwise, a transfer can be temporarily lost, and the books will show less cash than is actually available. Or a transfer may show up in two accounts, and the amount of cash available will then be overstated.

Important Indicators of Liquidity Problems

Converting a cash budget into a cash plan is the basic theme of this section. We have seen that the goal of cash management is to maintain the minimum cash balance that provides a firm with sufficient liquidity to meet its financial obligations and to enhance the company's profitability without exposing it to undue risk. We will begin by looking at signals or sources that seem to be important when identifying liquidity problems.

Various signals that may be indicative of liquidity problems in a company are listed below. Rate each of these on a scale of 1 to 5, depending upon how important you feel a particular indicator is (1 being very unimportant; 2, unimportant; 3, neutral; 4, important; and 5, very important). You will note that the indicators have been separated into three groups.

1. Sales and expense control

Declining sales orders	1	2	3	4	5
Sales below breakeven volume	1	2	3	4	5
Increased difficulty in expense control	1	2	3	4	5
Increased costs unable to be passed on	1	2	3	4	5
Difficulty in acquiring raw materials	1	2	3	4	5

2. Asset management

Declining daily cash inflows	1	2	3	4	5
Lower-than-normal cash balances	1	2	3	4	5
Increased accounts receivable	1	2	3	4	5
Declining turnover of receivables	1	2	3	4	5
Declining turnover of inventory	1	2	3	4	5
Buildup of inventories	1	2	3	4	5
Declining working capital	1	2	3	4	5

3. Liability management

Increased debt ratio	1	2	3	4	5
Dependence on one primary source of financing (only limited funding available)	1	2	3	4	5
Funding capital projects with short-term debt (incompletely converted into long-term funding)	1	2	3	4	5
All or most assets pledged to secure existing debt	1	2	3	4	5
Increased accounts payable	1	2	3	4	5

Professors Johnson, Campbell, and Wittenbach asked 400 *Fortune 1,000* treasurers to rate the same list of signals. The results of this survey are presented below so you can compare your opinion with these aggregate results.[1] It is interesting to note that most of the treasurers believed that the

---

[1] James M. Johnson, David R. Campbell, and James L. Wittenbach, "Identifying and Resolving Problems in Corporate Liquidity," *Financial Executive*, May 1982, pp. 41-46.

main source of liquidity problems was in the asset management group. The results and interpretation of this survey are included in the selected readings section in an article entitled "Identifying and Resolving Problems in Corporate Liquidity."

Comparing Your Responses with the Survey		
Indicators	Your Response	Average Response
1. Sales and expense control		
Declining sales orders	————	3.2
Sales below breakeven volume	————	2.8
Increased difficulty in expense control	————	3.0
Increased costs unable to be passed on	————	2.8
Difficulty in acquiring raw materials	————	3.6
2. Asset management		
Declining daily cash inflows	————	3.5
Lower-than-normal cash balances	————	3.2
Increased accounts receivable	————	3.6
Declining turnover of receivables	————	3.5
Declining turnover of inventory	————	3.9
Buildup of inventories	————	4.3
Declining working capital	————	3.5
3. Liability management		
Increased debt ratio	————	3.7
Dependence on one primary source of financing (only limited funding available)	————	2.6
Funding capital projects with short-term debt (incompletely converted into long-term funding)	————	2.7
All or most assets pledged to secure existing debt	————	2.3
Increased accounts payable	————	2.7

Resolving the Problem

When choosing the optimum solution to a liquidity problem, one must have a criterion on which to base the choice. Here, as always in financial management, the ultimate criterion is the maximization of stockholder wealth. An additional consideration is the impact that the choice has on the risk to the company. The cash manager must consider this balance of risk and return when making the decision as to which solution or technique is appropriate for solving a liquidity problem.

Using the same groupings of sales and expense control, asset management, and liability management as were used to identify liquidity problems, various suggested solutions or techniques that can be used to handle cash flow problems are presented. Rate the techniques listed below on the same scale of 1 to 5.

1. Sales and expense control

Delay new product offerings	1	2	3	4	5
Initiate greater cost control of overhead	1	2	3	4	5
Instruct purchasing to examine alternative sources	1	2	3	4	5
Reduce dividends	1	2	3	4	5
Freeze new hirings	1	2	3	4	5
Lengthen time between raises	1	2	3	4	5
Lay off personnel	1	2	3	4	5
Compensate operating managers largely on ability to generate cash flow	1	2	3	4	5

2. Asset management

Trim receivables	1	2	3	4	5
Use more rigorous collection policy	1	2	3	4	5
Reduce investment in inventories	1	2	3	4	5
Reduce capital expenditures	1	2	3	4	5
Close plants	1	2	3	4	5
Dispose of assets not meeting long-term profit objectives	1	2	3	4	5
Liquidate certain assets to meet operating and debt service needs	1	2	3	4	5
Educate nonfinancial personnel to significance of asset management	1	2	3	4	5

3. Liability management

Extend payables	1	2	3	4	5
Increase short-term borrowing	1	2	3	4	5
Establish revolving bank credit	1	2	3	4	5
Increase revolving bank lines	1	2	3	4	5
Place more emphasis on leasing assets	1	2	3	4	5
Increase long-term borrowing	1	2	3	4	5

Now compare your rating of each solution to liquidity problems with the average rating of 400 treasurers of companies in *Fortune 1,000*. The average of the replies to the Johnson, Campbell, and Wittenbach survey (see the selected readings) appear in the table that follows.[2]

Comparing Your Responses with the Survey

Solution	Your Response	Average Response
1. Sales and expense control		
Delay new product offerings	_____	2.1
Initiate greater cost control of overhead	_____	3.7
Instruct purchasing to examine alternative sources	_____	2.9
Reduce dividends	_____	2.0
Freeze new hirings	_____	2.1
Lengthen time between raises	_____	2.3
Lay off personnel	_____	2.9
Compensate operating managers largely on ability to generate cash flow	_____	2.2
2. Asset management		
Trim receivables	_____	3.7
Use more rigorous collection policy	_____	3.7
Reduce investment in inventories	_____	4.3
Reduce capital expenditures	_____	3.3
Close plants	_____	2.6
Dispose of assets not meeting long-term profit objectives	_____	3.1
Liquidate certain assets to meet operating and debt service needs	_____	2.5
Educate nonfinancial personnel to significance of asset management	_____	3.5
3. Liability management		
Extend payables	_____	2.9
Increase short-term borrowing	_____	3.6
Establish revolving bank credit	_____	3.2
Increase revolving bank lines	_____	3.0
Place more emphasis on leasing assets	_____	2.1
Increase long-term borrowing	_____	3.6

[2] Ibid.

Using Trade Credit

Almost all businesses make use of trade credit. That is, companies do not normally pay for supplies on a cash-and-carry basis. Invoices for materials, supplies, and services provided by outside suppliers are not received until some days after the materials are delivered or the services performed. Even if invoices are paid as soon as they are received, the lag between delivery and billing represents credit provided by outside suppliers. This credit can be increased by not paying bills immediately upon receipt. A financial executive's ability to manage liabilities is equally as important as that of managing assets, as can be seen by the responses to the Johnson, Campbell, and Wittenbach survey.

A very common reaction of a company that finds itself short of cash is to slow down the payment of its bills. This approach is costly, however, when figured on an annual interest rate basis, as discussed in Section 2 ("The Costs of Cash Inadequacy").

The real deadline for payments is not the nominal net 30 days; instead, it is the point at which further postponement of payment will bring a penalty in the form of damaged relations with the supplier, refusal of more supplies, a damaged credit rating, or even a lawsuit. It can even be argued that one valuable skill of a financial executive is the ability to sense when this deadline comes and to pay the bill one day before it.

In Section 5, under "Trade Credit" and "Stretching Accounts Payable," we will examine a number of specific ways in which trade credit can be utilized to maximize a company's cash.

Determining Short-Term Needs: An Example

XYZ Company is in a seasonal business—sporting goods—that has a mid-summer sales peak. In March, the company's financial vice-president is planning her financing strategy for the coming six months. In preparation for the seasonal demand for its products, the company starts to increase production in April and build up finished goods inventory. The financial vice-president has completed a six-month cash flow forecast and budget as seen below:

Cash Flow Budget—XYZ Company (000s Omitted)						
	April	May	June	July	Aug.	Sept.
Opening cash	250	320	260	75	(80)	125
Cash sales	5	10	15	20	10	5
Collections	620	650	660	740	850	890
Other inflows	0	10	0	0	0	0
Total inflows	625	670	675	760	860	895
Cash purchases	30	40	35	20	15	10
Payments due on accounts payable	275	420	450	470	400	250
Wages and salaries	200	210	210	210	180	150
Other expenses	50	60	65	65	60	50
Taxes on income	—	—	—	150	—	—
Cash dividends	—	—	100	—	—	100
Total outflows	555	730	860	915	655	560
Net changes in cash	70	(60)	(185)	(155)	205	335
Ending cash	320	260	75	(80)	125	460

These figures present a clear picture of what the vice-president expects to happen over the next six months. Production will be increased in April. This will immediately be reflected in higher wages. It will also mean that more materials will be bought from outside suppliers, resulting in increased payments to suppliers in May. The result is that the company's cash balance begins to fall in May.

Sales start to increase in May, increase more rapidly in June, and reach a peak in July. Collections, however, lag behind sales and show no marked change until July. Collections reach a peak in September. There is, therefore, a net cash outflow throughout June and July. This outflow creates even more of a problem because the quarterly cash dividend on common stock falls due in June and a tax payment is due in July. The expected result is a cash deficit of $80,000 by the end of July. Nevertheless, the need is clearly short-term. The upsurge in collections in August restores a positive cash balance, and by the end of September, the company will have a large cash balance.

At the very least, then, the company must find $80,000 in short-term funds to make up the deficit. In practice, XYZ Company will certainly need more than $80,000 to allow for uncertainties and to avoid the possibility of a zero cash balance—a situation no company likes to see. The financial vice-president likes to have a minimum cash balance of at least $100,000 on hand at all times. So she must borrow $180,000. She decides to round the figure and borrow $200,000 by the end of May or early June.

The next step is to review the sources of short-term credit that are open, their costs, and other relevant characteristics. In this case, we shall assume that the financial vice-president has already done this. She believes that there is almost no chance of speeding up the collections from credit customers. She knows, too, that the president and directors would be most unwilling to cut the cash dividend. The company does not qualify for help from the Small Business Administration, nor are funds available from any state or local development corporations.

One possibility, of course, is to stretch the company's accounts payable. Immediately after the summer sales peak, when the company is highly liquid, it pays all its bills promptly and takes all trade discounts. During spring and summer, however, available cash is always limited, and the company takes no discounts. The cash flow projection assumes that bills are paid when they fall due—usually after 30 days. As discounts are not being taken, then stretching the payables beyond their due date will not mean any financial loss.

The financial vice-president finds it difficult to decide just how far the payables can be stretched. She finally decides that about 50 percent of them can probably be stretched 30 days beyond the due date. She believes that it would be unwise to try to stretch any payables further than this. At this point, she recalculates the cash flow budget to show the effect of stretching of accounts payable. The revised cash flow budget appears below.

REVIEWING SOURCES OF FUNDS

First Revised Cash Flow Budget—XYZ Company (000s Omitted)

	April	May	June	July	Aug.	Sept.
Opening cash	250	320	260	300	155	125
Cash sales	5	10	15	20	10	5
Collections	620	650	660	740	850	890
Other inflows	0	10	0	0	0	0
Total inflows	625	670	675	760	860	895
Cash purchases	30	40	35	20	15	10
Payments due on accounts payable	275	420	225	460	635	250
Wages and salaries	200	210	210	210	180	150
Other expenses	50	60	65	65	60	50
Taxes on income	—	—	—	150	—	—
Cash dividends	—	—	100	—	—	100
Total outflows	555	730	635	905	890	560
Net changes in cash	70	(60)	40	(145)	(30)	335
Ending cash	320	260	300	155	125	460

The revised forecast shows that stretching accounts payable need start only in June and that the company will be able to pay all its overdue accounts and return to net terms in August. But the effect of the extra trade credit for just two months is quite dramatic. Expected cash balances never fall below $125,000 and no additional funds will be required.

Another possibility, if trade credit is not stretched, is to borrow the $200,000 from the company's commercial bank as a short-term loan. The financial vice-president does not foresee any problem in getting such a loan. Indeed, the situation is almost perfect for short-term bank lending. The amount is reasonable in relation to the size of the company. The loan will be required for no more than 120 days and will be self-liquidating at the end of that period. The cost of the loan will be 18 percent.

The financial vice-president has also looked at using intermediate-term funds, particularly a bank term loan. The immediate need is clearly short-term. However, the company plans to extensively modernize its facilities. The reconstruction and reequipment work is to be started in the fall, as soon as the sales peak is over, and funds will be needed to finance part of the cost. The bank has already been approached and has agreed to lend $300,000 with a five-year maturity. A third possibility, then, is to take out the term loan four months earlier than planned and use the funds to finance the short-term need as well as the construction. The interest rate on the term loan will be 20 percent. This alternative will make available more funds than the vice-president expects to need in the short-term, but the excess can be reinvested in marketable securities to yield a return of 14 percent.

A fourth possibility that has been studied is borrowing against inventory. But this does not provide a satisfactory solution. Finished-goods inventories will be at their highest in May and June, and it would certainly be possible to borrow against them at that time. Inventories will be drawn down in June, however, as sales build up, and will continue to run down throughout July. But this is exactly when the additional funds are needed. In other words, this source would make funds available, but the source would be at its lowest just when the need is greatest. Therefore, this particular source of funds is not being considered.

One more possibility has been examined—raising short-term funds by factoring the company's accounts receivable. Here the problems of timing encountered in borrowing against inventory do not arise. Accounts receivable will begin to rise markedly in June as finished-goods inventories drop, and the rise will continue throughout July when the funds are needed.

The next step, of course, is to determine whether enough funds would be available from this source. The financial vice-president estimates that about 80 percent of the company's accounts receivable would be accepted as good credit risks by a finance company and that the finance company would probably advance 85 percent of the face value of the invoices accepted. These assumptions have been used as the basis of yet another cash flow budget that follows.

Second Revised Cash Flow Budget— XYZ Company (000s Omitted)

	April	May	June	July	Aug.	Sept.
Opening cash	250	320	260	578	409	539
Cash sales	5	10	15	20	10	5
Collection/sale	620	650	1,163	726	775	178
Other inflows	0	10	0	0	0	0
Total inflows	625	670	1,178	746	785	183
Cash purchases	30	40	35	20	15	10
Payments due on accounts payable	275	420	450	470	400	250
Wages and salaries	200	210	210	210	180	150
Other expenses	50	60	65	65	60	50
Taxes on income	—	—	—	150	—	—
Cash dividends	—	—	100	—	—	100
Total outflows	555	730	860	915	655	560
Net changes in cash	70	(60)	318	(169)	130	(377)
Ending cash	320	260	578	409	539	162

The second revised forecast shows the results of factoring receivables for three months—the minimum period over which the vice-president believes any finance company will be willing to enter into such an agreement. The forecast indicates that there is a massive increase in net cash flow in the month in which the scheme goes into operation. Proceeds from sales then remain almost flat for two months, and finally, there is a large negative cash flow in September—the month in which the company stops selling its receivables and returns to normal collection. Nevertheless, the factoring achieves its purpose: Cash is available when it is needed, and even the large outflow in September does not bring the balance of cash on hand down to the vice-president's minimum of $100,000.

No other viable alternatives seem to be available. It would, of course, be possible to use some other form of intermediate- or even long-term funds to finance the planned modernization and to use some part of these funds to finance the needed short-term working capital. However, the financial vice-president has already made a firm decision to use a bank term loan for this purpose. Her choice for the source of short-term funds will be made from among those we've discussed.

MAKING THE CHOICE

In this case, the choice does not appear to be very difficult. There are four possibilities: stretching trade credit, short-term bank borrowing, a bank term loan, and factoring the receivables. Each choice will provide more than enough additional cash at the right time.

Two of the alternatives can be eliminated on the basis of cost. Factoring receivables is expensive, and there is no need to use this source if a less expensive source is available. Also, the term loan carries a slightly higher interest rate than the short-term loan. The real choice then, seems to be between stretching trade credit and using short-term bank funds.

Other things being equal, the best decision would be the one that costs the least. Stretching trade credit does not appear to have any quantifiable cost, because the company is not planning to take discounts for prompt payment anyway. But things are not equal, because stretching trade credit does have a cost in terms of the damage it may do to the company's relations with its suppliers, its bank, and its reputation in general. The decision, then, becomes a trade-off between the interest cost on a short-term bank loan and the qualitative costs to the company's reputation. The decision maker will have to use her judgement, and there is no way of saying with certainty which decision is right. We can say, however, that the costs of stretching trade credit, which there is no way of calculating, may be greater than the cost of the bank borrowing and that short-term bank borrowing therefore carries a lower risk.

ADDITIONAL FACTORS

The financial vice-president's analysis was less than complete, however. There are a number of other considerations. Once they are included, we can see that the problem is not as simple as it seemed to be in the first analysis.

First, the vice-president has not examined the possibility of using a combination of sources of funds. It might be possible, for instance, to stretch accounts payable to some extent and incur almost no danger of impairing the company's relations with its suppliers. Quite possibly, this limited stretching would not generate enough additional cash flow to meet the company's needs, but using limited stretching, it might be necessary to borrow only $100,000 from the bank, rather than $200,000. This might conceivably be the least expensive solution of all.

On the other hand, the assumption that stretching credit has no explicit cost for XYZ Company, because discounts for prompt payment are not taken, is misleading. Another possibility would be to take the term loan—or increase the size of the short-term bank loan—and use the funds to take discounts for prompt payment. If this is a possible strategy, then any other strategy that does not permit taking discounts for prompt payments should include the opportunity cost of not doing so. This changes the entire problem.

Most important of all, the financial vice-president has not planned for any contingencies. Her cash flow budget is based on what she believes is most likely to happen and is probably as realistic as any single forecast can be. The vice-president should at the very least repeat the analysis at a more pessimistic level to see whether her proposed solution is still viable under less favorable circumstances.

It will be useful to turn back and see how the vice-president's decision might be affected by such a contingency analysis. Her estimates of the expected outflows are probably fairly accurate; we assume that the company is not introducing a radically new product this summer and that production costs of the existing products can be predicted with reasonable certainty. The major uncertainty lies in sales. The vice-president's forecasts of cash sales and collections are based on a sales forecast provided by the marketing staff. This forecast is based on historical data plus a little optimism. But what if the summer proves to be unusually wet? What if one of the company's competitors cuts prices and forces XYZ to do the same? What if the economy suffers a severe recession with high unemployment? If any of these contingencies occur, it is conceivable that sales may be 20 percent lower than forecast. And this may happen too late to change the high production schedules.

A first assumption might be that, in such an event, the company will need considerably more additional financing than the vice-president has planned for. The third cash flow budget below shows how cash flows will be affected if sales fall 20 percent below forecast in the three peak months of May through July.

Third Revised Cash Flow Budget—
XYZ Company (000s Omitted)

	April	May	June	July	Aug.	Sept.
Opening cash	250	320	260	72	(235)	(155)
Cash sales	5	10	12	16	10	5
Collections	620	650	660	592	680	712
Other inflows	0	10	0	0	0	0
Total inflows	625	670	672	608	690	717
Cash purchases	30	40	35	20	10	5
Payments due on accounts payable	275	420	450	470	400	200
Wages and salaries	200	210	210	210	150	120
Other expenses	50	60	65	65	50	40
Taxes on income	—	—	—	150	—	—
Cash dividends	—	—	100	—	—	100
Total outflows	555	730	860	915	610	465
Net changes in cash	70	(60)	(188)	(307)	80	252
Ending cash	320	260	72	(235)	(155)	97

In this forecast, we assume that the company starts making plans to cut production as soon as the May sales figures are in—at the end of the first week in June. The cutback begins to take effect in August.

The new cash flow budget reveals a very different picture. The effect of the poor May sales begins to show in the July collections, and the cash deficit at the end of that month is now $235,000 instead of $80,000.

If the vice-president had decided on the basis of the first forecast to take out a 120-day loan from the bank for $200,000, under these new circumstances, this amount will not be enough. How much additional funding will be required? To maintain a minimum cash balance of $100,000 at all times, the company will need to borrow $335,000 and will not be able to retire this debt fully until October. But is it necessary to aim for such a high minimum balance under these adverse conditions? It can be argued that the purpose of the $100,000 minimum balance is to provide a buffer for just such emergencies as this and that, when the emergency actually arrives, cash should be expected to fall below the target minimum. If the vice-president had done a contingency forecast on the basis of a 20-percent decline in sales, then it might have been reasonable to borrow, say, $250,000, and to accept that cash on hand would fall to a low level for one month if the pessimistic forecast came true. In other words, a large minimum cash reserve is largely a substitute—and an inferior substitute—for contingency forecasting. It is superfluous to have both.

If the vice-president has not planned for such a contingency and is caught unaware, then she obviously must do something quickly. At this point, we must be realistic and acknowledge that there will not be time to do much systematic analysis. In circumstances such as these, good bank relations really prove their value.

Finally, we should also remember that decisions about short-term financing can never be completely independent of long-term financing and vice versa. The company is planning extensive modernization and has arranged a term loan to provide the cash for this project. But the amount of the term loan is based on the assumption that, as the initial cash flow forecast indicated, the company will have cash balances of almost $500,000 by the end of September. This sum is much more than the company needs for working capital and its minimum balance, and $250,000 of this cash is earmarked for use in the modernization. It will now be necessary to renegotiate the term loan to supply the missing funds. And indeed, it may now be that the company is chronically short of working capital and needs to acquire some permanent funds.

Summary

The main purpose of this section is to give you some ideas that you can use to turn a cash budget into a cash plan. In effect, once the problem has been defined, a financial executive must generate alternatives that will lead to a satisfactory solution. In most cases, there will be more than one way to solve a problem. Sometimes it is worth the extra effort to look for the best solution; sometimes it is not. As cash managers gain experience, one of the things that they learn is to know when to stop and use a satisfactory solution that may not be the best one theoretically.

The Case Study
Part Two

The Case Study: Part Two

Instructions: This case study consists of three parts. Each part has its own set of questions that you should answer as thoroughly as you can. Part One of the case study began on page 79, and Part Three continues on page 167.

SAN LARGO ORANGE BLOSSOM, INC.

ASSIGNMENT

The objective of this part of the case study is to allow the reader to convert a cash budget into a cash plan. After you have read this part of the case study, answer these questions:

3. *Evaluate Pam's proposed alternatives as possible solutions to San Largo's cash flow problem. Remember to consider cost, risk, suitability, flexibility, and control. Indicate which solution you feel will be the best approach based on the most likely assumptions you made in the first part of the case study.*

4. *Based on your selected solution to San Largo's cash flow problem, prepare a cash plan if the most likely scenario occurs.*

PAM'S THREE CASH BUDGETS

As Pam sits in her office just before Christmas, she gives a sigh of relief as she looks over the three cash budgets she has prepared. She has taken the assumptions and forecasts and created three possible scenarios—the worst case, the most likely case, and the best case. The cash budget that she believes reflects the most pessimistic case appears on the next page.

San Largo's Cash Flow Budget (Worst Case)

	Jan.	Feb.	Mar.	Apr.	May	June	July	Aug.	Sept.	Oct.	Nov.	Dec.
Sales	13	14	17	1	.5	.3	.3	.3	1	2	2	3
Cash Inflows												
Sales receipts [a]	3	12	13	16	.8	.5	.3	.3	.3	.9	2	2
Total cash inflows	3	12	13	16	.8	.5	.3	.3	.3	.9	2	2
Cash Outflows												
Salaries	1.65	1.65	1.65	1.65	1.65	1.65	1.65	1.65	1.65	1.65	1.65	1.65
Purchases	3.0	1.5	—	—	—	—	—	—	—	5.0	5.0	4.0
Utilities	0.55	0.55	0.55	0.55	0.55	0.55	0.55	0.55	0.55	0.55	0.55	0.55
Marketing expenses	—	—	—	—	—	—	—	—	0.77	0.75	—	—
Miscellaneous	0.3	0.3	0.15	0.15	0.15	0.2	0.1	0.1	0.3	0.2	0.5	0.3
New equipment	—	—	—	—	—	—	1.3	1.3	—	—	—	—
Interest	—	—	0.1	—	—	—	—	—	—	—	—	—
Loan repayment	—	—	4.0	—	—	—	—	—	—	—	—	—
Taxes	2.0	—	—	1.7	—	—	1.7	—	—	1.5	—	—
Dividends	—	—	2.0	—	—	2.0	—	—	2.0	—	—	2.0
Total cash outflows	7.5	4.0	8.45	4.05	2.35	4.4	5.3	3.6	5.25	9.65	7.7	8.5
Beginning cash balance	0.3	(4.2)	3.8	8.35	20.3	18.8	14.9	9.9	6.6	1.65	(7.1)	(12.8)
Net cash flow [b]	(4.5)	8.0	4.55	11.95	(1.5)	(3.9)	(5.0)	(3.3)	(4.95)	(8.75)	(5.7)	(6.5)
Ending cash balance [c]	(4.2)	3.8	8.35	20.3	18.8	14.9	9.9	6.6	1.65	(7.1)	(12.8)	(19.3)
Minimum cash balance	0.5	0.5	0.5	0.5	0.5	0.5	0.5	0.5	0.5	0.5	0.5	0.5

[a] Reflects an adjustment for possible bad debts. The historical experience with bad debts has been negligible, but Pam feels that, under the worst conditions, San Largo could have some problems.

[b] Cash inflows minus cash outflows.

[c] Beginning cash balances plus or minus net cash flow.

Pam's next step in the process is to prepare a list of possible alternatives. She feels that she should try to get as exhaustive a list of alternatives as possible before she begins to exclude those alternatives that don't offer much chance of solving the problem. Pam's list of alternatives is presented below. **PAM'S LIST OF ALTERNATIVES**

New product offerings were delayed
Greater cost control of overhead
Purchasing agents examined alternative sources of supply
Dividends were reduced
Lengthened time for raises
Personnel were laid off
Operating managers were compensated largely on ability to generate cash inflows
Receivables were trimmed
Used more rigorous receivables collection policy
Reduced investment in inventories
Reduced capital expenditures
Plants were closed
Assets not meeting long term profit objectives were disposed of
Liquidated certain assets to meet operating and debt service needs
Educated nonfinancial personnel on significance of asset management
Payables were extended
Increased short-term borrowings
Revolving bank credit arrangements were established
Revolving bank lines were increased
Greater emphasis placed on leasing assets
Increased long-term borrowings
Actively manage marketable security investments

As Pam begins evaluating the various alternatives, she realizes that she needs criteria to compare and rank them. She considers such factors as cost, risk, suitability, flexibility, and control as the major criteria upon which she can select the best course of action.

Pam has also gathered information on current short-term money market conditions, as she feels that San Largo should seriously investigate establishing an active strategy for investing in marketable securities. The results of her survey are tabulated below. **CURRENT INTEREST RATES**

Current borrowing rate for San Largo	10% on short-term funds
	15% on long-term funds
San Largo marginal tax rate	40%
Current money market rates	8% on short-term funds (less than 1 year)
	9% on funds (more than 1 year)

Pam has decided to finance the capital expenditures, which the company expects to make in July and August, with long-term sources of funds in order to follow the matching principle. She has arranged for a 20-year note to be issued on July 1 at 15 percent interest with semiannual interest payments due on December 31 and June 30. There is no repayment of principal scheduled for the first five years of the note.

5.

Short-Term Financing

Options for Obtaining Short-Term Cash

Companies do not have all the cash they need all the time. Very often, a firm needs to build up inventory. This reduces cash levels. Or customers may place unusually large orders and financing additional accounts receivable reduces the company's cash level. In this section, we will describe the many ways companies obtain additional short-term cash to restore cash balances to the required levels.

No company should incur debt haphazardly. Funds should be borrowed with a specific, well-defined purpose in mind. Short-term borrowing may be done to fill a gap in the cash flow cycle that is indicated in the cash budget, to facilitate growth, or to support a larger, more profitable level of working capital. Whatever the circumstances, a company should have a clear purpose to justify borrowing additional funds. The form, cost, and maturity of borrowed funds should be matched to the intended use. It would be foolish to borrow funds for 90 days for an investment in a machine with a life of 8 years. Likewise it would be unsound to borrow funds for 20 years to finance a seasonal buildup in inventory that is expected to last 3 months.

If maturities are not matched, the firm will be subject to unnecessary risk and to the burden of additional costs. If long-term assets are financed with short-term liabilities, the manager will have to continually refinance. Continued refinancing increases the risk the firm faces, because the funds may be unavailable or only available at substantially higher costs. In addition, repeated refinancing involves a great many transaction costs, in terms of both dollars and executive time.

On the other hand, if short-term needs are financed with long-term liabilities, the cost of long-term financing will, in general, be higher than the returns earned on the short-term assets. That is why we normally like to see a firm's current ratio (current assets/current liabilities) approximately equal to one.

This concept of ensuring that the maturities of current assets correspond to the maturities of sources of funds is called the matching principle. It is one of the few heuristics in financial management that will guarantee avoiding bankruptcy. And while following the matching principle, financial managers try at the same time to ensure that the return on the investment is sufficient to pay the cost of borrowing. (A detailed comparison between the aggressive and conservative approaches to the matching principle is presented in Section 1.)

As a general rule, financial managers look for short-term cash at the lowest possible rates. If they're unable to obtain cash at no cost or at a very small cost, they explore more expensive sources of cash. For example, a financial manager faced with a cash shortage might look first to the company's suppliers and customers. Suppliers extend credit by collecting for goods and services after those goods and services are supplied. A cash manager can enlarge this credit by paying bills more slowly. A cash manager can also obtain additional cash by collecting from the company's customers more quickly.

If these relatively low-cost options are unavailable (or if their cost is too high in terms of the ill will generated), a cash manager may turn next to the company's bank for a short-term loan. Various money market instruments are alternative sources of short-term financing.

Companies faced with a severe cash shortage can also try to convert into cash two working capital assets—accounts receivable and inventory. A company can pledge its accounts receivable to a finance company in exchange for a loan, or it can sell its accounts receivable to a factoring company for cash. Similarly, a company can pledge its inventory in exchange for a loan.

TRADE CREDIT

Trade credit is one important and often low-cost source of cash. Nearly all companies make use of trade credit to some degree by not paying suppliers immediately for goods and services. Instead, suppliers bill the company, and the company pays in 10 days, 30 days, or more. From the time when the supplier first provides the goods or services until the time when the customer pays for them, the supplier has, in effect, loaned the company money. The sum of all these bills is trade credit. By paying bills more slowly, a firm increases the amount of these loans from its suppliers.

One way a company can take more time to pay bills (or stretch its payables) is to stop taking discounts. For example, if your company normally takes advantage of all prompt-payment discounts, you can increase cash by passing up the discount and paying bills in 30 days. Of course, this is an expensive source of cash. (Refer to Section 2 ["The Costs of Cash Inadequacy"] for a detailed discussion of exactly how expensive this measure is in terms of its annual interest rate cost.)

This brings up the subject of late payments. As mentioned in the previous section, many cash managers do not consider 30 days or any other stated terms a real deadline. Instead, they try to determine the exact point at which further delay of payment will incur a penalty. For example, if a firm pays too slowly, a supplier may require payment in full on future orders; or report the company to a credit bureau, which would damage the company's credit rating with all suppliers; or even bring legal action against the company. Many cash managers believe, however, that as long as they pay bills just before incurring any of these penalties, they maximize the firm's cash at little or no cost. The hidden costs of this approach include such risks as damaged reputation, lower credit limits from suppliers, higher supplier prices to compensate for delayed payment, and the possibility of exceeding a final deadline and incurring a penalty.

However, if you want more trade credit and plan to stretch your payables, you do not always have to incur these risks. Very often, you can negotiate with suppliers for more generous credit terms, at least temporarily. If you and a supplier agree on longer terms (perhaps 60 or even 90 days), you get the extra trade credit without jeopardizing supplier relations or credit ratings.

Keep in mind that suppliers are trying to build up business and must compete with other similar suppliers. One way suppliers compete is through credit terms, and this can be used to advantage. Just as you get several price quotes before placing a major order, you may also want to encourage competition among suppliers for credit terms.

If you are in a highly seasonal business, such as many types of retailing, you will find a great variation in credit terms during different seasons. For example, as a retailer, you might be very short of cash in the fall as you build up for the Christmas season. Many suppliers understand this and will quite willingly extend their normal 30-day terms.

Furthermore, some suppliers will offer exceedingly generous credit terms to smooth out their own manufacturing cycle. Later in this section (under "Stretching Accounts Payable"), we will see an example of the sorts of credit incentives that may be offered by firms whose business is largely seasonal.

COLLECTING RECEIVABLES

You can see that stretching out accounts payable and collecting accounts receivable more quickly are really two sides of the same issue. Most companies try to stretch out bill payments as long as reasonably possible and to collect their bills as quickly as competitively possible. Your objective as a cash manager is to maximize company cash, using both these techniques—and to do this without antagonizing either suppliers or customers to such an extent that your working relationship with them suffers.

As we have just seen, the fastest way to collect receivables is to ask for the money regularly. But a company can also change its sales terms to collect cash more quickly. There are several options.

One option, noted in Section 4, is to introduce discounts. A company can initiate a discount for prompt payment—2 percent, say, for payment within 10 days. Similarly, a company that already offers a discount can increase it—for example, from 1 percent to 2 percent.

Or it's possible to reduce credit terms. A company can require full payment in 15 days, a deposit when the order is placed, COD orders (the customer pays on delivery), or even full payment with the order. But it will be difficult to institute these measures if competitors offer more lenient credit.

Another option is to emphasize cash sales. Some companies, particularly those selling directly to consumers, may be able to increase the percentage of their cash sales.

A fourth choice is to accept credit cards. Sales charged to credit cards are convertible immediately into cash. Credit card companies charge from 3 to 7 percent of the amount of the sale for this service.

A final option is imposing a penalty for late payment. Some companies now charge 1 percent or 1.5 percent of the unpaid balance per month as a penalty for late payment. But as Section 4 made clear, this approach has its disadvantages—including the federal and varying state laws governing the practice of charging interest as well as the fact that, again, competitive conditions may make it impossible to do so.

BANK LOANS

After a company has fully used its trade credit and collected receivables as quickly as competitively possible, it may next turn to a bank for a short-term loan. The most common bank loan is an unsecured loan made for 90 days. Standard variations of short-term unsecured loans include loans made for periods of 30 days to a year and loans requiring collateral. Interest charges on these loans typically vary from the prime rate to about 3 percent above the prime. (The prime rate is the amount a bank charges its largest and most financially strong customers.)

Very often, a company does not need money immediately but can forecast a definite need in, say, six months. This firm would not want to borrow the required money now and pay unnecessary interest for the next six months. Instead, the company would formally apply to its bank for a line of credit. A line of credit is an assurance by the bank that, as long as the company remains financially healthy, the bank will lend it money (up to a specified limit) whenever the company needs it. Banks usually review a firm's credit line each year. A line of credit is not a guarantee that the bank will make a loan in the future. Instead, when the company actually needs the money, the bank will examine the company's current financial statements to make sure that actual results coincide with earlier plans.

Banks also grant guaranteed lines of credit. Under this arrangement, a bank guarantees to supply funds up to a specified limit, regardless of circumstances. This relieves the company of any worries that money may not be available when needed. Banks usually charge extra for such a guarantee. Typically the charge is 1 percent a year on the unused amount of the guaranteed line of credit. For example, if a bank guarantees a credit line of $1 million and a company borrows only $300,000, the firm will have to pay a commitment fee of perhaps $7,000 for the $700,000 that wasn't borrowed.

In return for granting lines of credit, banks usually require that companies maintain a compensating balance. This is a specified amount kept in a checking account without interest. For example, if a company receives a $1 million line of credit with the requirement that it maintain a 15 percent compensating balance, the firm must keep at least $150,000 in its demand account during the year. The bank, of course, does not pay interest on money in a demand account. So the use of this money is the bank's compensation for standing ready to grant up to $1 million in loans during the year. Of course, when the bank actually makes the loans, it charges the negotiated rate of interest on them.

Banks use two factors to determine the interest rate they will charge to companies. These are the prime rate and the size and financial strength of the borrower. In the past few years, the prime rate has fluctuated from about 5 percent to 15 percent but has been as high as 18 percent, for short-term loans. Large, financially secure companies pay the prime rate. Smaller companies pay an amount over prime. The exact amount over prime depends on the financial strength of the borrower. It typically varies from 0.5 percent for large, strong companies to as much as 3 percent for smaller, but still creditworthy firms.

In order to reduce risks in making loans, banks may require collateral from borrowers. Collateral may be any asset that has value. If the borrower does not repay the loan, the bank then owns the collateral and may sell it to recover the amount of the loan.

Typical types of collateral include specific high-value items owned by the company (such as buildings, computer equipment, or large machinery) and all items of a particular type (all raw materials, all inventory, and so on). Banks use blanket liens as collateral in cases where individual items are of low value but the collective value of all items is large enough to serve as collateral.

When making loans to very small companies, banks often require that the owners and top managers personally sign for the loan also. Then, if the company does not repay the loan, the bank can claim the signer's personal assets—houses, stock investments, and so on—to satisfy the loan.

To maximize the chances of success when applying for a bank loan, a company should maintain good bank relations, as discussed in Section 2. Personal visits by the president and other senior officers as well as quarterly delivery of statements, balance sheets, and cash flow statements are useful means of doing this.

The actual process of obtaining bank credit must be conducted on a personal basis with the bank officer. The loan officer will be interested in knowing how much money the company needs, how it will use this money, how it will repay the bank, and when it will repay the bank. If you can answer these questions fully and support the answers with past results and realistic forecasts, you stand an excellent chance of obtaining a line of credit or a loan.

One important item that is often overlooked when applying for bank credit is a cash forecast. Many financial managers prepare only projected income statements and balance sheets if they want to negotiate bank credit. These projected financial statements are important, but as we have already seen, profits are not the same as cash, and the bank must be repaid in cash. Therefore, a cash manager would do well to bring cash forecasts to the bank.

It might also be important to prepare more than one cash forecast. If time allows, prepare a cash forecast that assumes optimistically high sales and another that assumes pessimistically low sales. These forecasts will enable the banker (and you) to see the effects of unexpected financial changes and to determine the company's future cash requirements under every possible condition.

SELLING COMMERCIAL PAPER

While many small- and medium-sized companies must look to banks for short-term funds, many large corporations have the option of selling commercial paper. Commercial paper is an unsecured IOU from a large corporation to the buyer. Corporations sell the commercial paper either directly or through recognized dealers to other corporations, insurance companies, banks, money market funds, and pension funds. Commercial paper sells in denominations from $25,000 to several million dollars. Maturities are always less than a year—usually between two and six months.

The interest rate for commercial paper falls between that of Treasury notes and the prime rate. Therefore, buyers willingly invest because they get a larger return than they could with Treasury notes. Similarly, corporations prefer to sell commercial paper rather than take out bank loans because their money costs less. Recognized dealers in commercial paper typically charge 0.25 percent. This amount, because of the large denominations involved, is sufficient to compensate the dealers for their services. It is also small enough to make the transactions attractive to both buyers and sellers.

Many corporations have another reason for preferring commercial paper over bank loans. Commercial paper is easily sold, once the corporation has fully established its strength and reputation in the financial community. Instead of going through lengthy negotiations with a bank, the company can sell commercial paper quickly and easily through established channels.

Today, corporations as a group sell about two-thirds of their commercial paper through dealers and one-third directly to buyers. Through direct sales, a company avoids the charges of commercial paper dealers.

ACCOUNTS RECEIVABLE FINANCING

We have already seen how a company can convert accounts receivable into cash more quickly through aggressive collection techniques. When a company fears that aggressive collection may offend customers to the point where they'll take their business to competitors, the firm may decide to convert its accounts receivable to cash through a financing company. The company can choose between two methods—pledging and factoring, both of which will be described later in this section (see "Converting Receivables into Cash"). In practice, finance companies or banks offer a long list of variations on these two financing methods.

INVENTORY FINANCING

A company's inventory is a valuable asset and can often be used as collateral for a loan. In this way, the firm can get the cash it needs while still retaining access to its inventory. There are four basic ways to use inventory as collateral, depending on how closely the lender controls the physical inventory. These are, first, a chattel mortgage (this means specific inventory is used to secure the loan); second, a floating lien (the loan is secured by all the borrower's inventory); third, field warehousing (the lender physically separates and guards the pledged inventory on the borrower's premises); and finally, public warehousing (the lender transfers the pledged inventory to a separate warehouse). These approaches are examined in depth later in this section (see "Turning Inventory into Cash").

OTHER OPTIONS FOR OBTAINING SHORT-TERM CASH

Insufficient borrowing capability often is a primary obstacle to profitability for a company. The obstacle is larger if the firm's credit standing precludes borrowing from one of the short-term sources discussed earlier. One alternative that may be available to such a company is a guaranteed loan from the Small Business Administration—the SBA. The SBA makes two types of loans—direct loans and indirect SBA-guaranteed loans.

Some firms are actually financed by their customers. This situation typically occurs on large, complex, long-term projects. Companies such as contractors, shipbuilders, and management consultants typically divide large projects into a series of stages and require payment as they complete each stage. This significantly reduces the cash such companies require, compared to firms that finance an entire project themselves and receive payment upon completion. In some companies, customers pay in advance for everything they buy. Many mail-order operations are financed this way.

SELECTING THE BEST FINANCING PACKAGE

A financial manager is interested in securing the required short-term funds at the lowest cost. The lowest cost usually means using a combination of trade credit, unsecured bank loans, accounts receivable financing, and inventory financing. While it is virtually impossible to evaluate every possible combination of short-term financing, financial managers can use their experience and subjective opinion to put together a short-term financing package that has a reasonable cost. At the same time, managers must be aware of future requirements and of the impact that using certain sources today may have on the availability of short-term funds in the future.

In selecting the best financing package, a cash manager should consider the firm's current situation and requirements, the current and future costs of alternatives, and the firm's future situation and requirements. For small companies, the options available may be somewhat limited, and the total short-term financing package may be of less importance. On the other hand, larger firms may be faced with a myriad of possibilities. Clearly, short-term borrowing decisions can become quite complex. But selecting the right combination of options can be of significant financial value to the company.

Sources of Financing and the Cash Flow Cycle

A financial manager's ability to manage liabilities is equally as important as his or her ability to manage assets. There are various sources of funds that can be used to improve cash flow. Not only can a cash manager deal directly with financial institutions, but he or she also has the option of managing the cash flows associated with receivables and payables.

Managing the company's cash flow cycle helps a financial manager determine the source of short-term financing that is most appropriate. The equation for calculating the cash flow cycle appears below. In addition, there is a list of the types of short-term financing that are appropriate for altering each component of the cycle.

$$\text{Cash flow cycle} = \text{Average age of inventory} + \text{Average age of accounts receivable} \quad \text{Average age of accounts payable}$$

Inventory	Accounts Receivable	Accounts Payable
Taking out trust receipts	Pledging	Stretching
Warehousing	Factoring	
Liquidating	Altering Credit Terms	

We will discuss each of these short-term sources of financing in turn. It is important to remember that the objective of using any one or a combination of these sources is to reduce the amount of funds tied up in the cash flow cycle.

Turning Inventory into Cash

Inventories are a major component of working capital. Inventories, like receivables or payables, can be converted into cash, but this conversion has a cost. Taking out a lien, warehousing, and selling or liquidating inventories are three ways of reducing the amount of cash tied up in this asset.

TAKING OUT TRUST RECEIPTS

A business that needs short-term funds, but finds that its general reputation and financial strength are inadequate to support unsecured borrowing, may be able to raise cash by using its physical assets to secure the loan. The lender takes out a trust receipt—that is, a lien against these assets. Inventory is the most commonly used asset to secure borrowing in this way.

A chattel, or property, mortgage is a loan secured by specific assets. For example, a borrower might pledge 5,000 new refrigerators as collateral for a loan. In order to guarantee the lender's position as a secured creditor in case of bankruptcy, a chattel mortgage must precisely describe the items pledged as collateral. If refrigerators are used, the loan agreement will include the serial numbers of the specific refrigerators pledged by the borrower. If the borrower sells some of these refrigerators or receives a new shipment of refrigerators, the chattel mortgage must be rewritten to include these changes.

Because a chattel mortgage describes the collateral so specifically, it offers fairly high security to a lender. Lenders further reduce their risk by lending only a fraction of the estimated market value of the collateral. This fraction depends on how easily the assets can be transported and sold. In the case of refrigerators, which are easy to sell, a borrower might obtain as much as 90 percent of the wholesale cost. On the other hand, a borrower with a highly specialized inventory, such as bulldozer scoops, might get 50 percent or less of the fair market value because the lender would have difficulty selling such items to recover the money. Since chattel mortgages describe the collateral so specifically, lenders limit their use to high-value items.

Instead of naming specific items of inventory to secure a loan, borrowers may pledge all their inventory. This is a floating, or blanket, lien. Because such an arrangement does not describe specific inventory items, it does not have to be rewritten each time the borrower sells or receives inventory. But this flexibility makes it extremely difficult for the lender to maintain the security for the loan. For example, the borrower might sell most of the inventory and not leave enough to secure the loan. For this reason, banks and finance companies will usually lend only a small fraction of the inventory's market value in the case of a floating lien.

WAREHOUSING

Taking out a trust receipt is not necessary if the warehousing method of financing is used. There are two variations of this method—field warehousing and public warehousing.

When field warehousing is used, the finance company—usually an organization that specializes in warehousing—is given the use of a certain part of the borrowing company's premises. This floor space—the "warehouse"—must be segregated from the borrower's other operations so it can be kept locked. Only the warehousing company has the right of access to this space. The inventory to be used as collateral is transferred to the segregated area, and the warehousing company advances the discounted cash value of the inventory to the borrower. In return, the warehousing company gets a warehouse receipt giving it title to the inventory.

This inventory cannot be sold or used without the warehousing company's permission. This permission is given only when a corresponding portion of the funds that were advanced is repaid. Thus, the lender is able to ensure that the collateral is adequate to secure the loan at all times. The warehousing company maintains a member of its own staff—the custodian—on the borrower's premises to ensure that its rights are respected.

Public warehousing, which is sometimes called terminal warehousing, is similar to field warehousing except that the physical inventory is transferred to and stored in a warehouse operated by an independent warehousing company instead of in a segregated section of the borrower's premises. The mechanics of the financing remain the same: Inventory is not released to the borrower until a corresponding part of the loan has been repaid.

There are many variations of warehousing. For example, some bonded warehouses accept checks in payment for loans and then forward these checks to the finance company while simultaneously releasing the appropriate amount of inventory to the borrower. If such an arrangement is acceptable to all parties, it helps the borrower regain title to the inventory more quickly.

Warehouse financing is very widely used in the food and lumber industries. Canned goods, in particular, account for almost 20 percent of all field warehouse loans; however, almost any nonperishable and easily marketable commodity may be used. Warehousing, like receivables financing, is a flexible source of short-term credit that automatically grows as the company's working capital needs expand. But its cost is fairly high. Typically, the warehousing company makes a service charge—usually a fixed minimum plus 1 to 2 percent of the funds loaned—in addition to charging an interest rate of 8 to 12 percent or more. The fixed costs of warehousing—the minimum service charge plus the cost of providing the field warehouse facilities or moving goods to a public warehouse—render it unsuitable for very small companies; the minimum feasible inventory is probably about $100,000.

SELLING

The simplest way of turning inventory into cash, of course, is by selling it, and in extreme situations, this is a possible source of funds. But such a source may be very costly indeed. If the company has finished goods on hand, presumably the company has not been able to sell them at the regular price, or they are being accumulated to meet a future seasonal demand that does not yet exist. In either case, to sell the goods immediately, the company would probably have to offer especially attractive terms of sale—that is, either a lower than normal price or unusually attractive credit terms. And a company that is itself short of cash is in no position to offer more credit to customers. To sell the finished goods, then, it will probably be necessary to reduce the price substantially— perhaps to a point where the sale is completely unprofitable. But this may still be an acceptable strategy—in a liquidity crisis, cash flow is much more important than profit.

If the company has an inventory of raw materials in excess of its immediate needs, it may be possible to generate cash by selling some of the inventory. A chocolate manufacturer, for instance, that bought large stocks of cocoa bean when the price was unusually low may be able to resell some of this stock to generate cash. Such a policy is likely to be less expensive than selling off finished goods at fire-sale prices and is well worth considering.

Converting Receivables into Cash

Accounts receivable are a major item of working capital for most companies. But we have seen that working capital is not the same as cash. Receivables themselves cannot be used to pay bills. However, one way in which a company can increase its cash flow in a financial crisis is to convert receivables into cash more quickly than the normal method of collection would. There are two ways of doing this—pledging and factoring.

PLEDGING

Pledging is using receivables as security for an advance of funds. The lender who accepts and discounts the receivables may be a commercial bank or an industrial finance company, specializing in pledging. The schematic process of pledging accounts receivable is illustrated on the next page.

The first step in setting up a pledging relationship is to negotiate a formal agreement between the borrower and the lender. Once agreement has been reached and a legal contract has been signed, the borrower begins to present receivables. The lender gives the borrower the face value of the invoices less charges. That is, the lender discounts the invoices and pays less than the amount it hopes to collect.

A pledging agreement almost always has two important characteristics. One is that, in the event that the customer defaults and fails to pay the sum invoiced, the lender has the right of recourse to the borrower. Assume, for example, that a toy manufacturer is short of cash and pledges its receivables with a finance company. One customer, a local department store, buys toys worth $10,000. The toy manufacturer invoices the sale and sends a copy of the invoice to the finance company. The finance company gives the manufacturer the discounted value of the invoice, probably about $8,500. If all goes well, the department store will pay the bill after 30 days or so by sending a check to the manufacturer. The toy manufacturer, in turn, sends the check to the finance company. But if the department store fails to pay on time, and if inquiry reveals that the store is about to liquidate and will never be able to pay the bill, then the manufacturer is legally obliged to pay the full face value of the invoice—in this case, $10,000—to the finance company.

There are many variations on this basic pattern. Sometimes the borrower, instead of borrowing against individual invoices, is virtually given a line of credit by the finance company and assigns all its receivables as collateral for the credit line. Sometimes the borrower assigns individual invoices but without recourse. In such cases, the lender holds back an agreed-on portion of each payment as a reserve for losses from bad debt and charges any invoices it is unable to collect against this reserve.

The second important characteristic of a pledging agreement is that, except in those cases in which all invoices are assigned as blanket collateral, the lender retains the right to examine the invoices submitted and to discount only those it considers to be acceptable credit risks. Clearly, this reduces the lender's risk.

I. Pledging

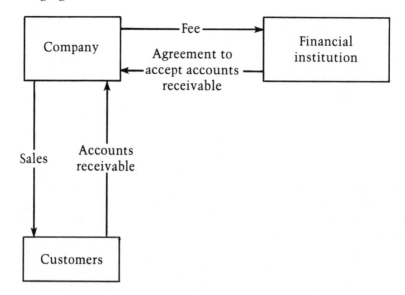

II. Payment by Customer

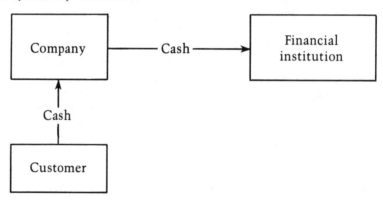

III. Nonpayment by Customer

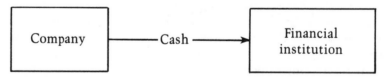

Pledging (or discounting) receivables is not a cheap source of credit. During most of the 1970s, when the usual commercial bank rate was between 8 and 15 percent, the cost of discounting was about 20 percent. Similar rate differentials exist today. An additional charge is often made to cover the lender's expenses incurred in appraising the credit risks. Consequently, this source is used mostly by companies that have no other source of funds open to them— primarily smaller companies. But for such companies the pledging method offers two advantages. First, after the initial agreement has been reached, the method is fairly informal and automatic, except when invoices are rejected as bad risks. Second, the customer being invoiced is in no way made aware that the borrowing company is in financial trouble; he or she simply sends a check in the normal way and never knows that it has been assigned to a third party. For this reason, pledging receivables is sometimes called nonnotification financing.

Factoring is a transaction that is essentially an outright sale of a company's **FACTORING** accounts receivable to a finance company or the factoring department of a commercial bank. In a factoring situation, the finance company has no recourse to the borrower in the case of bad debts. The steps involved in factoring are illustrated on the following page. A factoring arrangement clearly increases the lender's risk. To reduce this risk, the finance company virtually takes over the work of the borrower's credit department. All orders received from customers (Step 1) are first sent to the finance company (Step 2) for a credit appraisal. If the finance company rejects a customer as an unacceptable credit risk, the borrower must either turn down the order or fill it on a cash basis. If the lender approves the customer's credit (Step 3), the sale is made (Step 4), and the customer pays the finance company (Step 5).

Factoring, like pledging, is fairly costly. The overall cost has a number of distinct components. A charge is made for the credit appraisal. This charge varies between 1 and 3 percent of the face value of the invoice. The interest charge depends on whether the finance company has agreed to forward the funds as soon as the goods are shipped or only at the end of the net due date. In the former case, the cost may well be as high as 15 to 20 percent.

The advantages of factoring are that, like pledging, it is a relatively easy and flexible source of funds once the initial negotiations have been completed. Factoring also provides additional funds as the borrower's scale of operations—and therefore its needs—grows. Factoring has always been widely used by small companies in the textile industry. For a small company, factoring allows the borrower to avoid the cost and trouble of setting up its own credit department, and to this extent factoring may be preferable to pledging. Against this, however, must be set the possible damage to the borrower's reputation when customers learn that their accounts have been sold to a finance company.

Another example of factoring is the use of a credit card. In effect, the selling company is factoring its accounts receivable to a bank or other sponsoring agency, and the credit card holder pays the issuer of the credit card directly.

There are several considerations when a firm is deciding whether or not to use factoring. Many companies are not able to duplicate the services for the same cost. For example, costs would be significantly reduced by eliminating the expense of credit investigation, uncollectable accounts, record keeping, and other expenses of maintaining a credit department. The company could then devote more management time to production and marketing and let credit professionals take care of accounts receivable collection.

Factoring is excellent for companies that have growth potential and seek increased cash flow to enhance expansion. It is also beneficial to companies that want to reduce bad debts. Factoring can accommodate the needs of small- to medium-sized businesses that require working capital or have seasonal selling patterns.

Users of factors receive many benefits. A factor's scale of operations and extensive credit files provide information on new customers quickly and efficiently. This prevents lost sales. Extensive files on the client's customers facilitate approving credit on a more liberal basis and in larger amounts. This increases the client's volume. A factor is able to incur greater risks because of its large financial resources. A factor may also increase the sales volume by advising a client of potentially desirable customers. Because the factoring firm is involved with many businesses, it may also identify customers that are undesirable.

The client may benefit from improved relations with customers as well, because the responsibility of collection rests with the factor. The client no longer risks causing tension by pressuring for payment. Customers may also pay their bills faster when they know a factor is involved. They realize that one factoring firm may handle the accounts of several of their suppliers and that nonpayment to one may jeopardize their credit with several firms.

Factoring is not appropriate for all companies, however. Although the benefits of factoring are great, for some businesses the cost of factoring may outweigh the value of the services they receive. A company with adequate cash resources that deals with a few customers with excellent credit standings would probably not gain much by using factoring. From the factor's point of view, some companies may be unacceptable as clients—for example, firms that depend heavily on one or two customers, those with unsound management or extremely limited working capital and sales volume, and those whose product quality is subject to frequent disputes or that incur heavy returns.

In general, factoring is more expensive than pledging. On the other hand, factors do provide services, such as credit checking and collection, that a company would otherwise have to carry out itself.

Processes Involved in Factoring Accounts Receivable

I. Factoring

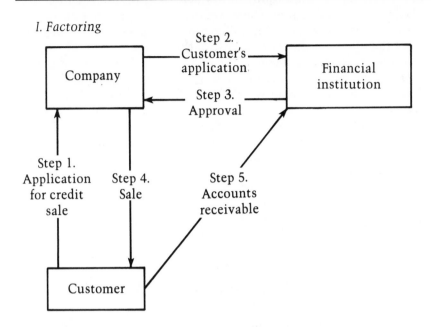

II. Payment by Customer

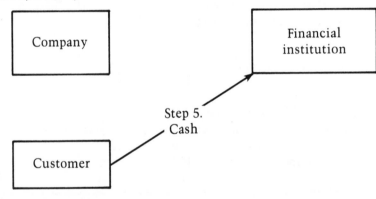

III. Nonpayment by Customer

There is no recourse, except to the customer.

SETTING CREDIT TERMS

The terms of credit include both the length of time allowed before payment is due and the discount given for prompt payment. The first factor to be considered is the size of the discount. The size of the discount depends on whether a cash discount really does speed up collections and on whether the opportunity cost of the funds justifies the expense of this action.

Assume, for example, that a company's terms are 2/10, net 30 and that 25 percent of its customers actually take advantage of the 2 percent discount. Annual sales are $72 million, of which $18 million are discounted, and the company recognizes profits when sales are made. The discount cost is, therefore, 2 percent of $18 million, or $360,000. Assuming that 25 percent of the customers pay in 10 days and the rest pay in 30, the average collection period, including both discount and nondiscount sales, is 25 days, given average accounts receivable of $5 million, as shown in the following equation.

$$\text{Credit sales} \div \frac{360}{\text{Average collection period}} = \text{Average accounts receivable}$$

$$\$72,000,000 \div \frac{360}{25} = \$5,000,000$$

If the company did not give a discount, none of its customers would pay within 10 days, and the average collection period would increase from 25 to 30 days. This would increase the cash flow cycle by 5 days. In this case, average accounts receivable would increase to $6 million:

$$\$72,000,000 \div \frac{360}{30} = \$6,000,000$$

The question is, then, whether the added return the company makes on the $1 million, by which the discount policy has reduced the average accounts receivable, exceeds $360,000, the cost of the discount policy.

A change in the number of days in which the firm expects payments is likely to make a greater difference to the average accounts receivable balance than giving or withholding a discount for prompt payment. A change of 2/10, net 30 to 2/10, net 45, assuming 25 percent of the company's customers take advantage of the discount, causes the average payment period to increase from 25 days to 36 days. This change will increase the cash flow cycle, thereby tying up greater amounts of cash. The average accounts receivable will now be $7.2 million, as shown below:

$$\$72,000,000 \div \frac{360}{36} = \$7,200,000$$

A company's accounts receivable depend not only on the terms of credit offered, but on how well those terms are enforced through the company's collection policy.

Some of a company's accounts receivable will be paid after the stated limit in the credit terms. Others will never be paid at all and will have to be written off as bad debts. Both can be controlled to some extent through the company's collection policy.

One generalization that can safely be made is that collection procedures are expensive, and their use is justifiable only when the expected results exceed the cost. Collection operations, in fact, are an excellent demonstration of the economists' law of diminishing returns. For a given volume of overdue accounts, the first few thousand dollars spent on collections will probably produce worthwhile results. Further expenditure is likely to yield less and less return. In the Selected Readings, an article entitled "Solving the Cash Crunch Through Credit Control" by Mark Goodman offers an interesting approach to collection problems.

Stretching Accounts Payable

Managing payables involves the same procedures as managing receivables. But these procedures are looked at from the opposite viewpoint—that is, the company is a user rather than a provider of credit. In fact, both processes go on simultaneously. Almost all companies, having accounts receivable and accounts payable, both provide and use trade credit at the same time.

Difficult though it may be to determine exactly how much credit a supplier will be willing to extend, it will almost certainly be more than the nominal net terms. The prime objective of suppliers is to sell products, and they will be very reluctant to do anything that will endanger sales. Few suppliers are monopolists; suppliers who try to enforce net 30 terms will quickly lose business to competitors. Any company selling on terms of net 30 days expects some of its customers to stretch their payments beyond 30 days. If a high percentage of these customers are small companies that rely heavily on trade credit, the company's average receivables will probably exceed 30 days. Usually, the company monitors its receivables closely and institutes a general tightening up if average receivables increase beyond a certain limit—say, 45 days—but even this depends to some extent on what policy rival suppliers have adopted.

Some suppliers actively use generous terms of trade credit as a form of sales promotion. This is especially likely in the case of a distributor, trying to enter a new geographical area, for example, that is faced with the need to lure customers away from established rivals. In such circumstances, generous credit may well be more effective than an intensive advertising campaign or a high-pressure sales team. The credit may be a simple extension of the discount and/or net terms, or it may take a modified form such as an inventory loan. The most extreme case might be the manufacturer or distributor that finds no suitable outlets for its product in the new territory and is forced to encourage local people to start up in business as company agents. Almost the entire working capital of such new ventures might have to be provided in the form of trade credit.

CREDIT AND SEASONAL BUSINESS

Special circumstances arise in highly seasonal businesses. Think again of the toy manufacturer, whose business has a very marked pre-Christmas seasonal peak. This manufacturer's customers, toy distributors or retail stores, probably have an even more severe seasonal fluctuation in their sales and probably find themselves acutely short of working capital from August through November of each year, when they must build up their stocks in preparation for Christmas. Even though the toy manufacturer's terms of sale are nominally 2/10, net 30, the company may give extended credit to its customers during difficult periods.

The toy manufacturer might be better advised to do whatever can be done to encourage customers to start building up their stocks well before the August-November peak, so that production can be smoothed out over a longer period. This can be done through seasonal dating, a policy of offering more generous credit terms on orders placed outside the usual peak period. The toy manufacturer may decide to offer terms of net 90 days on June orders, net 60 days on July orders, and net 30 on August through November orders. This produces advantages for both the manufacturer and its customers. Toy distributors are able to start buying earlier and enjoy a longer lead time, but they still do not have to pay for the toys until the selling season begins. The manufacturer, on the other hand, is able to spread toy production for the seasonal sales peak over a longer period without having to accumulate and store a large inventory of finished goods. But this policy clearly has a cost to the manufacturer: the funds invested in a large increase in accounts receivable. As usual, there is a trade-off to be made between the economics of smoothing production and the cost of financing these receivables.

This brings us to another important question. Who, in general, pays the costs of trade credit? Clearly, there is a cost, because funds are tied up in a use that produces no direct return on investment. The obvious conclusion seems to be that the supplier, who gives the credit, must pay the cost. But this is not always true. A supplier who gives unusually generous credit terms may be passing some of the costs on to customers as higher prices, which customers pay because they have no other source of credit. The extent to which this happens depends on the supplier's competitive position. If its product is in some way unique—perhaps because it is a powerful brand—the demand will be relatively inelastic, and it may well be possible to pass on some of the cost of trade credit in the form of higher prices. When demand is elastic, this will probably not be possible. But as we have already mentioned, the availability of other sources of short-term funds may be more important than the availability of alternative suppliers.

WHO PAYS THE COST?

Trade credit has two important advantages that justify using it extensively. First, it is convenient and readily available. Because it is not negotiated, it requires no great expenditure of executive time and no legal expenses. If a supplier accepts a company as a customer, the usual credit terms are automatically extended, even though the maximum line of credit may be low at first. Second, and closely related to the first advantage, is the fact that the credit available from this source automatically grows as the company grows. As sales expand, production schedules are increased. This in turn means that larger quantities of materials and supplies must be bought. In the absence of limits on credit, the additional credit becomes available automatically simply by placing orders for the extra material. Of course, if the manufacturing process is long and the supplier's payment deadline is reached before the goods have been sold, some additional source of credit will also be needed. But the amount required will still be very much less than it would have been if no trade credit had been available.

ADVANTAGES OF TRADE CREDIT

We should always remember, however, that a company is actually using trade credit as a source of financing only to the extent that its accounts payable exceed its accounts receivable. That is, a company is using trade credit to finance its operations only if it is using more credit granted by its suppliers than it is in turn granting to its own customers; we might call this positive net trade credit. Some companies are never able to achieve this. The toy manufacturer may buy its raw materials from two or three major suppliers, who offer terms of net 30 days and monitor their receivables closely to ensure that their customers pay fairly promptly. But the toy manufacturer's own customers are perhaps small distributors—or even retailers—who rely on trade credit to supply much of their working capital, especially during seasonal peaks. If the manufacturer were to try to restrict their credit, they would probably place their orders elsewhere. Thus, the toy manufacturer will almost certainly find itself having to give more trade credit than it receives and will have to look elsewhere for short-term funds to bolster its working capital.

Summary

Some of the methods of obtaining short-term funds have been discussed in this section. It must be remembered that the primary source for most businesses is short-term borrowing at a commerical bank. The other sources described here are meant to be additional and supplementary sources and not substitutes for bank borrowing.

By using a company's cash flow cycle as the standard of measure, a financial manager should be able to analyze the effects of various combinations of short-term financing on the firm's cash flow. In addition to the benefits derived from these sources, some attempt should be made to evaluate the cost, so that the least costly combinations can ultimately be selected.

6.

Investing in the Money Market

A Guide to Money Market Investment

The process of managing company cash is clearly interrelated with managing the investment of funds in the short-term money market. For the sake of simplicity, we are arbitrarily defining the money market as that market where securities having maturities of one year or less are issued and traded. This chapter offers guidelines for investment and describes eight types of securities that a company might consider as investment options.

We have seen that the most important strategies of cash management are speeding up cash inflows and slowing down cash outflows so the company will have liquid funds available. Generating these funds would not be worth the effort if the cash were then to pile up in checking accounts that offer minimal or no returns. Instead, idle funds, which are not being used to pay off current liabilities or carry on day-to-day operations, should be invested in the money market. Selecting which marketable securities to invest in can significantly affect a company's risk, growth, profitability, and liquidity objectives. Therefore, financial managers should be well versed in the fundamentals of the money market.

Managing the balance between cash and marketable securities is directly tied to balancing return and illiquidity. All assets—inventory or accounts receivable, for example—are managed to provide a contribution toward achieving corporate objectives of growth, profitability, and reduced risk. So it is with managing marketable securities.

Managers know that the risk of insolvency is related to the variability of cash flows and the fixed-cost structure of the firm. Company management establishes an objective of minimizing insolvency risk, subject to achieving other corporate objectives. The strategy for managing the marketable securities account is then adjusted to contribute both to corporate profitability and to liquidity.

Illiquidity becomes imminent when the cash flow generated is not sufficient to meet the current objectives of the company. Since the cash account is held at a minimum level—only enough cash to meet normal outflows and minimum-balance requirements—no cash is available from this source. Therefore, the more funds the company has invested in marketable securities, the less likely that illiquidity will be a problem. At the same time, remember that the term structure of interest rates slopes upward. This means that under normal conditions, the rate of return on assets or investments with short maturities will be lower than the return on assets with longer maturities. Hence, trade-offs must be made between the demand for profitability and the need for liquidity.

An interesting parallel can be made between how businesses and individuals should manage their cash positions. Everybody knows that it is necessary to keep funds for a rainy day to cover expenses in emergencies. Most personal financial consultants recommend that an individual keep an amount equal to six months of income in a liquid form. The most liquid form is a checking account. But the return on this investment is very low. It rarely exceeds 5.5 percent. Because of this low return, a savings account, money market fund, or certificates of deposit represent much more profitable opportunities for individuals. Securities or investments in bonds, stock, or real estate with longer maturities present an opportunity for greater returns but mean sacrificing liquidity. For a corporation, the parallel is to invest in long-term equity or fixed assets instead of marketable securities.

SOURCES OF SURPLUS CASH

Very often, a company has surplus cash that is not needed for immediate business activities. If the corporation leaves this surplus cash in a checking account, it earns no return or a very small return. For this reason, corporations try to invest surplus cash so it will earn interest. This cash may come from any of several sources.

One source could be a seasonal sales peak. If a company's strongest selling season is during the summer and its customers pay within 30 to 60 days, the company is likely to have surplus cash in the fall.

A second source is obtaining a large loan. Frequently, companies negotiate bank loans for more than their immediate needs. For example, if a company sees that it will need $600,000 over the next six months to build up inventory, it may borrow the entire amount the first month instead of borrowing $100,000 each month. This simplifies bank negotiations, but it leaves the company with surplus cash that must be invested profitably in order to offset bank interest charges.

Another source is the result of leasing equipment. A company may decide to lease equipment that it had planned to buy. Or the company might sell an existing piece of equipment to a leasing company and then lease it back. Either way, the firm will find itself with surplus cash.

A fourth source could be the sale of stock or the placement of bonds. A company may raise money by selling additional shares of its own stock or by placing its bonds with outside investors. Either way, the company probably will be unable to use the sudden influx of cash immediately and must invest the surplus.

In addition to these situations, a firm may have surplus cash simply from its day-to-day activities. For example, if several large customers pay sooner than expected, the company may have extra cash a week earlier than it had planned. An efficient cash manager can profitably invest this money for one week.

Very often, a company may have surplus cash at the same time that it owes money to banks or has bonds outstanding. Why not simply pay back the bank? Sometimes this is the correct thing to do, but more often the company's cash surplus is temporary. This means the cash manager should look for a temporary investment. If the company prepaid part of its bank loan with temporary surplus cash, it might have to go back to the bank for an additional loan in a week or two.

CRITERIA FOR INVESTING SURPLUS CASH

Cash managers use four criteria when they invest surplus cash: safety, liquidity, return, and taxability.

The first responsibility of cash managers is to prevent the loss of capital. They must analyze each investment in terms of the risk of default by the borrower. They must carefully assess the probability that the borrower will pay all contracted interest and repay the principal at maturity. In the case of marketable securities, cash managers must also assess the risk of a drop in the market value of the security.

Liquidity refers to how quickly the investment can be converted back into cash. Many marketable securities can be changed back into cash overnight. Other investments require anywhere from a few days to 90 days. In general, the cash manager must either select very liquid (quickly convertible) investments or match the maturity of investments to the company's needs. For example, if a company has surplus cash that it will need in 30 days, a cash manager may give preference to an investment that matures in 30 days.

A cash manager must look at the return—or profit—that each potential investment offers. In order to calculate the return accurately, the cash manager must include such expenses as commissions to brokers and handling time.

Finally, the cash manager must assess the taxability of each investment. Some investments offer a lower apparent return, but the income from them is taxed at a lower rate, so that the after-tax return is fully competitive with that of other investments.

Companies are often tempted to misuse a marketable securities account to generate profits at the expense of reduced liquidity. As these firms become more aggressive with cash management programs, they tend to appreciate and take for granted the additions to the bottom line. They lose sight of the volatile nature of short-term rates. They forget that the basic purpose of a marketable securities account is to preserve liquidity. Paramount in the mind of a financial manager must be the realization that liquidity in the marketable securities portfolio must be preserved at all costs. The primary purpose of investing in marketable securities is not to generate profits. That is only a side benefit. The main objective is to have an immediate source of funds that ensures that liquidity is maintained even if cash outflows exceed cash inflows.

KEEPING THE CASH MANAGEMENT FUNCTION IN PROPER PERSPECTIVE

If a company takes more risk and lengthens the maturity of an investment, the result will be illiquidity. This happens because the lower the credit standing of a security, the harder it is to sell—especially on short notice. Also, the longer the maturity of the portfolio, the greater the swing in market value of the investment for a given change in interest rates. As rates rise, the value of a portfolio with an average maturity of two years will fall much further than the value of a portfolio with an average maturity of three months.

Remember, cash managers are responsible for providing the wherewithal to ensure the smooth, uninterrupted functioning of the company's main business. They must not subvert this task by speculating on interest rate changes or other risky investment practices, which could detract from the firm's main line of endeavor. It is very important for cash managers to keep a proper perspective, not only with respect to their own actions but also when describing the cash management program to other officers of the company.

Financial managers who are responsible for investing in marketable securities should be aware of the types of securities available in the money market. They must understand the characteristics, maturities, denominations, and so on of marketable securities. We will turn our attention to the specific types of investments and securities that the cash manager should be familiar with.

BANK SAVINGS ACCOUNTS

Most corporations hold some funds in a demand deposit in a commercial bank. These funds are immediately available. But the bank is not permitted to pay interest on corporate demand deposits. An alternative to a demand deposit is a time deposit. In exchange for a return, the corporation must be willing to give up the immediate availability of funds that demand deposits offer. Time deposit accounts are extremely safe because so few banks fail. Moreover, bank deposits are insured up to a governmentally determined maximum amount by the Federal Deposit Insurance Corporation.

There are several types of time deposits. Regular savings accounts are used predominantly by individuals and small companies. Savings accounts do not usually offer a high return. In fact, the interest allowed is limited by law. Also, many banks are not chartered to offer interest paying savings accounts to corporations. The maturity of savings accounts is indefinite. Money can be kept in a savings account for as long or as short a time as you want. As an alternative to savings accounts, many banks now offer money market accounts. These accounts pay higher interest than regular savings accounts and can be used by corporations as well as individuals.

Another type of time account is a certificate of deposit—called a CD. CDs are the interest paying obligations of commercial banks. The two major differences between a CD and a regular savings account are maturity and amount of interest. The maturity of a CD is fixed. The rate of interest at the point of inception can vary. We'll discuss details of negotiable CDs later in this section.

SELECTING AN APPROPRIATE MIX OF MARKETABLE SECURITIES

Although cash managers may hold some surplus cash in a bank savings account, most prefer to earn a significantly higher return by investing in some of the many types of marketable securities. In order to select the appropriate mix of marketable securities, a cash manager should first divide the available surplus funds into three classifications: backup, predictable needs, and free cash.

A company may need extra cash quickly to serve as a backup if anything goes wrong. Therefore, a portion of any surplus funds should be invested in securities that can be readily converted into cash—that is, securities with high liquidity.

A company can predict many of its cash needs in advance. Thus, some surplus cash can be invested in securities with longer maturities that will yield cash for such predictable needs as payrolls, taxes, and dividends.

Once a company has provided for emergency backup needs and predictable needs, its remaining cash is free. Therefore, the securities in this part of a company's portfolio are not earmarked for any specific immediate purpose, and the cash manager is able to invest these funds in securities offering a higher return. Short-term liquidity is not as important for these investments.

The most important factor in the decision regarding which securities you should buy for each classification of cash is the liquidity of the investment. Obviously, the backup cash portfolio must be instantly convertible into cash. Securities bought for predicted cash needs should ideally have maturities that closely match dates when the cash will be needed. And finally, the free-cash portfolio may have any reasonable maturities.

Going back to the four guidelines for investing surplus cash—safety, liquidity, return, and taxability—we can now outline the three steps to follow in selecting marketable securities. First, every security must offer a very high degree of safety and liquidity or you must discard it from further consideration. Second, you should match the liquidity or maturity of each security to its purpose. Third, within the constraints of safety, you should seek the security offering the highest return—remembering, of course, to consider commissions, handling time, and taxes.

There are eight important types of marketable securities: U.S. Treasury bills, federal agency issues, commercial paper, certificates of deposit, banker's acceptances, tax-exempt obligations, money market funds, and Eurodollar deposits. We will discuss each of these instruments in turn.

TYPES OF MARKETABLE SECURITIES

U.S. Treasury securities account for the largest fraction of the money market. The Treasury issues several forms of securities, including Treasury bills, tax-anticipation bills, notes, and bonds.

U.S. Treasury Securities

Treasury bills—called T-bills—are extremely popular because of their safety, high trading volume, and variety of maturities. T-bills are considered completely safe because they are backed by the U.S. government. But T-bills are traded on the open market and, if sold before maturity, may suffer from temporary market fluctuations. The Treasury auctions T-bills weekly and offers standard maturities of 91 days and 182 days. Subsequently, T-bills are traded in a broad secondary market handled by registered securities dealers and banks. Because of this broad secondary market and the weekly auctions, you can purchase T-bills that mature almost any week during the coming year. The Treasury sells three-month and six-month bills every week. In addition, it periodically sells nine-month and one-year bills.

T-bills do not pay interest. Instead, they are sold at a discount from the par or face value. The holder then collects the full face value at maturity and, in this way, earns a return on his or her investment. For example, a 91-day T-bill might sell for $98.50. That is, you buy the T-bill now for $98.50, and you will receive $100.00 in 91 days. This $1.50 profit for 91 days (one-fourth of a year) is roughly equivalent to $6.00 annually, or 6 percent.

The Treasury occasionally sells tax-anticipation bills. Most corporations must pay taxes quarterly in March, June, September, and December. Tax-anticipation bills mature near these quarterly tax-due dates, so a corporation can use them at full face value to pay taxes. For example, a company may know that it has to pay $2 million in taxes on March 15. This company could buy tax-anticipation bills that mature in the middle of March and use them to pay its taxes when it files its quarterly return.

The Treasury also issues obligations with longer maturities. Treasury bonds have maturities of more than ten years, and notes have maturities of one to ten years. Unlike Treasury bills, these Treasury securities pay interest. If the market rates of interest have risen above the interest rate printed on the securities, they will sell at a discount. This discount brings the effective interest rate closer to the short-term T-bill rate. The safety and liquidity of longer-term Treasury securities are fully equal to that of T-bills.

Federal Agency Issues

Other federal agencies also issue securities. Like T-bills, most of these securities are sold at a discount price that gives an effective return very close to that of T-bills. The same securities dealers and banks that maintain a secondary market in T-bills also maintain a secondary market in federal agency securities. These issues are not a legal debt of the U.S. Treasury and are not guaranteed by the government. Because of the close association of these agencies with the government, many people feel that they are government-guaranteed. Perhaps because of their slightly higher risk, short-term issues of federal agencies usually offer a yield that is 10 to 40 basis points higher than the current T-bill rate. (A basis point is equal to one-hundredth of a percentage point of an interest rate. The term is used to make it easier to compare rates of return on various investments. In the case of short-term federal agency issues, 10 to 40 basis points are equivalent to a 0.1 to 0.4 percent higher yield.)

There are six principal federal agencies that issue short-term securities. First, the Federal National Mortgage Association—known as "Fannie Mae"—buys and sells mortgages guaranteed by the Federal Housing Administration and the Veterans Administration. Second, the Government National Mortgage Association—called "Ginnie Mae"—provides mortgage money for home owners. Third, Federal Land Banks extend long-term credit to Federal Land Bank Associations. These associations then make long-term loans to farmers. Typical Federal Land Bank bonds mature in about 10 years. Then there are Federal Home Loan Banks, which sell notes with 9- and 12-month maturities, as well as bonds with 3- to 5-year maturities. These banks then lend the funds to their member savings and loan associations. Fifth, Federal Intermediate Credit Banks sell 9-month debentures each month and lend the funds to credit associations and agricultural credit corporations. And finally, the 13 Banks for Cooperatives issue 6-month debentures once or twice a month.

Commercial Paper

Commercial paper is the popular name for short-term, unsecured promissory notes issued by corporations. Corporate paper is issued by industrial, commercial, financial, and banking firms. Because commercial paper is unsecured, only the largest and most creditworthy corporations can successfully sell these promissory notes. The maturities on corporate paper range from a few days to nine months. The most popular maturities are three to six months, or nine months. Most commercial paper is sold at a discount and offers an effective interest rate somewhat higher than the current T-bill rate. Corporations occasionally issue commercial paper in denominations as small as $25,000. The denominations for most commercial paper range from $100,000 to $5 million.

Corporations sell their commercial paper either directly to buyers or to dealers. Only the most financially sound corporations can sell their paper directly, but this route accounts for the largest dollar volume of transactions. Smaller corporations sell their paper through dealers. These dealers very carefully investigate the financial strength of all potential issuers. They select only issuers that meet the dealers' high standards of size, financial condition, and reputation.

Because a large percentage of commercial paper is placed directly, there is very little secondary market for commercial paper. Therefore, cash managers should buy commercial paper expecting to hold it for predictable cash needs or as free cash. Although the secondary market for commercial paper is small, direct sellers of commercial paper will usually repurchase paper they have sold if requested to do so.

Certificates of Deposit

Negotiable certificates of deposit (CDs) are, as noted earlier, the interest paying obligations of commercial banks. They are very similar to time deposits except that they are negotiable. In other words, the original buyer can sell a CD to a third party. A CD proves that the owner has a specified amount of money on deposit at the named bank for a specified period of time and at a specified interest rate. Generally, the maturity of CDs ranges from 30 to 360 days. However, since CDs are negotiable, you can buy them with almost any maturity you want.

CDs offer a greater yield than Treasury bills and roughly the same yield as commercial paper. However, the interest range from the lowest-quality to the highest-quality CD can be as much as 75 basis points, or 0.75 percent. Three factors determine the quality of a CD. The first factor is the size and reputation of the issuing bank. The second is the maturity date. Companies prefer CDs that mature just before monthly and quarterly tax payment dates. So because the demand is higher for these CDs, the yield on them is lower. The third factor is the denomination. The most popular denomination is $1 million.

There is a large, deep secondary market for CDs. Therefore, substantial holdings may be traded in a single transaction. This makes large-denomination CDs very liquid but decreases the liquidity of smaller CDs. In fact, some dealers will not buy CDs in denominations under $500,000, nor will they buy the CDs of smaller banks.

Banks initially sell CDs at par and offer to pay interest at maturity. If the original buyer then decides to sell the CD, market forces determine the price.

Banker's Acceptances

A banker's acceptance is a draft that instructs a bank to pay a specified amount of money to the owner of the draft at a specified future date. The bank signs the draft in acceptance of its obligation to make this payment. There are four types of banker's acceptances, which are usually connected with foreign trade. The first type is used to finance exports or imports; the second, to finance the storage of goods in international trade; the third, to finance the storage of goods in domestic trade; and the fourth facilitates foreign currency exchange.

Banker's acceptances are considered very safe because almost everyone connected with them is responsible for their ultimate payment. Primary responsibility rests with the accepting bank, of course, but the original maker (often a foreign trader) is also responsible. Furthermore, if a dealer buys an acceptance from a bank and later sells it to an investor, the dealer is also responsible in case either the bank or the original maker defaults.

The standard maturity for banker's acceptance is 90 days. Because acceptances are actively traded, an investor can usually purchase an acceptance on the open market with any needed maturity less than 90 days. Bond dealers and many large banks maintain a market in banker's acceptances, and this provides excellent liquidity. Banker's acceptances typically yield 20 to 50 basis points (0.2 to 0.5 percent) above the prevailing T-bill rate.

| **Tax-Exempt Obligations** | Tax-exempt obligations are also a type of marketable security. City and state governments and their agencies can issue bonds on which the interest is exempt from federal income tax. For an investor in the 50 percent tax bracket (this includes most corporations), tax-exempt interest is worth double its stated value. For instance, if a company invests $100,000 in an 8 percent taxable bond, it earns $8,000 in a year and must pay $4,000 in taxes. This leaves a net profit of $4,000. But if the company invests the same $100,000 in a 5 percent tax-exempt security, it receives $5,000 in one year but pays no federal tax. The net profit in this case is the full $5,000. In other words, the 5 percent tax-exempt security supplies a greater net profit than the 8 percent taxable security. |

The creditworthiness of tax-exempt securities ranges from excellent to completely unacceptable. You can find estimates of the credit risk of tax-exempt obligations in standard bond-rating tables such as those prepared by Moody's or Standard & Poor's. The liquidity of tax-exempt obligations ranges from very good to none at all.

| **Money Market Funds** | In 1973 and 1974, the interest rates on 90-day commercial paper and CDs rose substantially above 10 percent. Many smaller investors wanted to obtain these high yields but did not have the $100,000 minimum amount necessary to purchase these investments. To meet this need, several investment companies formed money market funds, which pooled the small investments of thousands of investors to purchase short-term money market instruments. |

Money market funds offer several advantages to investors: First, these funds require a low minimum investment. A typical investment is $1,000 to $5,000. They also offer complete liquidity. In most funds, investors can withdraw at will. Another advantage is relatively high safety. Most funds invest in a wide variety of very safe securities. The variety of investment also helps to decrease the risk by eliminating the investor's dependence on a small number of securities. Money market funds offer a high yield because they can afford to buy high-denomination investments that offer the highest yields. In addition, since securities are bought in large quantities, commissions as a percentage of transaction size are reduced. The fund itself, however, adds its own service charges that offset some of these savings. And finally, money market funds are convenient. Professional money managers make all investment decisions, thus relieving the individual investor or small-company cash manager of this job. In this way, money market funds allow smaller companies to earn a high return on their surplus funds, just as very large corporations do.

Unfortunately, many portfolio managers overestimate the complexity of money market trading. They believe that only an experienced Wall Street financier can buy and sell certificates of deposit or banker's acceptances. In fact, whatever can be done on Wall Street can be done in any major city of the country.

The easiest and safest way for a company to buy money market securities is through the investment department of its bank. The larger banks in all big cities have money market departments that are fully prepared to purchase whatever securities you want. Alternatively, a cash manager can buy securities directly. For example, a company can purchase commercial paper directly from several large corporations and finance companies, such as

General Motors Acceptance Corporation and Household Finance Corporation, both of which issue commercial paper directly. The aggressive cash manager can purchase certificates of deposit and banker's acceptances directly from issuing banks. In addition, many brokerage firms will assist a cash manager with a purchase of money market securities.

Eurodollars are deposits denominated in dollars in foreign banks or foreign **Eurodollars** branches of U.S. banks. These banks are not under the jurisdiction of the Federal Reserve, so they can issue time deposits that are not allowed in the United States, at rates not subject to Federal Reserve regulations. The market is largely a wholesale one. Eurobanks will accept deposits from well-known corporations, banks, and governments. A unique feature of the Euromarket is that, because of the myriad nationalities, financial practices, and varying degrees of information disclosure, an informal channel of information has emerged. For these reasons, depositors tend to place their money with the largest and best known Eurobanks rather than with smaller, obscure banks. This has helped to reduce somewhat the riskiness of the investment.

When corporations have surplus cash to invest, the cash manager must carefully evaluate the safety, liquidity, and yield of each investment. Investment possibilities include bank savings accounts and the eight principal money market investments that were discussed in detail.

Investing Surplus Cash

An alternative to holding cash is investing in marketable securities. Unlike cash, these investments earn interest but are not immediately available to use as payments. One requirement of a good cash management program is that the manager maintain as much of the company's liquid funds in the form of marketable securities as possible without endangering the company's ability to pay its bills on time. Another aspect of sound cash management is managing the investment portfolio to ensure that the company gets the best possible combination of return and protection of capital from invested funds. A financial executive in a small company with limited funds may simply accept advice from the company's commercial banker or leave the task of portfolio management entirely to a professional. But when the sums to be invested are large, skilled investment in marketable securities can make a significant contribution to the bottom line.

Various types of securities that are normally considered money market investments are listed on the following pages.

To test your judgment about the importance of various characteristics of marketable securities, indicate below on a scale of 1 to 5 how much significance each factor has when selecting a marketable security for investment purposes (1 being most important; 2, important; 3, neutral; 4, unimportant; and 5, least important).

1. Liquidity	1	2	3	4	5
2. Time to maturity	1	2	3	4	5
3. Status (market recognition)	1	2	3	4	5
4. Price stability	1	2	3	4	5
5. Risk	1	2	3	4	5

A survey by Lawrence Gitman and Mark Goodwin lends some insight into the thinking of cash managers associated with 182 companies in the middle range of the *Fortune 1,000* list.[1] The average responses to the survey are given below. These responses show that risk is the most important factor to be considered when selecting marketable securities. Liquidity and time to maturity were ranked as the second and third most important. The article entitled "An Assessment of Marketable Securities Management Practices," which contains the results of this survey, is included in the selected readings at the end of this book.

---

[1] Lawrence J. Gitman and Mark D. Goodwin, "An Assessment of Marketable Securities Management Practices," *The Journal of Financial Research*, Fall 1979, pp. 161-169.

Surplus Cash Investment Opportunities

Investment	Description	Denominations	Safety
U.S. Treasury bills (T-bills)	U.S. government obligations	$10,000 to $1 million	Virtually complete
Federal agency issues	Bonds, notes, and debentures from 6 major federal agencies	Most are $10,000 and up	Considered to be government guaranteed
Commercial paper	Unsecured interest-bearing notes of large corporations	$25,000 to $5 million	Very high; backed by financially strong corporations
Certificates of deposit (CDs)	Interest-bearing obligations of banks; similar to time deposits but negotiable	$100,000 to $1 million	High to very high; backed by large banks
Banker's acceptances	Draft instructing bank to pay acceptance holder	$25,000 to $1 million	Very high; backed by 2 or 3 financially strong parties
Tax-exempt obligations	Bonds and notes from state and city governments; exempt from federal income tax	$1,000 and up	Ranges from excellent to unacceptable
Money market funds	Private funds pooling investor's money to purchase money market securities	$1,000-$5,000 minimum	Usually high; depends on fund's investments
Eurodollar deposits	A time deposit, denominated in dollars in a bank outside the U.S.	$1 million minimum	Very safe

Surplus Cash Investment Opportunities

Maturity	Liquidity	Yield	State Taxation	Basis
3 and 6 month, sold weekly; 9 month and 1 year, sold monthly	Large active market	Varying recently from 6% to as high as 10%	No	Sold at discount; traded at market value
6 months to 10 years	Large active market	10-40 basis points (0.1% to 0.4%) above T-bills	Varies	Either discounted or interest bearing
3-270 days	Lack liquidity	Above T-bills and below banks' prime rate	Yes	Sold at discount
3 months to 1 year	Active market for large denominations and major banks	Above T-bills. Wide variation between different CDs	Yes	Sold at par; interest bearing; traded at market value
30-270 days	Market centered in New York	20-50 basis points (0.2% to 0.5%) above T-bills	Yes	Discounted
2 months to several years	Ranges from high to none	Tax exemption can lead to very high effective yield	No, if issued in own state	Usually interest bearing
All investments 1 year or less	Often completely liquid without prior notice	Typically 0% to 0.5% below commercial paper yields	Yes	Sold and redeemed at par; interest bearing
1 day or more	No secondary market	Above domestic CDs	No	Sold at par

Comparing Your Responses with the Survey

Characteristics	Your response	Average response
1. Liquidity	_____	2.50
2. Time to maturity	_____	2.90
3. Status (market recognition)	_____	4.36
4. Price stability	_____	3.55
5. Risk	_____	1.38

Another factor that was evaluated by the Gitman and Goodwin survey was the length of time a marketable security should be held. The results of the survey are given below.

Holding period	Average response*
1. Less than one week	2.1
2. One week to one month	1.83
3. One to three months	2.0
4. Over three months	3.3

* 1 = most frequent, 2 = next most frequent . . . , 4 = least frequent.

The most frequent holding period was one week to one month, followed closely by one to three months. It is interesting to note that most cash budgets are done on a monthly basis, and the response indicates a very aggressive posture of investing idle funds even for short periods of time.

Next, try ranking various types of marketable securities listed below on the basis of the risk each involves. The scale for ranking is from 1 to 7 (1 being least risky; 2, next least risky; 3, little risk; 4, neutral; 5, some risk; 6, next most risky; and 7, most risky).

1. Treasury securities	1	2	3	4	5	6	7
2. Federal agency issues	1	2	3	4	5	6	7
3. Federal funds	1	2	3	4	5	6	7
4. Repurchase agreements	1	2	3	4	5	6	7
5. Money market funds	1	2	3	4	5	6	7
6. Bankers acceptances	1	2	3	4	5	6	7
7. Negotiable CDs	1	2	3	4	5	6	7
8. Commercial paper	1	2	3	4	5	6	7
9. Foreign securities	1	2	3	4	5	6	7

In the Gitman and Goodwin study, a similar question was asked of cash managers, and the results of the survey are presented below. It is interesting to note that the risk rank corresponds quite closely to the yield factor for these same securities on pages 156 and 157.

Survey Results of Marketable Security Risk Ranking

Type of Security	Your Response	Average Response
1. Treasury securities	————	1.09
2. Federal agency securities	————	1.89
3. Federal funds	————	2.55
4. Repurchase agreements	————	3.07
5. Money market funds	————	3.13
6. Bankers acceptances	————	3.43
7. Negotiable CDs	————	3.53
8. Commercial paper	————	4.18
9. Foreign securities	————	4.33

Hedging with Interest Rate Futures

Because future interest rates cannot be predicted with precision, techniques have been developed to reduce the price risk of investing in marketable securities. Hedging was originally used to reduce the risk of price fluctuations in grains and other commodities.

Commodities were being traded in active markets in China, Egypt, Arabia, and India 1,200 years before the birth of Christ. Futures contracts for commodities as we know them today were probably developed in Japan in the seventeenth century. In 1848, Chicago became the center of commodity trading in the United States. Financial futures were first traded in October 1975, when trading in Government National Mortgage Association (GNMA) certificates was started in Chicago. As the markets developed by increasing the depth of trading and the types of securities that were traded, opportunities for hedging became available. Hedging is defined as taking a position so that one's wealth is unaffected by changes in the market rate of interest.

Like contracts for other commodities, interest rate futures contracts are traded on exchanges. These exchanges consist of a clearing agency or corporation. The clearing houses play a central role in every futures transaction. Buyers of futures contracts are obliged to make payment to the clearing house, while sellers are entitled to receive payment from it. Hence, buyers and sellers of futures contracts need not worry about the creditworthiness of the other party.

The types of instruments on which futures contracts are based have increased dramatically since 1975. The following pages list these financial instruments, the basic trading units, the exchanges where they are traded, the delivery method, and the price quotation associated with futures trading.

The real usefulness of futures markets is that they provide a relatively low-cost method for transferring the risk of unanticipated changes in interest rates. From the viewpoint of a corporate treasurer, two types of hedges are advisable—the long hedge and the short hedge. The long hedge involves purchasing futures contracts as protection against falling interest rates. The sale of futures contracts or a short hedge can be used as protection against rising rates on the value of an investment or transaction.

A long hedge entails purchasing a futures contract with the intention of offsetting it later by selling an identical contract. This type of hedge can be used to lock in the return on an investment planned for some future date. An example of a long hedge is outlined below.

Example of a Long Hedge

A long hedge is used when an investor wishes to lock in today's relatively high rates, but will not have the funds to invest until some future date.

	Cash Market	*Futures Market*
1 October	Expect to have $1 million to invest by 1 December. Wish to lock in current yield of 13% on T-Bills. Cost of $1 million in 90-day T-Bills at 13% is $967,500.	Purchase 1 December, 3-month T-Bill contract for $967,000 at 13.20%
1 December	Buy $1 million of 3-month T-bills for $968,625 (12.55%)	Sell 1 December, 3-month T-Bill contract for $968,125 at 12.75%
Net result	Opportunity loss = $1,125	Gain = $1,125

The example indicates that if a treasurer expects interest rates to fall and plans to make investments in the future, he or she can protect the funds by locking in the current high rate through the use of a long hedge. This is done by purchasing a 3-month T-bill futures contract for delivery in December. By December 1, if rates have fallen as anticipated, the treasurer would have suffered an opportunity loss by not investing on October 1st. The loss of $1,125 in the example is caused by a drop of T-bill rates from 13 percent to 12.55 percent. This loss can be offset by the purchase of a futures contract when the rates are 13.20 percent and the sale of that contract when the rates drop to 12.75 percent, yielding a gain of $1,125. The net effect of this hedge is that it allows the treasurer to invest at the higher rates available in October even though the funds are only available in December.

A short hedge involves the initial sale of a futures contract with the intention of offsetting it later by buying another contract for the same instrument with the same delivery date. This type of hedge is useful if interest rates are expected to rise. The example on page 164 illustrates the need for borrowing in the future when rates are expected to rise.

	Financial Futures		
	30-Day Commercial Paper	*90-Day Commercial Paper*	*Treasury Bills*
Basic trading unit	$3 M face value A-1 commercial paper	$1 M face value A-1 commercial paper	$1 M par value T-bills
Exchange where traded	Chicago Board of Trade	Chicago Board of Trade	AMEX Commodity Exchange Commodity Exchange International Monetary Market
Delivery method	Financial receipt backed by commercial paper in approved vault	Financial receipt backed by commercial paper in approved vault	Federal Reserve Book entry wire transfer system
Price quotation	Index: 100 minus annualized discount, e.g., 100 – 6.54 = 93.46	Index: 100 minus annualized discount, e.g., 100 – 6.54 = 93.46	Discounted interest based on actual days in 360-day year

Financial Futures		
4- to 6-year Treasury Notes	*GNMA*	*Long-Term Treasury Bonds*
$100,000 noncallable Treasury Notes	$100,000 GNMA 8% certificates	$100,000 U.S. Treasury Bonds, at least 15-year maturity
Chicago Board of Trade International Monetary Market	Chicago Board of Trade AMEX Commodity Exchange Commodity Exchange	Chicago Board of Trade AMEX Commodity Exchange
Federal Reserve Book entry wire transfer system	Actual GNMA Certificates	Federal Reserve Book entry wire transfer system
Percentage of par of a nominal instrument: 8% coupon, 6-year maturity	Percentage of par of a nominal instrument: 8% GNMA certificate	Percentage of par of a nominal instrument: 8% coupon, 15-year maturity

Example of a Short Hedge

A short hedge is used when a borrower wishes to lock in today's relatively low rates.

	Cash Market	*Futures Market*
1 May	Anticipate issuing $10 million in commercial paper in September; current rate is 5.38%	Sell 10 September, Commercial Paper contracts at 5.2%. Total funds received = $9,870,000
1 Sept.	Issue $10 million in commercial paper at 6.63% Value of Contract = $9,834,250	Buy 10 September, Commercial Paper contracts at 6.59% Value of Contract = $9,835,250

Cost of Issue:

Interest cost	$165,750
Less hedge profit	34,750
	$131,000

Gain: $34,750

$$\text{Effective annualized rate} = \frac{131,000}{9,834,250} \times 4 = 5.32\%$$

In the case of either rising or falling rates, the long or short hedge will benefit a treasurer by locking in a return on an investment or guaranteeing an interest rate for future financing. In effect, these transactions are insurance against future fluctuations in interest rates. A caveat must be entered at this point. The examples presented above assumed that there was no change in the basis, which is defined as the cash market price minus the futures market price. This simplification allows the gain in the futures market to exactly offset the loss in the cash market. However, this is not always the case. Thus a crucial element to the success of hedging with interest rate futures is what happens to the basis. It is beyond the scope of this book to become embroiled with this issue.

Summary

This section has provided the groundwork for an understanding of the money market. The various types of securities and their characteristics were discussed.

The relatively new technique of hedging applied to managing marketable securities was discussed, with the objective of showing how it could be used to reduce the risk of interest rate fluctuations.

The Case Study
Part Three

The Case Study: Part Three

Instructions: This case study consists of three parts. Each part has its own set of questions that you should answer as thoroughly as you can. Parts One and Two of the case study began on pages 79 and 113.

SAN LARGO ORANGE BLOSSOM, INC.

ASSIGNMENT

The objective of this part of the case study is to allow the reader to formulate an investment strategy for San Largo. After you read the case, respond to the following questions.

5. *How should Pam meet the short-term cash deficit in January? Be sure to discuss the costs and benefits of various short-term alternatives. A cost analysis worksheet is provided on page 171.*

6. *Prepare a plan or investment strategy for using the excess cash for February through December. Be sure to indicate the types of marketable securities and their maturity that you propose for investment of San Largo's excess cash. (For the sake of uniformity use the cash balances shown in the chart entitled "Excess Funds Available for Investment in 1986" on page 173, instead of the cash balances from your cash plan.)*

THE DECISION TO OBTAIN SHORT-TERM FUNDS

Because of the seasonal nature of San Largo's business, Pam believes that she will have to obtain short-term funds each year. Based on last year's experience with the bank, Pam feels that the change in bank policy requiring personal guarantees from the Grants will not be acceptable in the future. After discussing the situation with the loan officer at the bank, Pam is offered three alternatives for consideration.

The first alternative is to factor the company's accounts receivable. The second is to use the company's inventory as collateral for a field warehousing arrangement. The third alternative is a line of credit personally guaranteed by the Grants. If the factoring arrangement is used, the bank acts as the factor and assesses a 2 percent factoring commission based on total monthly credit sales. On any funds advanced to the company, the bank charges interest at an annual rate of 10 percent.

If San Largo uses its inventory as collateral, the bank requires that a field warehouse be established and controlled by a third-party agent. The field warehousing agent charges a one-time fee of $500 and a warehousing commission of 1.5 percent per month on all credit extended by the bank against the inventory. In addition, the bank charges interest at an annual rate of 10 percent on the actual funds lent to San Largo.

The line of credit would be established for $5 M with a 10 percent compensating balance and a standby fee of 0.5 percent on the amount of the line. Any

---

The Case Study: Part Three

169

borrowing would be at a 10 percent annual rate with a 10 percent compensating balance on the borrowed amount. The bank feels that a personal guarantee is justified in San Largo's case and is unwilling to concede on this point.

EVALUATING THE ALTERNATIVES

To make an objective decision, Pam knows that she should look at the costs and benefits as well as the advantages and disadvantages of each financing alternative. Before she makes her recommendation to the board of directors, she prepares a worksheet similar to the one that follows.

Cost Analysis Worksheet for Financing Alternatives

Amount of funds required in January 1986 $ _____

Source of Funds	Cost	Benefits	Disadvantages
Factoring accounts receivable			
Factor commission	_____		
Credit sales × 0.02	_____		
Interest cost (10% annual)	_____		
Credit sales × 0.10 × 1/12	_____		
Total cost	_____		
	$ ======		
Inventory Financing			
Base fee	_____		
Warehouse commission	_____		
Credit × 1.5%	_____		
Interest cost (10% annual)	_____		
Credit × 0.10 × 0.05	_____		
Total cost	_____		
	$ ======		
Line of credit			
Fee	_____		
Amount of line × 0.005	_____		
Interest on borrowing	_____		
Credit × 0.10 × 0.5	_____		
Minimum balance	_____		
Amount of line × 0.10	_____		
Credit × 0.10	_____		
Total cost	_____		
	$ ======		

In evaluating the plan for the investment of excess cash in marketable securities, Pam gathers data on the current state of the money market. She hopes to use this information to formulate an investment strategy that will minimize risk and other costs at the same time and add something to the bottom line. The information on money market conditions is tabulated on the next page.

Money Market Conditions, January 1986

Securities	Maturities Available	Annual Yield
T-bills	1 month	8.00
	3 month	8.25
	5 month	8.30
	6 month	8.50
	7 month	8.60
	8 month	8.60
	9 month	8.80
	12 month	9.00
Federal agencies	1 month	8.20
	3 month	8.30
	5 month	8.40
	6 month	8.60
	7 month	8.70
	8 month	8.80
	9 month	8.90
	12 month	9.20
Federal funds	1 day	7.00
	2 day	7.00
	3 day	7.00
	1 week	7.50
	2 week	7.50
Negotiable CDs	1 month	8.25
	2 month	8.30
	3 month	8.40
	4 month	8.45
	5 month	8.45
	6 month	8.60
	7 month	8.70
	8 month	8.80
	9 month	8.90
	10 month	8.90
	11 month	9.10
	12 month	9.20

Securities	Maturities Available	Annual Yield
Commercial paper		
	1 month	8.15
	2 month	8.20
	3 month	8.25
	4 month	8.30
	5 month	8.35
	6 month	8.40
	7 month	8.45
	8 month	8.50
	9 month	8.60
	10 month	8.70
	11 month	8.70
	12 month	8.80

Note: For the sake of simplicity, you can assume that these rates will stay fairly constant for each month in 1986. Actually, you should have a forecast of expected rates for each month at each maturity. This complication, although desirable and necessary in real life, would greatly increase the number of possible alternatives.

In formulating her investment strategy, Pam expects to have excess cash balances available from February to December. The amounts that she anticipates will be available are presented below.

Excess Funds Available for Investment in 1986 (Dollars in Millions)

	Feb.	Mar.	Apr.	May	June	July	Aug.	Sept.	Oct.	Nov.	Dec.
Amount of new funds	8.9	11.1	17.8	0.8	(2.7)	(2.7)	(2.6)	(4.0)	(8.8)	(5.6)	(6.9)
Cumulative funds available	8.9	20.0	37.8	38.6	35.9	33.2	30.6	26.6	17.8	12.2	5.3

Selected Readings

Introduction to Selected Readings

Each of these selected readings is meant to amplify or extend the discussion of a particular topic. The first two readings by Professors Johnson, Campbell, and Wittenbach are presented in order to give the views of the practitioner. What are the problems that treasurers face in the liquidity area? And what are some of the techniques and alternatives that are currently being used in the real world?

The Goodman article on credit control offers an alternative procedure for speeding up the inflows and collections of accounts receivable. This offers a defensive move for treasurers as more and more managers become involved in cash management.

The "Alternative Cash Transfer Mechanisms and Methods" article presents some views on the methods used to move cash in a more efficient fashion. It offers an explanation of the various techniques as well as a least cost transfer analysis that allows users to evaluate the best technique, given their situation.

The Nauss and Markland article dealing with lockboxes is meant to demonstrate a sophisticated use of computer analysis in solving what can become a very complex problem: Where should a firm locate its lockboxes? Of particular interest is the computer output that shows the best solution for the firm's given problem. It is not intended that the reader replicate or do the programming analysis, but rather the purpose of this article is to make the reader aware of some of the types of techniques that can be used to solve these problems.

The Gitman and Goodwin survey presents some interesting findings with respect to managing marketable securities. Although the results of the survey are not surprising, they tend to reinforce what we expect to find.

The interest rate futures article is offered as an example of the type of innovation and creativity that is available in the cash management field.

Problems in Corporate Liquidity

James M. Johnson, David R. Campbell, and James L. Wittenbach

Corporate liquidity, or the lack of it, has been renewed as a serious topic over the past five years. Violent swings in short-term interest rates and credit availability, high inflation rates, thinning profit margins, and unencouraging forecasts for these and other factors suggest that liquidity will remain a problem for some time.

In reaction, many articles have appeared in the financial press and journals over the past few years which deal directly or tangentially with corporate liquidity. Although many facets of liquidity have been examined from a diversity of viewpoints, there is a lack of information regarding how executives manage it. How big a problem is it? What is their objective? What is the relative importance of various tools?

The following survey presents research findings which address these questions.

THE SURVEY

A questionnaire was developed by the authors, based upon their own knowledge of liquidity and the results of pilot interviews conducted on-site with executives of ten major corporations. Several executives in the pilot interviews stated that some questions could not be given unqualified responses, because they depended on whether short-run or long-run implications were being sought. Accordingly, half the final surveys requested that the respondent answer questions from a short-term (less than one year) perspective.

The survey was sent to the treasurer of each company listed in the *Fortune 1,000* of 1978. Executives were asked to evaluate the relative importance of five factors which might be considered objectives of liquidity management. They were then asked to rate the relative importance of 35 factors that might affect liquidity planning or management. For each of the 40 questions, executives were requested to rate their degree of importance on a scale ranging from one (very unimportant) to five (very important). Executives also had the option of designating a question as not applicable to their situation. Information was also solicited regarding the degree of liquidity problems encountered by the business at any time over the past five years (i.e., including the last recession).

The initial mailing plus one follow-up request resulted in 418 returned questionnaires, a 41.8 percent response rate. Executives evaluating liquidity from a short-term perspective numbered 220, while long-term responses totaled 198.

Severity of Problems

Executives were asked to evaluate the worst degree of liquidity problems experienced by their businesses during or since the 1974 recession. Their responses are summarized in Figure 1. . . .

Eleven percent of the executives indicated their business had faced substantial liquidity problems during at least some portion of the past five years. An additional 21.3 percent admitted moderate problems, while 16.3 percent had few problems and 51.4 percent had virtually no difficulties. Although it would be somewhat questionable to generalize these findings, it is a fact that at least

Source: Reprinted with permission of publisher and authors from the March 1980 issue of *Financial Executive*, published by Financial Executives Institute, Morristown, N.J.

Figure 1   Degree of Liquidity Problems Encountered

Degree of Problem	Number of Responses	Percent of Total
Substantial	46	11.0%
Moderate	89	21.3
Few	68	16.3
Virtually none	215	51.4
Total	418	100.0%

13.5 percent of corporations comprising the *Fortune 1,000* have experienced liquidity problems of moderate degree or worse during the past five years. Had all businesses responded, this percentage would undoubtedly be higher.

This is quite good evidence that for a sizeable number of major U.S. businesses, illiquidity has been a very real problem. Although the percentage would perhaps be higher for smaller businesses, it is apparent that they do not face the problem alone.

Management Goals

Five definitions which might be regarded as liquidity management objectives were presented to executives for their evaluation. They were also invited to contribute their own description, though few did. Figure 2 summarizes the average rankings of these definitions.

Figure 2   Objectives of Liquidity Management

Description of Objective	Short-Term Survey		Long-Term Survey	
	Number of Responses	Average Rank[1]	Number of Responses	Average Rank[1]
1. Ability to meet creditor obligations with existing assets	212	3.8	192	3.5
2. Ability to meet creditor obligations with unused bank credit lines	204	3.7	190	3.5
3. Ability to meet temporary financial problems as they arise	216	4.4	191	4.2
4. Ability to generate long-term debt or equity financing when needed	212	3.9	194	4.5
5. Ability to convert assets into cash in a reasonable time	217	3.6	191	3.6

[1] 1 = very unimportant; 5 = very important.

The data reported in Figure 2 indicates that executives view all liquidity definitions as at least somewhat important, although some are ranked considerably higher than others.

Definitions 1 and 5 might be described as "existing asset" solutions, definition 2 as a "line of credit" solution, definition 3 as an "ability to meet temporary financial problems as they arise" solution, and definition 4 as a "capital market" solution.

Liquidity objectives evaluated from a short-term standpoint rated definition 3 appreciably higher than the remaining four, when clustered together. This indicates executives view short-run liquidity management as one that may require a diversity of tools and actions, with no single factor overwhelming the others. The remaining definitions are all indicative of "one-pronged" solutions to liquidity management, which executives deemed of lesser importance.

The picture is somewhat different for executives who rated liquidity objectives from a long-term viewpoint. Here, capital market access was rated most important, followed quite closely by definition 3 (which was rated number 1 as a short-term objective). Because many finance texts and articles stress the importance of bank financing as a tool in working capital management, it is significant that managers rate long-term financing accessibility as considerably more important. (Although bank lines were ranked relatively low, this is not to say that executives attach little value to banking relationships in general.) While this may sound counter-intuitive, a permanent financing capability does allow a business to avoid refinancing and higher interest rate problems during the course of a business cycle. Accordingly, cash demands that could be made at precisely the time they are least affordable should be reduced.

The remaining definitions were not considered as significant from a long-term perspective.

Factors in Planning and Management

Because 36 factors were evaluated in importance to liquidity management, they are divided, for simplicity, into forecasting, ratio analysis, asset management, liability management, and other groups. Although opinions will differ regarding which factors are most logically grouped together, it is not material to the results or conclusions presented, and is designed to facilitate comprehension.

The average importance rankings for each factor, ranging from 2.6 to 4.7 are presented in Figure 3. The average ratings given each group for its short-term and long-term importance are coded S and L, respectively. If a factor is given the same average rating by each group, it is coded B.

Forecasting

Of the forecasting factors presented in Figure 3, managers rated cash-flow forecasts of greatest importance when the projection is for the coming year. The value of cash-flow projections declines as they extend further into the future.

Projected earnings are also rated quite highly from both short-term and long-term perspectives, but planning models are given low marks. Because the term "planning models" may convey the notion of mathematical or computerized forecasting, it appears that managers either feel such methods are of questionable value or else have not been used and thus do not play a significant role in liquidity management.

Figure 3 The Importance of Various Factors in Liquidity Mangement

Factor and group	Average rankings*																					
	4.7	4.6	4.5	4.4	4.3	4.2	4.1	4.0	3.9	3.8	3.7	3.6	3.5	3.4	3.3	3.2	3.1	3.0	2.9	2.8	2.7	2.6
Forecasting:																						
Cash-flow projections for:																						
1 year or less	S																					
1-3 years								L					S									
more than 3 years																L						S
Projected earnings of the firm					L	S																
Planning models																L			S			
Ratio analysis:																						
In general														L		S						
Current ratio															L		S					
Quick (acid test) ratio																		L	S			
Inventory turnover									L		S											
Receivables turnover									B													
Payables turnover															S	L						
Total asset turnover																L				S		
Return on total assets								L						S								
Return on owners' equity							L					S										
Profit margin ratio					L						S											
Times interest earned						L												S				
Debt-to-equity ratio												L			S							
Importance of ratio analysis when business is:																						
Highly liquid																		L	S			
Moderately liquid												L		S								
Barely liquid									S	L												
Illiquid						L		S														
Asset management:																						
Management of cash surplus						S																
Receivables management		S			L																	
Inventory management		S		L																		
Budgeting for capital expenditures					L		S															

Liability management:											
Good relations with bankers	B										
Aggregate lines of credit		L	S								
Bond ratings				L				S			
Short-term interest rates					S			S			
Longer-term interest rates					L				S		
Other factors:											
Current operating earnings		S	L								
Timely, accurate management reporting system		L	S								S
Operating management's awareness of the impact of their decisions on liquidity				L	S						
Macro-economic factors (inflation, energy needs etc.)				L				L			S
Firm's accounting and/or tax policies				L				S			S
Financial strength of customers					S	L					

* S = average short-term management response.

L = average long-term management response.

B = short-term and long-term average responses were the same.

Ratio Analysis

Most finance and accounting texts devote at least a full chapter to ratio analysis, and numerous articles have discussed their importance in evaluating the condition of a business, not the least of which is its liquidity position. Accordingly, executives were asked to rank ratio analysis in general and in 11 specific ratios, and to measure their usefulness in various liquidity situations.

Perusing the ratio analysis section of Figure 3 it is seen that its general importance is rated quite low, from both short-term and long-term management viewpoints.

One of the greatest surprises of the study concerns the rankings of ratios designed to measure liquidity. Both the current and acid test ratios were rated as being among the *least important* liquidity management factors included in the survey. Although this result was not expected, it is consistent with the liquidity objective rankings discussed previously (Figure 2). It will be recalled that existing asset coverage and asset conversion objectives were not considered as important as access to capital markets and the ability to meet temporary financial problems. Thus, even though these two liquidity ratios (current and acid test) may be a staple of external analysts, corporate executives find them of little value as a management tool.

Four turnover, or asset productivity ratios, were included for evaluation: inventory, receivables, payables, and total assets. Of these, inventory and receivables turnover were evaluated to be considerably more important management tools than payables and total asset turnover. This would seem appropriate, since receivables and inventory are the two major accounts which will convert (directly and indirectly) into cash, yet must be managed to insure they are turned over and at the proper rate. Nevertheless, payables are more predictable and controllable, and thus should require less management attention.

Of the three profitability ratios examined—return on total assets, return on equity, and profit margin on sales—profit margin was considered to be the most important in liquidity management. In all cases, however, evaluations from a long-term perspective rated each profitability measure significantly higher than managers assessing their short-term value. Because the most important long-term liquidity objective was found to be capital market access, the higher long-term rating given all profitability measures is probably attributable to its importance in maintaining that long-term funding capability. In other words, the greater importance of profitability as a long-term liquidity tool is in large part indirect; higher profitability may enhance a firm's ability to procure capital market funds. Higher profitability will also tend to increase liquidity directly in many cases, but the desire for capital market access would offer an explanation for the differential rankings of profitability from short-term and long-term viewpoints.

Two leverage ratios were included in the study, since financial leverage can affect liquidity in several ways, directly and indirectly. The ratios to be evaluated were times interest earned and debt/equity. Both ratios were considered to be more important as long-term tools than short-term tools. But, from either perspective, debt/equity was credited with significantly greater importance than interest coverage.

The priority given both leverage ratios as long-term tools may again be due to the greater significance attached to capital market access as a long-term liquidity objective. An explanation for the greater importance of debt/equity from short-term and long-term perspectives may be a concern about meeting restrictions in banking line agreements and bond indentures. Interest earned may not be considered as important because it does not reflect total debt service repayment ability or because respondents may not have encountered coverage problems. Alternatively, debt/equity may be viewed by external analysts as more important because it does reflect the degree to which creditors are financing the business. Also, industry norm data is more readily available for debt/equity than interest earned, which may account for the greater reliance placed on the former. (For example, Dun and Bradstreet periodically reports debt/equity ratios for industries, but not interest coverage averages.) Should any combination of these reasons be valid, it would indicate that both ratios have greater importance because of the reliance placed upon them by external parties rather than their ongoing value as management tools.

Finally, managers were asked to evaluate the importance of ratio analysis when their company is highly liquid, moderately liquid, barely liquid, and illiquid. The rationale was to determine whether ratio analysis might be of situational importance. First, it may be observed that ratio analysis is credited with more importance as a business becomes less liquid. This was the case from both short-term and long-term perspectives. This may be attributed to a firm's need to place greater reliance on external financing (from either money or capital markets, or both) as it becomes progressively less liquid and depletes internal resources at its disposal. Because external suppliers of funds will necessarily place considerable weight on ratio analysis of the firm's condition, the relatively illiquid business will also be compelled to attach importance to ratios.

A second observation regarding the situational importance of ratio analysis is that it is always credited with somewhat greater long-term importance than short-term importance, although significantly so only in the "barely liquid" category. Even though greater dependence may be placed on money market access for both short-term and long-term management in illiquid situations, the greater overall importance attached to capital market access for long-term management may explain the consistently higher rankings for long-term purposes; that is, if accessibility to capital markets is an important long-term liquidity objective to a business, and since capital suppliers will evaluate the business in no small part by ratio analysis, it is reasonable to presume that such a business would always be more sensitive to ratios (and thus credit them with more importance). Indeed, of the 11 ratios, nine were rated as being more important as long-term management tools.

Asset Management

Four factors are presented in the asset management group in Figure 3. Executives were asked to rate the degree of importance they would attach to cash, receivables and inventory management, and budgeting for capital expenditures. Although all four factors were rated highly for their short-term importance in liquidity management, receivables and inventory were rated significantly above cash and capital expenditures. This might be attributed to the greater internal control which may be exercised over cash and the timing of capital expenditures. Receivables and inventory will be more heavily influenced by external forces and thus may be viewed as more important because they are more difficult to control for liquidity purposes.

When the four factors were rated for their long-term significance, receivables, inventory, and capital expenditure management were considered to be among the most important of all factors in the survey. Still of importance, but significantly less so, was management of cash surplus. Here, executives may be indicating that management of a pure liquid asset is not as vital as controlling assets, which will contribute to or make demands on cash in the future.

Liability Management

Managers were requested to appraise the significance of good relations with bankers, aggregate lines of credit, bond ratings, and short-term and longer-term interest rates.

For both short-term and long-term liquidity management, good relations with bankers was considered to be among the most important of all factors included in the study. Although aggregate lines of credit (with banks) was also given a high ranking, the total banking relationship was more important.

Because capital market accessibility was found to be a higher ranked long-term objective than a short-term one, it is appropriate that bond ratings and long-term interest rates were credited with greater long-term management value, and that short-term interest rates were valued more highly for short-term management. An interesting point to note here is that executives are not nearly as interested in the price (interest rate) of funds as in an ability to acquire them.

Other Factors

In the pilot interviews, executives considered several factors to be important in their operations. These items were included in the final survey, and the responses are summarized in the "other factors" grouping in Figure 3. Two items were ranked as very important from both short-term and long-term management viewpoints: current operating earnings and a timely, accurate management reporting system. Of slightly less value was operating management's awareness of the impact of their decisions on liquidity. The remaining factors were rated as having moderate to low value in the management of liquidity.

SUMMARY

The following points highlight some of the more important findings of this study:

1. Almost one-third of the companies surveyed have encountered moderate liquidity problems or worse during at least some portion of the past five years.
2. Liquidity is not just an ability to pay tomorrow's bills tomorrow, but is viewed as having short-term and long-term management dimensions.
3. The major objective of short-term liquidity management is seen as a general multi-faceted ability to resolve financial problems.
4. The major long-term liquidity goal is capital market access.
5. Contrary to the importance attached to liability coverage with existing assets by external analysts, corporate managers do not see this as a major goal of liquidity management.
6. The most important factors in managing liquidity were found to be:
   - Cash flow projections.
   - Current and projected earnings.
   - Good relations with bankers.
   - Management of receivables, inventory, and capital expenditures.
   - A timely, accurate management reporting system.

7. Factors credited with the least importance in liquidity management include
   - Ratio analysis in general.
   - Current and quick ratios.
   - Planning models.
   - Long-term cash-flow projections.

Identifying and Resolving Problems in Corporate Liquidity

James M. Johnson, David R. Campbell and James L. Wittenbach

Illiquidity is a problem faced periodically by many large and many more small businesses. Although numerous articles have been written about the subject, little has been known about how executives actually manage liquidity.

To develop a better understanding of liquidity management in practice, the authors reported the results of their survey of Fortune 1000 treasurers in the article, "Problems in Corporate Liquidity" (*Financial Executive*, March 1980). It focused upon the degree of illiquidity experienced by major companies during and since the recession of the mid-1970s, the objectives of liquidity management, and the factors that executives should consider in managing liquidity.

This article is a continuation of the authors' investigation of liquidity management. The purpose is to address the dynamic issues of how executives *identify* liquidity problems—i.e., what are the important signals, and what measures are taken to *resolve* a condition of illiquidity. The results reported are taken from a survey conducted by the authors.

THE SURVEY

The treasurers were asked to indicate the degree of liquidity problems encountered by their businesses over the past five years and to evaluate the relative importance of numerous liquidity problem awareness and resolution statements. For each of the 17 awareness and 22 resolution items, executives were requested to rate their degree of importance on a scale ranging from one (very unimportant) to five (very important). Executives also were given the option of designating a question as not applicable.

In response to the question of liquidity problem severity, 46 respondents indicated their companies suffered substantial problems; 89 experienced moderate problems; 68 reported few problems, and 215 indicated no liquidity problems were encountered. Those companies experiencing at least a few problems comprise this study (a total of 203 businesses).

The results were examined to determine whether companies which experienced different degrees of liquidity problems responded differently. With only one exception (which will be noted), companies that experienced from substantial to few problems did not respond in a meaningfully different fashion. Accordingly, average responses ranged across the spectrum of degree of liquidity problems experienced.

IDENTIFYING THE PROBLEMS

Executives were requested to rate the importance of 17 factors which could trigger their awareness of a liquidity problem. For the convenience of discussion, the factors have been (somewhat arbitrarily) grouped into three categories: sales and expense control, asset management, and liability management. The results are shown in Table 1.

In the area of sales and expense control, it is interesting to note that sales control ("sales orders declining") and expense control ("increased difficulty in controlling expenses") are virtually tied at moderate importance in triggering

Source: Reprinted with permission of publisher and authors from the May 1982 issue of *Financial Executive*, published by Financial Executives Institute, Morristown, N.J.

Table 1 Identifying Liquidity Problems

Factor and group	Average rankings																						
	2.0	2.1	2.2	2.3	2.4	2.5	2.6	2.7	2.8	2.9	3.0	3.1	3.2	3.3	3.4	3.5	3.6	3.7	3.8	3.9	4.0	4.1	4.2	4.3
Sales and expense control																								
Sales orders were declining												●												
Sales were below break-even volume									●															
Increased difficulty in controlling expenses										●														
Increased costs could not be passed on																	●							
Raw materials more difficult to acquire									●															
Asset management																								
Daily cash inflows were declining															●									
Cash balances were lower than normal												●												
Accounts receivable increased																	●							
Receivables turnover declined																●								
Inventory turnover declined																			●					
Inventories built up																								●
Working capital declined																●								
Liability management																								
Debt ratio increased																		●						
Firm was dependent upon one primary source of financing and more funds from such sources became limited							●																	
Firm was funding capital projects with short-term debt which could not be completely converted into long-term funds								●																
All or most assets were pledged to secure existing debt				●																				
Accounts payable increased								●																

an awareness of illiquidity. The number one factor of importance in this group is an inability to pass increasing costs along to customers. Two areas, below break-even sales and difficulty in procuring materials, were rated as least important in flagging liquidity problems. When viewed collectively, the responses suggest that an awareness of illiquidity was brought about by a condition truly described as "stagflation." Although a decline in revenue was evident, the liquidity crunch was attributable to unit costs increasing more rapidly than unit prices—a condition brought about by a slump in demand. By its low ranking, executives apparently felt below break-even volume was a trivial indication of illiquidity, an explanation more symptomatic than problematic.

Executives rated a buildup in inventories as by far the most important signal of liquidity problems in this group. The second most important signal was a decline in inventory turns. These two factors, of course, are not addressing the same issue. One may envision a company which is reducing its inventory levels but still experiences a reduction in turns because sales are dropping at a more rapid rate than the inventory reduction. The fact that executives *simultaneously* gave high ratings to *both* increasing inventory levels and decreasing turns suggests that the decline in product demand was difficult to predict. Had the slump been predictable, one would expect a winding down of production, a concomitant *decrease* in inventory levels, and thus a low rating to have been given to the "inventories built up" factor.

A reduction in daily cash inflows, receivable turns, and working capital levels, along with an increasing level of receivables, were all rated as important signals of liquidity problems. Below-normal cash balances was the factor deemed least important of all asset signals, which indicates that executives attach more importance to the *flow* of cash ("daily cash inflows were declining") than to the *stock* of cash ("cash balances were lower than normal").

LIABILITY MANAGEMENT

An increasing debt ratio was clearly the most important liability management signal in the opinion of responding executives; all other signals in this group were rated as relatively unimportant. It is reasonable to conclude that an increasing debt ratio is considered a powerful illiquidity signal because the increase *itself* makes it increasingly difficult to tap debt markets for additional financing that may be required.

RESOLVING THE PROBLEMS

For the convenience of discussion, measures taken to remedy liquidity problems are grouped into three categories. The results are shown in Table 2.

SALES AND EXPENSE CONTROL

To control expenses, executives ascribed the greatest importance to greater cost control of overhead. Two moderately important tactics implemented to accomplish this were to examine alternative supply sources and to begin personnel layoffs. It is significant to note that four of the five tactics given low importance ratings could be considered to have substantial detrimental repercussions over time. Delaying new product offerings could compromise a company's image and market position well beyond the delay period, and cutting dividends could affect its cost of financing. A new hire freeze or delay in compensation adjustments might damage morale, adversely affect turnover, or have other undesirable human capital consequences.

Table 2 Resolving Liquidity Problems

Factor and group	Average rankings																							
	2.0	2.1	2.2	2.3	2.4	2.5	2.6	2.7	2.8	2.9	3.0	3.1	3.2	3.3	3.4	3.5	3.6	3.7	3.8	3.9	4.0	4.1	4.2	4.3
Sales and expense control																								
New product offerings were delayed	•																							
Greater cost control of overhead																		•						
Purchasing agents examined alternative sources of supply									•															
Dividends were reduced	•																							
New hirings were frozen	•																							
Lengthened time for raises				•																				
Personnel were laid off									•															
Operating managers were compensated largely on ability to generate cash inflows		•																						
Asset management																								
Receivables were trimmed																	•							
Used more rigorous receivables collection policy																		•						
Reduced investment in inventories																								•
Reduced capital expenditures															•									
Plants were closed							•																	
Assets not meeting long-term profit objectives were disposed of												•												
Liquidated certain assets to meet operating/debt service needs						•																		
Educated nonfinancial personnel on significance of asset management																•								
Liability management																								
Payables were extended										•														
Increased short-term borrowings																	•							
Revolving bank credit arrangements were established													•											
Revolving bank lines were increased											•													
Greater emphasis placed on leasing assets	•																							
Increased long-term borrowings																	•							

Liquidity crunches are predominantly viewed as short-term phenomena, and thus companies tend to adjust to them with flexible or reversible tactics (e.g., layoffs and cost reductions). They are reluctant to tamper with what might be called pipeline processes (flow of new personnel, dividend payments, new product introductions)—activities whose present level, stature, or position take considerable time to achieve and therefore must continue to be "fed" or suffer potential repercussions far beyond the period during which the action itself was taken.

The most important asset management action taken by executives to resolve illiquidity was to reduce investment in inventories. In fact, this was the most important action taken among all of the three groups. It is appropriate that inventory reductions be given this status because it will be recalled that the number one signal of illiquidity was a buildup of inventory. Also consistent with illiquidity remedies are the high ratings given to trimming accounts receivable and putting in use a more rigorous receivables collection policy.

Moderate importance was attached to educating non-financial personnel on the significance of asset management and on the reduction of capital expenditures. The educational thrust was undoubtedly an important tactic necessary to implement receivables, inventory, and capital expenditure actions taken. Reducing capital outlays represents the most significant pipeline action taken to bring liquidity under control.

The three actions considered to be least important in resolving illiquidity should also be considered the most drastic measures proposed: plant closings and two kinds of asset liquidations. The only factor in the study where companies facing different degrees of liquidity problems gave a significantly different response was the "liquidated certain assets to meet operating/debt service needs." Here, companies reporting few liquidity problems gave an average response of 1.8 (an unimportant liquidity remedy). However, companies that faced substantial problems rated it 3.3 in importance. Thus, companies facing the worst liquidity problems were forced to take the most drastic remedial action.

LIABILITY MANAGEMENT

Executives indicated that increasing the level of borrowings, from both short- and long-term sources, was the most important liability management action taken to resolve liquidity problems. This may appear somewhat curious because executives indicated that debt ratio increases were considered an important signal of illiquidity. However, recognizing that a condition of illiquidity can occur fairly rapidly, executives may quite justifiably interpret a rising debt position simultaneously as a sign of, and a cure for, a liquidity shortage. It may be viewed as a sign because it compromises further borrowing and (thus) ideally would not be done. It is also a cure, as in the short run it must be done.

Establishing or increasing bank lines were only of modest importance in resolving liquidity problems, as was extending accounts payable. A shift to leasing was considered by far to be the least significant debt financing action employed. Executives were much more prone to use more financing from traditional sources than to seek out new forms.

CONCLUSION

In the opinion of surveyed executives, the most important signs of illiquidity were asset-based in general, and an inventory buildup was considered to be the single most important monitoring device. A reduction in inventory turns and an increasing debt ratio were rated second and third, respectively in importance as signs of illiquidity.

To resolve liquidity problems, reducing inventories was the most important action taken. This, of course, is consistent with inventory buildups being considered the most important sign of a liquidity crunch. Greater cost control of overhead, collecting and trimming receivables, and increasing borrowings were rated next in importance as corrective actions.

In descending order of importance, executives rated the following as being the most important factors in liquidity problem identification and resolution.

- Working capital (inventory most important).
- Overhead costs.
- Debt financing.

Solving the Cash Crunch Through Credit Control

Mark R. Goodman

In this era of high interest rates, spiraling inflation, and economic recession, the most important function of many businesses has switched from sales, production, or even personnel management, to credit control.

For companies who extend credit, the problem of cash flow has become one of the financial executive's chief concerns. Control and collection of the accounts receivable is now a life or death matter during these uncertain economic times—even for those companies selling to large corporations.

With the prime interest rate again near 20 percent, many companies have learned to use their creditors' money by delaying payment. Usual collection procedures are becoming less effective. In the past, one or two statements, or at most a phone call, to the accounts payable department was enough to motivate payment. Today nothing seems to work; statements, phone calls, letters, even personal visits bring nothing more than promises.

The financial executive, faced with the prospect of rising receivables and the reality of collecting only a percentage of his depreciated dollars, has been caught in a quandary. Does he get tough with credit and extend it only to those who pay according to terms—(an unlikely choice because it would drastically reduce revenue in an already slumping economy)—or does he resort to outside help to bring the receivables in line?

The alternative of professional help has traditionally been viewed as a last resort. The use of conventional collection agencies, credit bureaus, and attorneys has historically yielded very low recovery rates along with high costs and, in most cases, the loss of the debtor's future business.

The typical agency, credit bureau, or attorney charges a percentage of the debt, which usually ranges from 25 up to 50 percent of the original balance. If these high cost were not enough, the recovery rate reported by the typical collection agency is between 15 and 20 percent of the accounts referred to them. In other words, the financial executive seeking an alternative to his rising receivable problem can anticipate recovering only about 60 percent of his dollars on 20 percent of his slow accounts. In addition, once a debtor settles through one of these typical sources, it is unlikely they will be a source of future business.

With these facts in mind, it is easy to see why many corporate financial executives are turning to credit control professionals.

BRIDGING THE GAP

The field of credit control, relatively new in the financial industry, fills a needed void between the time when a company's own internal procedures prove ineffective and the real need for costly old-fashioned collection techniques arise.

U.S. Department of Commerce studies have shown that a company's own billing and followup procedures are most effective during the first 75 days; once a bill has passed the 90-day point, only about 5 percent of the accounts

Source: Reprinted with permission of the publisher and the author from the July 1982 issue of *Financial Executive,* published by Financial Executives Institute, Morristown, N.J.

can be recovered through a company's own efforts. To refer an account to a typical collection source at this time would be too costly in both dollars and future business. This is the point that a credit control service can be used for optimum results.

A credit control company is a licensed and bonded collection agency, but this new generation of collector is a financial executive's dream, offering the same "third party" influence that motivates payments from debtors, but doing so diplomatically so that they may be retained for continued future business. Two key factors in the success of credit control companies are their practice of not handling the creditor's money (all payments are sent directly to the original creditor, not to the collector) and their low cost. Unlike their old-fashioned predecessors, the company offering credit control charges a flat rate for its service and not a costly percentage. By handling slow-paying accounts for a nominal fee (from $5 to $10 per account), creditors can afford to use a credit control service at the early stages of delinquency when the third party can be most effective. When a credit control service is used at 90 to 120 days, the creditor's own credit department can concentrate on accounts in the early stages of delinquency (where they are most effective) and actually allow fewer accounts to be referred to the credit control company.

The use of a credit control company will not completely eliminate the need for a typical agency or attorney, but it will greatly reduce the need for such steps. Where corporate attorneys cannot be used, many credit control companies can also offer a legal alternative for the firm dealing with debtors in more than one state.

A three-phase program for keeping more of your dollar should include a good internal credit department, a professional credit control service, and a typical collection or legal phase (see Table 1).

The first step falls under the financial executive's domain; he must re-examine corporate credit policies. Terms must be explicit, and the credit department must stay on top of accounts in the early stages of delinquency.

CREDIT CONTROL FORMULA

Once the account slips into the 90-day stage, company billing and followup should stop (this move alone can save up to 20 to 40 percent of a company's billing cost) and a credit control service should be employed. Used at this point, 75 to 90 percent of the receivables should be recovered at a cost of less than 5 percent. The typical credit control company works accounts for only 90 days and during that time contacts each debtor from five to nine times. Contacts from a credit control company have proved to have a greater impact than those from a typical agency or from an attorney. This is because of three basic factors. First, the initial contact is usually made within a few days and, in many cases, by way of the "Urgent Message" media. Second, the contacts received by the debtor are "customized" and appear to be personally typed letters as opposed to pre-printed form letters. Third, and finally, is the "third party psychology," a motivating factor that makes any collection source effective. The credit control service not only provides this quickly and constantly but, most importantly, in a professional manner. Many times, the bulk of your receivables will be recovered within the first few weeks; in any case, results will be evident very quickly.

The credit control company also offers other benefits that their predecessors lack. These include an ability to work a great volume of accounts efficiently (because of computerization), accurate monthly reporting on collec-

Table 1   Cost and Result Comparison of the Two-Phase and Three-Phase Accounts Receivable Programs

Two-Phase Program	Cost*	Three-Phase Program	Cost*
Internal Phase			
Invoice	–3.40		
30-day statement	3.40		
60-day statement	3.40		
Phone call	—		
90-day statement	3.40		
Phone call	—	Invoice	–3.40
120-day statement	3.40	30-day statement	3.40
Collection letter no. 1	6.63	60-day statement	3.40
Collection letter no. 2	6.63	Phone call	—
180-day final notice	6.63	Final notice	6.63
Total Cost Phase I	$36.89	Total Cost Phase I	$16.83
Internal Cost 90 to 180 Days (U.S. Dept. of Commerce shows internal followup is 5 percent effective.)	$23.29	*Control Phase:* Credit control co. 90 to 180 days. Used at this point, the credit control company will collect on 89 percent** of the outstanding debts.	7.00*
Collection Phase: 25 to 50 percent of the balance plus possible filing fees.		*Collection Phase:* 25 to 50 percent of the total balance plus possible filing fees.	
Collection phase should return approximately 20 percent used after the 180-day internal phase.		Collection phase should return approximately 8 percent used after the credit control phase plus internal phase.	

Notes: An increased collection rate of 18 percent in the 90- to 180-day range at a cost almost equal to one business letter will be realized by installing a control phase.

By using a control phase, writeoffs can be reduced by approximately 7 percent and the cash flow can be stepped up so the average turnaround time on receivables can be cut significantly.

The collection phase is still used at the same point, but is effective on a smaller percentage because the control phase collected many accounts that would pay at the introduction of a third party.

* Average cost of credit control system.
** This is the current recovery rate on commercial claims referred to Capax Credit Control at the 90-day point (based on results for 12 months in 1981).

tions and activity, personal service, national coverage, and guaranteed results.

When accounts reach 6 months using this three-phase program, 95 percent of all collectable accounts should have been recovered by either the credit control company or by a company's internal efforts, and at a minimal cost. Now is the time, at this point, to employ the old-fashioned percentage house and let them earn their high fees.

By adding the second phase to a company's collection practices, the cost of recovering money can be reduced by almost 90 percent, and far more money can be recovered.

Credit control companies offer a viable alternative to the corporate financial officer looking for a modern answer to an old problem. When implemented, the three-phase collection program not only allows a company to keep more of their dollars, but keeps long-standing customers coming back to purchase again (now trained to pay on time) and, most importantly, improves a company's cash flow and profit line.

Alternative Cash Transfer Mechanisms and Methods: Evaluation Frameworks

Bernell K. Stone and Ned C. Hill

INTRODUCTION AND OVERVIEW

The selection of a transfer mechanism is a major decision in the design of a cash concentration system along with the selection of a company's concentration bank or banks. It is the design decision that has received the most practitioner attention during the past decade.

This paper deals systematically with the selection of a concentration transfer mechanism. Section I describes alternative mechanisms and their properties. Section II presents the conventional breakeven analysis that is usually set forth as the appropriate framework for evaluating two alternative transfer mechanisms. Sections III to V criticize the conventional breakeven framework and show that it is both incomplete and biased. Sections VI and VII present a correct framework. Section VIII synthesizes the analysis. An appendix providing technical detail is available from *The Journal of Bank Research.*

I. ALTERNATIVE TRANSFER MECHANISMS

A transfer mechanism is a means for moving money between two accounts at different banks. Until recently, there were two primary transfer mechanisms—a wire and a depository transfer check (hereafter DTC). A wire is an electronic same-day transfer.

A DTC is a check restricted for deposit at a particular bank. The "deposit-only" restriction mitigates problems of check control. Other than the deposit-only restriction, a DTC is an ordinary check. It moves money between accounts by being written on the account from which money is to be removed and being deposited into the account to which money is to be added. In cash concentration, the DTC is written on each depository bank and deposited at the concentration bank.

The New ACH-Based Electronic Image Transfer

In the spring of 1979, the Federal Reserve announced a later cut-off time for presentation of tapes to the automated clearinghouses (ACHs) for intracompany transfers. These later cut-off times were phased into the various ACHs during 1979. When translated into bank cut-off times, this generally meant that the electronic ACH based transfers had a later cut off than DTCs. Since the ACH based transfers cost less than DTCs, the ACH electronic image transfer had become a viable alternative to the DTC for many companies.

In many ways, the electronic image transfer is a hybrid of a wire and a DTC. It is paperless like the wire but involves a time delay like the DTC. In essence, it looks like a paperless check with a uniform one-day availability and clearing time and generally a lower cost than an ordinary check. It is commonly called a "paperless DTC" or "electronic DTC." This article will use the currently popular "electronic DTC" and hereafter use the abbreviation EDTC.

Transfer Methods

A transfer method is a way of using a transfer mechanism that affects its cost, clearing time and availability time. There are many variations to the ways each mechanism is used, but there are a number of generic methods that characterize each mechanism. For instance, DTCs may be field initiated or

Source: Reprinted with permission of the publisher from the Spring 1982 issue of *The Journal of Bank Research,* published by the Bank Administration Institute, Rolling Meadows, Il.

centrally initiated.

1. *Mail Based Field Initiation.* Personnel at the company's field units prepare the DTC and mail it and a deposit slip to the concentration bank. Or alternatively, the field unit personnel mail the DTC and an appropriate deposit slip to a "lockbox gathering bank" rather than directly to the concentration bank. A lockbox gathering bank functions as an "intermediate concentration bank." It subsequently transfers the funds to the central cash pool in the primary concentration bank along with other items received at the lockbox.

2. *Company Managed Central Initiation.* Company field units call a central company location and report on deposits. At this location the company accumulates the deposit data, organizes them, and then prepares a "DTC tape image." The tape is sent (or possibly teleprocessed) to the concentration bank, which then prepares the DTCs and enters them into the check clearing system. Or, less often, the company itself prepares the DTCs and deposits them at the concentration bank.

   A variant to company managed central initiation arises with point-of-sale (POS) terminals. Rather than a phone call, the terminal communication link is used to transmit deposit data to a central location. As another variant, some companies have their depository banks (rather than field units) communicate deposit information.

3. *Third-Party Central Initiation.* Rather than calling a central company location, the company field units (and less frequently depository banks) call deposit information into a third-party deposit information gathering service. It accumulates the deposit data and sends the information to the company's concentration bank at a company specified time. The concentration bank then prepares and initiates the transfers.

   The third-party service eliminates the need for a company to develop and operate a deposit information gathering system. Otherwise, it looks like company managed central initiation.

EDTC Methods

Mail based field initiation is not pertinent for EDTCs. They can be initiated centrally just like DTCs, i.e., with central company management or a third-party gathering service.

Figure 1 summarizes cost and delays for various transfer methods.

EDTC and Corporate EFT

Because EDTCs involve company-to-company transfers, they do not involve some of the legal issues that arise in intercompany electronic funds transfer (EFT). Hence EDTCs may have the potential for being one of the pioneering areas of corporate EFT. In fact, the Federal Reserve (see, for instance, Coldwell [1979]) apparently plans to use both pricing and regulatory action to induce companies to switch to EDTCs in place of DTCs.

Contemporary Pertinence of Mechanism Evaluation

The issue of mechanism selection is particularly pertinent now. Besides the usual issue of wire versus DTC and the merits of alternative wire based and DTC based transfer methods, there is now the issue of wire versus EDTC and EDTC versus DTC. Moreover, even for companies adopting EDTCs, there is the issue of appropriate method.

Besides a new mechanism, three other factors are changing transfer economics. First, there is intensive Fed effort to reduce float drastically, including now the possibility of check truncation and electronic check presentment.

Figure 1. Transfer Methods: Key Attributes

Transfer Methods	Delay (Days)	Typical Cost Range[1]	Cost Components
Wire	0	$6.00-$20.00	1) Outgoing wire 2) Wire receipt
DTC: Third-party assisted	1-2	$.60-$1.00	1) Third-party charge 2) Deposit charge 3) DTC preparation charge 4) Check charge
DTC: Centralized company initiation	1-2	$.05-$.40 plus the cost of bank and/or company preparation of either the DTCs and/or the DTC tape image and any communication costs	1) Deposit charge 2) Check charge 3) Bank processing charge 4) Company processing cost 5) Communication cost
DTC: Mail based	2-7	$.30-$.55	1) Deposit charge lock-box 2) Check charge 3) Postage/envelope
EDTC: Third-party assisted	1	$.24-$.36 plus any bank preparation charge	1) Third-party charge 2) Electronic transfer charge 3) Bank preparation charge
EDTC: Centralized company initiation	1	$.03-$.06 plus any bank preparation charges and/or the cost of company preparation of the EDTC tape and any communication costs.	1) Electronic transfer charge 2) Bank preparation charge 3) Company processing cost 4) Communication cost

[1] Cost ranges reflect variation in charges across banks and third-party information gathering services.

Second, there is the requirement of the 1980 Monetary Control Act that the Fed "price float." Finally, there is now the possibility of interest on field deposits (or at least *de facto* interest via automatic transfer accounts) so that field balances in excess of levels necessary to compensate the bank are no longer necessarily "idle balances."

The availability of a new transfer mechanism and changing transfer economics mean that, over the next few years, virtually every large multi-bank company will have to look systematically at the role of EDTCs in their cash concentration and disbursement funding systems and compare EDTC methods with their current transfer methods. Having a mechanism evaluation framework that correctly incorporates all aspects of the problem is more important than ever.

II. THE CONVENTIONAL BREAKEVEN ANALYSIS

The conventional analysis of alternative transfer mechanisms and/or methods assumes that evaluation is just an issue of transfer speed versus cost. The wire is more expensive but provides a same-day transfer. The wire, therefore, presumably provides an opportunity for greater interest income. Hence, the conventional evaluation is couched in terms of seeing whether the value of extra interest arising from faster transfers justifies the extra cost.

To quantify the conventional comparison of interest versus cost, let I denote the appropriate daily interest rate, let ΔT denote the difference in transfer time in days and let S denote the size of the transfer in dollars. The value of extra interest is $IS\Delta T$. If the cost difference is denoted by a $\Delta COST$, the net advantage of the faster, higher-cost mechanism is, in the conventional argument, asserted to be the interest income for the days of extra availability less the added cost, i.e.:

$$\text{Net advantage} = IS\Delta T - \Delta COST. \tag{1}$$

The Breakeven Transfer Size

The net advantage of the faster mechanism increases with the amount transferred. Figure 2 shows this dependency by plotting net advantage versus transfer size for a given interest rate and cost difference.

The indifference size S^* occurs when the net advantage is zero. The formula for this "breakeven size" is:

$$S^* = \Delta COST / I \cdot \Delta T \tag{2}$$

The mechanism selection rule implied by this breakeven analysis depends on transfer size in the conventional analysis. For transfer sizes greater than S^*, the faster, higher-cost mechanism is preferred. Conversely, for transfer sizes less than S^*, the lower-cost but slower mechanism is preferred.

Typical Breakeven Sizes: Wires Vs. DTCs

To illustrate typical breakeven sizes, assume that the cost difference between a wire and a DTC is $6.00, that the time difference is one day and the interest value of funds at the concentration bank is .03% per day (about 11% per annum). Then the breakeven transfer size would be $S^* = \$6.00/.0003(1) = \$20,000$. If the time differences were one day and the interest value were .02% per day (about 7.3% per annum) rather than .03%, then the decision rule would be to wire amounts over $30,000, i.e., $6.00/(.0002)(1) = $30,000.

These examples explain the common rule of thumb for deciding between wires and DTCs, namely to wire whenever the amount to be transferred exceeds $20,000 to $30,000 and to use a DTC whenever the transfer amount is less. These breakeven levels reflect about a 7-11% interest value, one day delay and roughly $6.00 difference in net cost. The dependence on interest rate and transfer amount for a given cost difference is often illustrated graphically by a

Figure 2. Net Advantage for the Faster Higher Cost Mechanism as a Function of Transfer Amount.

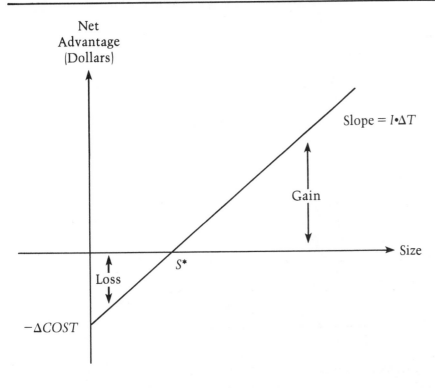

plot such as that given in Figure 3. Such an indifference curve can be plotted for each cost difference and time delay.

The conventional breakeven analysis is a widely used analysis framework. The authors have, for instance, found it in the brochures of many money-center banks. They do not, however, explain the behavior of many companies in deciding between wires and DTCs. As noted previously, typical breakeven sizes for comparing wires with centrally initiated DTCs are not more than $30,000.

Limitations of the Conventional Breakeven Analysis

Yet the authors have encountered companies using DTC transfers for deposits well over this amount, e.g., often well over $100,000 per day and in some cases over $1,000,000 per day. When these cash managers are asked to explain their use of DTCs, virtually all answers are given in the context of breakeven analysis but assert some factor not incorporated in the standard treatment. One common explanation is that "back float value" offsets the interest loss. Another is that the company has somehow "accelerated" its DTC flow so that the nominal delay is not the true delay. Often both reasons are given. Further discussion reveals that these companies have used DTCs for large transfer amounts despite the conventional breakeven rule because of more extensive analysis. However, there is not a systematic framework for making the decision.

These cash managers have recognized that the conventional breakeven analysis ignores several important factors that require consideration in eva-

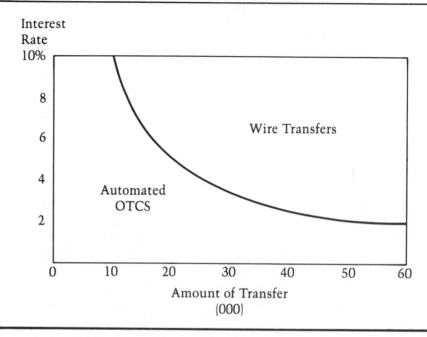

Figure 3. The Dependence of Breakeven Size on Interest Rate and Transfer Size

luating transfer alternatives, namely: (1) The fact that most companies use compensating balances at depository banks to pay for various services, (2) the ability to "anticipate" the deposits to reduce or to eliminate time delay completely and (3) DTC "back float" that arises from differences between granted availability time and actual clearing time. The next three sections elaborate on these deficiencies.

III. COMPENSAT-ING BALANCES AND SERVICES CREDITS

The conventional breakeven analysis assumes no value for funds in the depository bank. In effect, it assumes that the only usable funds are deposits in the concentration bank. In practice, most companies compensate their depository banks with balances, which earn "service credits" to pay for bank services. Thus, there is no interest opportunity cost unless a company has excess balances, i.e., more balances than required to compensate the depository bank.

IV. ANTICIPATION

The conventional breakeven analysis assumes that interest opportunity cost is the interest that can be earned for the difference in availability times for the two transfer alternatives. The nominal delay is not necessarily the effective difference for earning interest. For instance, with knowledge of time delays, a company can initiate a DTC or EDTC sooner than it would initiate a wire and have the same effective fund arrival time and, thus, the same effective opportunity to earn interest.

The generic term for the techniques used to accomplish the delay shift is "anticipation." There are several variations in anticipation technique. The objective here is not an exhaustive presentation of the various techniques.

Rather the intent is to illustrate how its use can reduce or even completely eliminate delay differences and show how its use complicates the evaluation of alternative transfer mechanisms.

The Adjusted Target Technique

The most common form of anticipation is the so-called "adjusted target technique" for coping with transfer delays. To illustrate its use, assume that a company needed to maintain an average balance of $10,000 to compensate a particular depository bank. The cash manager made DTC transfers with $10,000 target but then observed from bank statements that the actual average balance was $16,000, the extra $6,000 being due to "transfers in process." Hence, the cash manager makes a one-time transfer of $6,000 out of the depository bank and thereafter manages the transfers with an effective target balance of $4,000 on the company books. However, the actual average balance is $10,000—the $4,000 effective target plus the $6,000 of transfers in process.

The removal of the $6,000 of transfers in process means that the company has available to earn interest the very money that the conventional breakeven analysis assumes to be idle. Hence, the one-time withdrawal has effectively eliminated the time delay effect by making the investable funds from a DTC-based transfer system equivalent to the investable funds from a wire-based transfer system. In this example, it has completely eliminated the excess field balance and thus eliminated any issue of interest opportunity cost.

Time Varying Anticipation

In many cases of a time varying deposit level, a company cannot remove all of the average transfers in process via a one-time transfer without being exposed to an overdraft. Then companies can use "time varying anticipation," i.e., they reflect knowledge of how transfers in process vary. While administratively more complex, the effect is the same as the simple adjusted target, namely the removal of some or all of the transfers in process.

Anticipation-Delay Synthesis

To the extent that transfers in process can be removed so that there is no excess balance at the depository bank, a DTC-based system dominates a wire-based system, i.e., same investable funds and lower transfer cost. When anticipation cannot remove all deposits in process and there is an excess balance, differences in interest value and transfer cost must be compared. However, this comparison requires a more complex analysis than the conventional breakeven treatment.

V. DUAL BALANCES

When the DTC clearing time exceeds the availability time granted at the concentration bank, then a company can receive credit for having available balances in two places at once—the concentration bank and the depository bank from which funds are being transferred. The common terms for this situation are "back float" or "clearing float." However, because of imprecision in the popular usage of the various float terms, the term "dual balance" is used here to refer to the additional available balances arising when actual clearing time exceeds granted availability time.

To illustrate how dual balances arise, assume that the availability time granted at the concentration bank is one business day but that the actual DTC clearing time back to the depository bank upon which the DTC is written is two business days. Thus, if a $10,000 DTC were deposited in the concentration bank on Tuesday, the result would be a $10,000 available balance addition at the concentration bank on Wednesday with the $10,000 also residing in the depository bank on Wednesday. The same $10,000 are available balances in both the concentration and the depository bank on Wednesday. The company has the benefit of a "dual balance." Hence, it has the potential to earn extra interest.

While the example above assumed faster availability than clear time, the reverse can also occur, namely faster clearing than granted availability although this situation is less frequent. In this case there will be a time period for which the company has no available balance at either the depository bank or the concentration bank. Hence, there is a net loss in available balances and thus a loss in ability to earn interest.

Dual Balances and Mechanism Evaluation

Positive dual balances clearly make DTCs even more attractive than they would otherwise be. In terms of the conventional breakeven framework, positive dual balances mean more money able to earn interest and/or compensate banks for services. However, reflecting the value of positive dual balances (or the absence of any balances) correctly within the breakeven framework is virtually impossible. It requires more complex analysis.

VI. NEED FOR A CORRECT EVALUATION-COMPARISON FRAMEWORK

The conventional breakeven analysis naively assumes that the mechanism selection is an issue of the interest earned over the period of the nominal transfer delay versus the transfer cost. This framework omits a variety of important complicating factors—compensating balances, anticipation and back float.

These omissions are generally biased against DTCs and in favor of selecting wires. Hence, the use of the conventional analysis would generally cause a company to use wires far more than is economically justifiable. In fact, the use of anticipation can make a DTC or EDTC absolutely dominate a wire in the sense that the wire would never be used for any size transfer. Likewise, positive dual balances can make a DTC absolutely dominate either a wire or an EDTC. Negative dual balances can make an EDTC dominate a DTC.

The presentation of these complicating factors establishes deficiencies of the conventional breakeven framework for evaluating transfer alternatives.

Further Criticism: Cash Transfer Scheduling

Cash transfer scheduling is the task of specifying the time and amount of transfers. Up to this point the criticism of breakeven analysis has been couched in the context of the common practice of a daily transfer of each day's deposits. It has not reflected the fact that good transfer practice today means scheduling to reduce transfers and/or accelerate cash flows rather than automatically making a daily transfer of each day's deposits.[1] Such scheduling generally means fewer transfers than would be made with daily transfers. Thus, there is no longer a well defined fixed transfer cost. Likewise, the transfer size depends on the transfer frequency and not just the amount deposited. Further, the effective transfer delay varies from transfer to transfer. Such improvements in transfer practice undermine even further the conventional breakeven framework.

The Need for a Correct Criterion

Many cash managers recognize the deficiencies of the conventional framework. Yet they have no systematic alternative for making mechanism deci-

[1] For a nontechnical overview of cash transfer scheduling, readers are referred to Stone, Ferguson, and Hill (1980).

sions. Moreover, the authors have encountered others who still embrace the breakeven framework and incorrectly use wires "because they have deposits much larger than the breakeven size," often thereby unnecessarily incurring significant costs for their companies. There is a clear need for a complete and correct evaluation criterion and a procedure for using it to evaluate mechanism alternatives systematically.

VII. A CORRECT EVALUATION PROCEDURE

As noted above, cash transfer scheduling is the task of deciding when and how much to transfer. The common practice of a daily transfer of each day's reported deposits is a simple (and often costly) solution. The best transfer schedule is the one that minimizes the cost of transferring subject to bank and company constraints. The cost of using a particular transfer mechanism will depend on the transfer schedule, i.e., on (1) the number of transfers, (2) the amount of excess or underutilized balances and (3) any usable dual balance benefits.

To express the components of the transfer scheduling cost quantitatively, let CPT denote the cost per transfer, let $EXCESS$ denote the amount by which average balances exceed the required compensating balance at the depository bank over an appropriate time period and let $DBAL$ denote the average dual balance benefit over the same time period. Then, if I measures the opportunity value of balances, the transfer scheduling cost (TSC) is:

$$TSC \equiv CPT \cdot (\#\text{Transfers}) + I \cdot EXCESS - I \cdot DBAL. \qquad (3)$$

Note that positive dual balances are treated as a benefit (negative cost). They have value only to the extent they can be removed from the depository bank. If an increase in dual balances just increased the average excess, there would be no effect on the total scheduling cost. For instance, a $5,000 increase in average dual balances that could not be removed would just increase the average excess by $5,000 and there would be no impact on the total cost in Equation (3). The point here is that the formulation of the total cost in (3) counts only usable (removable) dual balances.

If there were a negative dual balance, then this term would be positive in (3) and would be properly counted as a cost. Again it would affect the total cost only if it reduced removable balances.

The interest rate in (3) should be an "opportunity rate." Hence, if there were interest earned of 6% on an account, then the opportunity rate in (3) should be the value of funds at the concentration bank less the 6% earned at the depository bank. Thus, (3) can reflect interest at the depository bank.

In summary, the formulation of the total transfer scheduling cost incorporates all the costs associated with a transfer schedule for a given mechanism and trades them off properly.

Comparison with the Formulation of the Breakeven Framework

It is insightful to compare the statement of the transfer scheduling cost in Equation (3) with the costs implicit in the net benefit comparison of Equation (1).

First, dual balance benefits are included here but absent in the breakeven treatment of (1). Second, while both approaches use interest rates to compare direct costs with balances, the measures of both direct costs and interest values are different. Costs in (1) are for a single transfer while (3) uses the total costs over some time period and thus reflects the number of transfers that are actually made. Interest value in (3) is based on average excess balances rather than the dollar amount of transfers in process used in (1). Thus (3) measures the true interest opportunity cost and reflects any effect of anticipation while the interest measure in (1) has no necessary relation to the interest opportunity cost. In fact, (1) often falsely imputes a cost when there is no excess balance and no interest opportunity cost at all.

Role of Optimal Scheduling in Mechanism Selection

This article is not concerned with the details of cash transfer scheduling *per se*. Nor does it concern the development of the problem as a mathematical program.[2] Rather, the concern here is the selection of an appropriate transfer mechanism. For selection of a transfer mechanism, what is important is an ability to solve the cash transfer scheduling problem for each alternative mechanism and compare solutions, i.e., compare optimal scheduling costs. Hence, for the purposes of evaluating alternative transfer mechanisms, the mathematical program can be viewed as a "black box" that converts mechanism attributes, deposits schedules, and problem parameters into optimal transfer schedules with an associated value for the minimum transfer scheduling cost for that mechanism.

Besides using the appropriate cost measure, the basic evaluation principle used here is that cost comparisons should be based on the "best version" of each alternative. For instance, it would clearly be meaningless to compare the cost of an optimal wire system with a very poor DTC-based transfer schedule and vice versa. Rather, the relevant comparisons in an evaluation of wires versus DTCs in the least-cost wire system versus the least-cost DTC system. Thus, intelligent cost comparisons require an ability to obtain the least-cost version of each alternative and then compare costs.

Evaluation Procedure for Mechanism Comparisons

Once it is possible to solve the cash transfer scheduling problem, ascertaining the least-cost mechanism is a simple three-step procedure.

Step 1: Input. Each mechanism is characterized by 1) an availability time at the concentration bank, 2) its clearing time back to the depository bank and 3) its cost.

Step 2: Schedule Optimization. The best transfer schedule is found for each mechanism.

Step 3: Evaluation. Scheduling costs are compared. The best mechanism (before consideration of administration-control issues and fixed costs) is the one with the smallest transfer scheduling cost. Figure 4 illustrates a report comparing the costs for the optimal schedules for a DTC, EDTC and wire.

Fixed-Cost Considerations

So far, there has been no explicit treatment of the information-control-administrative costs associated with alternative mechanisms and alternative ways of using mechanisms. To a great extent, these costs are independent of a particular schedule (amount and timing of transfer).[3] Thus, they can be viewed as "fixed costs" for a given mechanism transfer system.

When there are differences in information-control-administrative costs for alternative mechanisms or ways of using mechanisms, then these costs can be added to the total transfer scheduling costs (the transfer scheduling costs over

---

[2] The formulation as a mathematical program is summarized in an appendix available from *The Journal of Bank Research* and developed in detail in Stone and Hill (1980).

[3] This independence is true "by definition." If any information-control-administrative costs depended on the number of transfers, it would be part of a properly specified direct transfer cost, *CPT*.

all depository banks) to obtain a grand total cost for each alternative. Then grand total costs can be compared to see if alternative frameworks are justified.

VIII. SUMMARY AND SYNTHESIS

The mechanism selection problem is a practical decision task that is implicitly involved in the design of every cash concentration system. It is widely recognized and has been the major focus of much cash concentration.

This paper has noted the deficiencies of the conventional breakeven framework and set forth a correct alternative. The essence of the correct evaluation framework is the comparison of optimal scheduling costs for each alternative. Obtaining the least-cost schedule requires the solution of the mathematical program. However, carrying out the evaluation does not require proficiency in mathematical programming. Rather, with appropriate software, all that is involved is specification of the appropriate inputs (deposit schedules, costs, mechanism parameters) and the comparison of the least-cost schedules as summarized in a report such as Figure 4. Thus, once a decision support system is available for use, the correct least-cost comparison framework is as easy to use as the incorrect breakeven framework.

CITED REFERENCES

Coldwell, Philip E., "The FED's Role in Defining the Payments System," Remarks at the Bank Administration Institute Conference, New Orleans (September 13, 1979) and reprinted in part in *The Cash Manager*, Vol. 2, No. 10 (October 1979).

Stone, Bernell K., Daniel M. Ferguson and Ned C. Hill, "Cash Transfer Scheduling: Overview," *The Cash Manager*, Vol. 3, No. 3 (March 1980).

Stone, Bernell K. and Ned C. Hill, "Cash Transfer Scheduling for Efficient Cash Concentration," *Financial Management* (Fall 1980).

An earlier version of this paper was presented at the annual meetings of the Southwestern Finance Association (San Antonio, March 1980). This paper is

Figure 4. A Report Giving the Current Transfer Schedule and the Optimal Schedule for Wires, DTC, and EDTCs.

Schedule Description	Transfer Amount (% of weekly deposit)					Excess Balance	+ Direct Transfer Cost (in balances)	− Dual Balance Benefit	= Total Scheduling Cost
	M	T	W	T	F				
Current schedule (Wire)	20	15	25	20	20	18,900	1,800	0	20,700
Optimal schedule (Wire)	20	15	25	20	20	0	1,800	0	1,800
Optimal Schedule (DTC)	0	0	0	100	0	0	35	8,690	−8,655
Optimal Schedule (EDTC)	0	55	0	0	45	0	25	0	25

an outgrowth of research on the cash concentration problem supported by The First National Bank of Chicago. While the authors are responsible for the content and exposition, they acknowledge the ideas and criticism provided by other members of the team, and thank both Daniel M. Ferguson, vice president and manager of the consulting services group, and John E. Coblentz, vice president and manager of the cash management division, for the faith and patience necessary to see a major research and development project from idea to model to computer programs and, finally, to a computer based decision support system.

Solving Lock Box Location Problems

Robert M. Nauss and Robert E. Markland

"Cash management is being given a priority throughout U.S. business today
that it has never enjoyed before, and company after company is being swept
along," according to a recent *Business Week* article [4]. Need for more efficient
cash management has concentrated attention on more sophisticated computer-based methods for managing corporate cash flows. During the last few
years, more and more corporations have begun using computer-based management science approaches to cash management.

One of the most important aspects of cash management is development of
an efficient receivables collection system that makes it possible to collect
payments quickly from a number of wide-spread customers. A company that
must collect payments from such customers generally maintains "lock box"
accounts with banks in several strategically-located cities. The company
wants to select a *set* of lock box banks to minimize both the opportunity costs
of uncollected funds and lock box service charges. The increased profits
resulting from such a use of lock box collection systems have been very
significant to many companies.

Researchers have dealt with the lock box problem. Levy [13] developed a
heuristic procedure for the selection of a low cost combination of lock boxes
from a given set of possible locations. Kramer [11] evaluated various lock box
plans by simulating their mail- and clearing-time for a representative sample
of checks. Stancill [24] developed a procedure for determining the costs and
benefits for a given lock box. McAdams [14] provided a critique of Stancill's
work, arguing for a more rigorous definition of the opportunity benefits accru-
ing to the funds released through the use of a lock box. Kraus, Janssen, and
McAdams [12] later designed an integer programming formulation of the lock
box problem, but did not show any computational results. Shanker and
Zoltners [23, 24] extended the formulation proposed by Kraus, Janssen, and
McAdams, again with no actual computational results. More recently, Maier
and Vander Weide [15, 16] have specified a different approach to this problem,
also failing to present computational results. Cornuejols, Fisher, and Nemhauser [6] have produced an excellent theoretical treatise and survey of the
state of the art in lock box location modeling. There are very brief discussions
of computational results in working papers by Ciochetto *et al.* [5] and by Bulfin
and Unger [2].

The basic objective of this article is to describe the development and
application of an efficient model for solving large-scale lock box location
problems. The discussion deals with the practical aspects of implementing
this model, using sophisticated computer programs that provide the user with
modeling flexibility. The model presented is an improvement over existing
models in terms of its ability to solve large problems in a reasonable amount of
computer time.

•
•
•

Source: Reprinted (abridged) with permission of the publisher and authors from the Spring 1979
issue of *Financial Management,* © 1979 by the Financial Management Association.

LOCK BOX CHARGES

Charges for lock box services vary from bank to bank. Most charges are based on two components: a fixed charge that is independent of lock box activity and a variable charge that depends on the number of checks processed. Fixed charges are assessed on a periodic basis (daily, weekly, monthly, etc.) regardless of the number of checks processed. Examples of fixed charges include monthly account maintenance, daily deposit fees, depository transfer checks, and/or daily wire transfer charges.

One important point should be made concerning daily wire transfer charges. A single wire transfer is assessed an outgoing charge by the originating bank as well as an incoming charge by the receiving (concentration) bank. To calculate an annual figure for wire transfers for a non-concentration bank, both the originating wire transfer charge and the receiving charge by the concentration bank should be included in the non-concentration bank's annual figure. The reasoning for this is quite simple. If all customer checks were mailed directly to the concentration bank's lock box, no wire transfer charges would be incurred. Wire transfer charges are incurred only if a non-concentration bank's lock box is selected, and hence the incoming wire transfer charge assessed by the concentration bank must rightly be attributed to the non-concentration bank in the calculation of fixed charges.

Generally, payment for lock box charges may be on a cash basis or a compensating balance basis, or some combination of the two. The method of payment affects the cost to the corporation (in opportunity dollars) of maintaining a lock box at a particular bank, since this cost includes not only cash payments made to the bank, but also the cost of keeping compensating balances at the bank when in fact these balances could be invested elsewhere to earn additional funds.

•
•
•

COMPUTATIONAL RESULTS—A TYPICAL LOCK BOX LOCATION PROBLEM

Let us now consider the solution to a typical lock box location problem, where there are 46 potential lock box sites and 99 customer zones (in this case zip codes from which customer checks are received.) The first solution in Exhibit 3 is the optimal solution for the unconstrained lock box location problem (with no upper limit on the number of lock boxes allowed to be open in a solution). The optimal solution calls for seven lock box locations, with a resultant opportunity cost of dollar-float plus bank cash charges equal to $100,805. The solution indicates customer zones to be served by each of these seven banks, and it summarizes the various costs associated with each of the banks. Marginal cost associated with closing each of the seven lock boxes is also indicated. Following the optimal solution are three "next best" solutions based on a one-for-one swap of lock boxes that were open in the optimal solution. For example, in the first one-for-one swap solution, lock box #36 has been replaced by lock box #40, with an increase in the minimum objective function value to $100,810. Other one-for-one solutions have a similar interpretation.

Following the optimal solution, the lock box model determines a sequence of solutions in which the number of lock boxes open is successively reduced by one. For example, consider the solution shown in Exhibit 4 for a constrained problem where six lock boxes (one less than the unconstrained optimal solution) are allowed to be open. The minimum objective function value increases to $100,999. All the additional cost information is again provided, and the three next best solutions, based on a one-for-one swap of lock boxes that were open in the optimal six lock box solution, are indicated.

The process of reducing the number of lock boxes is then continued, until we are down to a one lock box solution. As can be seen in the summary in Exhibit 5, as the number of lock boxes allowed open is reduced, the (minimum) value of the objective function increases. Such an analysis allows the manager to determine the marginal cost associated with a fixed number of lock boxes.

Exhibit 5   Summary Table—Lock Box Solutions

Solution #	Description	Value of Objective Function	Lock Boxes in Solution
1	Unconstrained*— 7 Lock Boxes	$100,805	1, 10, 33, 36, 37, 41, 43
2	6 Lock Boxes	$100,999	1, 10, 33, 37, 41, 43
3	5 Lock Boxes	$101,398	1, 10, 33, 41, 43
4	4 Lock Boxes	$102,735	1, 33, 41, 43
5	3 Lock Boxes	$104,116	1, 33, 41
6	2 Lock Boxes	$107,126	1, 41
7	1 Lock Box	$123,257	10

* Optimal solution to original unconstrained problem.

Exhibit 6 presents a summary of our computational experience for a number of problems that have been solved to date. It depicts quite clearly the speed and efficiency of this model in determining solutions to problems that are quite large. These results are quite encouraging, because until recently it was thought that finding optimal solutions to such problems required an inordinate amount of central processing unit (CPU) time and was thus very costly. Our results suggest that even larger problems can be solved using a modest amount of CPU time.

SUMMARY AND EXTENSIONS

Several large banks and corporations are now using the lock box location model utilizing the branch and bound algorithm and the corresponding computer programs. We feel that this model offers an improved means of solving the lock box location problem in the context of more efficient cash management. Among the improvements are the following: (1) Improved calculation of expected total float; (2) Increased user flexibility: input options that allow the determination of solutions for several differing bank charging arrangements; (3) Improved output capability: output that provides the user with valuable sensitivity and incremental analysis information; (4) Greater computational efficiency: the ability to solve large problems (more than 45 potential lock boxes) using only a small amount of computer time (less than 40 seconds CPU time); and (5) Greater computational accuracy: the ability to always determine an optimal solution to the lock box location problem, with no restriction on the number of lock boxes allowed in solution.

Exhibit 3 Optimal Solution—Unconstrained Lock Box Problem

LOCK BOX OPTIMIZATION MODEL

FIGURES ARE ON AN ANNUAL BASIS UNLESS OTHERWISE NOTED

CORPORATE INTERNAL RATE OF RETURN= 0.060
THIS SOLUTION IS CONSTRAINED TO HAVE NO MORE THAN 46 LOCK BOXES OPEN

BANKS IN SOLUTION
AND ZIP CODES SERVED

****

BANK	AVERAGE $=FLOAT PER DAY	DISCOUNTED $=FLOAT PER DAY	EXPECTED CHECKS PER DAY	VARIABLE CHARGES PER YEAR	FIXED CHARGES PER YEAR	TOTAL CHARGES PER YEAR	VARIABLE COMP BAL PER MONTH	FIXED COMP BAL PER MONTH	TOTAL COMP BAL PER MONTH
1	915216.	54913.	960	96.	1000.	1096.	20833.	2000.	22833.
10	161592.	9696.	125	13.	1000.	1013.	19583.	245.	19828.
33	95158.	5710.	110	16.	1000.	1016.	21667.	357.	22024.
36	34073.	2044.	70	6.	1000.	1006.	19167.	107.	19274.

BANK 1
ZIP CODES

```
 1   2   3   4   5
 6   8   9  11  12
13  16  17  19  20
24  25  26  33  34
38  43  48  49
51  53  54  55  56
57  58  59  60  61
63  64  65  67  69
70  72  73  74  76
78  79  80  81  82
83  84  85  86  87
88  89  90  91  92
93  95  96  97  98
99
```

MARGINAL COST OF CLOSING
LOCK BOX IS   4309.
****

BANK 10
ZIP CODES

```
 7  10  14  15  46
47  77
```

MARGINAL COST OF CLOSING
LOCK BOX IS   1326.
****

BANK 33
ZIP CODES

```
21  28  29  37  50
52  68
```

MARGINAL COST OF CLOSING
LOCK BOX IS   1215.
****

BANK 36
ZIP CODES

```
22  27  66  75
```

MARGINAL COST OF CLOSING
LOCK BOX IS   194.
****

```
BANK
ZIP CODES 37  18  23  44  94

MARGINAL COST OF CLOSING
LOCK BOX IS   220.
************************
                              29017.   1741.   25   3.   63.   1000.   21000.   1003.   21063.

BANK
ZIP CODES 41  30  31  32  39  40
             42  62
MARGINAL COST OF CLOSING
LOCK BOX IS   8855.
************************
                             287316.  17239.  130  13.  271.   1000.   20833.   1013.   21104.

BANK
ZIP CODES 43  35  36  71

MARGINAL COST OF CLOSING
LOCK BOX IS   1381.
                              38450.   2307.   60   9.  195.   1000.   21667.   1009.   21862.


TOTALS FOR LOCK BOX SYSTEM  1560819.  93649.  1480 156. 3238.   7000.  144750.   7156.  147988.


TOTAL DISCOUNTED $-FLOAT                          93649.
TOTAL BANK CASH CHARGES                            7156.
DISCOUNTED $-FLOAT PLUS BANK CASH CHARGES        100805.

NOTE: MARGINAL COST OF CLOSING A LOCK BOX IS COMPUTED BY ADDING THE ADDITIONAL DISCOUNTED FLOAT INCURRED IF THE
LOCK BOX WERE CLOSED (AND THE LOCK BOXES IN THIS SOLUTION REMAIN OPEN) AND SUBTRACTING THE FIXED AND VARIABLE CHARGES
INCURRED BY THE LOCK BOX


3 NEXT BEST SOLUTIONS BASED ON ONE-FOR-ONE SWAP OF BANKS OPEN IN OPTIMAL SOLUTION.

(BANKS FIXED OPEN OR CLOSED ARE NOT INCLUDED)


TOTAL DISCOUNTED $-FLOAT PLUS BANK CHARGES= 100810.00     TOTAL DISCOUNTED $-FLOAT PLUS BANK CHARGES= 101105.00

BANKS IN SOLUTION ARE                                      BANKS IN SOLUTION ARE

    1                                                           1
   10                                                          10
   33                                                          33
   37                                                          36
   40                                                          40
   41                                                          41
   43                                                          43


TOTAL DISCOUNTED $-FLOAT PLUS BANK CHARGES= 100951.00

BANKS IN SOLUTION ARE

    1
   10
   33
   37
   41
   43
   45
```

Exhibit 4 Optimal Solution—Constrained Lock Box Problem

```
LOCK BOX OPTIMIZATION MODEL

FIGURES ARE ON AN ANNUAL BASIS UNLESS OTHERWISE NOTED

CORPORATE INTERNAL RATE OF RETURN= 0.060
THIS SOLUTION IS CONSTRAINED TO HAVE NO MORE THAN   6  LOCK BOXES OPEN

BANKS IN SOLUTION
AND ZIP CODES SERVED
```

	AVERAGE $-FLOAT PER DAY	DISCOUNTED $-FLOAT PER DAY	EXPECTED CHECKS PER YEAR	VARIABLE CHARGES PER YEAR	FIXED CHARGES PER MONTH	TOTAL COMP BAL PER YEAR	COMP BAL PER MONTH	TOTAL COMP BAL PER MONTH

```
**************************

BANK       1
ZIP CODES  1   2   3   4   5
           6   8   9  11  12
          13  16  17  19  20
          22  24  25  26  33
          34  38  43  45  48
          49  51  53  54  55
          56  57  58  59  60
          61  63  64  65  66
          67  69  70  72  73
          74  75  76  78  79
          80  81  82  83  84
          85  86  87  88  89
          90  91  92  93  95
          96  97  98  99
                         942249.   56535.   1010   101.   2104.   1000.   20833.   1101.   22938.
MARGINAL COST OF CLOSING
LOCK BOX IS    4519.
**************************

BANK      10
ZIP CODES  7  10  14  15  46
          47  77
                         161592.    9696.    125    13.    245.   1000.   19583.   1013.   19828.
MARGINAL COST OF CLOSING
LOCK BOX IS    1326.
**************************

BANK      33
ZIP CODES 21  27  28  29  37
          50  52  68
                         122058.    7324.    130    19.    422.   1000.   21667.   1019.   22089.
MARGINAL COST OF CLOSING
LOCK BOX IS    1309.
**************************

BANK      37
ZIP CODES 18  23  44  94
                          29017.    1741.     25     3.     63.   1000.   21000.   1003.   21063.
MARGINAL COST OF CLOSING
LOCK BOX IS     399.
**************************
```

BANK
ZIP CODES 41 30 31 32 39 40
             41 42 62   287316.   17239.   130   13.   271.   1000.   20833.   1013.   21104.

MARGINAL COST OF CLOSING
LOCK BOX IS   8855.
****

BANK
ZIP CODES 43 35 36 71   38450.   2307.   60   9.   195.   1000.   21667.   1009.   21862.

MARGINAL COST OF CLOSING
LOCK BOX IS   1381.

TOTALS FOR LOCK BOX SYSTEM   1580679.   94841.   1480   158.   3300.   6000.   125583.   6158.   128884.

TOTAL DISCOUNTED $-FLOAT   94841.
TOTAL BANK CASH CHARGES   6158.
DISCOUNTED $-FLOAT PLUS BANK CASH CHARGES   100999.

NOTE: MARGINAL COST OF CLOSING A LOCK BOX IS COMPUTED BY ADDING THE ADDITIONAL DISCOUNTED FLOAT INCURRED IF THE
LOCK BOX WERE CLOSED (AND THE LOCK BOXES IN THIS SOLUTION REMAIN OPEN) AND SUBTRACTING THE FIXED AND VARIABLE CHARGES
INCURRED BY THE LOCK BOX

3 NEXT BEST SOLUTIONS BASED ON ONE-FOR-ONE SWAP OF BANKS OPEN IN OPTIMAL SOLUTION.
(BANKS FIXED OPEN OR CLOSED ARE NOT INCLUDED)

TOTAL DISCOUNTED $-FLOAT PLUS BANK CHARGES= 101025.00

BANKS IN SOLUTION ARE

1
10
33
36
41
43

TOTAL DISCOUNTED $-FLOAT PLUS BANK CHARGES= 101172.00

BANKS IN SOLUTION ARE

1
10
33
41
43
45

TOTAL DISCOUNTED $-FLOAT PLUS BANK CHARGES= 101389.00

BANKS IN SOLUTION ARE

1
10
33
41
42
43

Exhibit 6   Summary of Computational Results

Problem Type	Number of Potential Locations	Number of Customer Zones	Number of Locations in Optimal Solution	Value of Objective Function	CPU Time in Seconds*
Lock Box	15	115	6	143,382	4.4
Lock Box	15	99	5	145,016	7.2
Lock Box	47	120	24**	199,134	36.5
Lock Box	47	120	26**	202,861	30.1
Lock Box	45	31	2	46,876	1.4
Lock Box	46	99	7	100,805	35.1
Lock Box	46	100	10	58,063	4.5
Lock Box	46	100	10	129,416	36.4
Lock Box	46	100	9	81,531	12.2
Lock Box	92	100	7	98,748	38.7
Lock Box	94	120	6	227,013	32.3
Lock Box	45	101	1	14,326	10.9

* Includes input/output time for runs made on IBM 370/168.

** Problems involving very small fixed charges, thus resulting in a large number of open lock boxes in the optimal solution.

We have also developed and implemented a similar model for remote disbursing account location analysis (see references 3, 5, 8, 19, and 21 for details). The remote disbursing account location problem is essentially the converse of the lock box location problem. The objective of a remote disbursement system is to maximize the $-float associated with payments made to suppliers minus associated bank charges. We have solved several large-scale disbursement account location problems that are not presented here.

We are now working with several banks and corporations to implement the model using the latest bank availability schedules, bank charging schemes, and expected mail times. These programs, associated documentation, and illustrative examples are available from the authors.

REFERENCES

1. Norman Agin, "Optimum Seeking With Branch and Bound,"*Management Science* (December 1966), pp. B176-85.

2. R.L. Bulfin and V.E. Unger, "Computational Experience With An Algorithm For the Lock-Box Problem," *Proceedings of the 28th Association For Computing Machinery National Conference*, Atlanta, August 1973.

3. Robert F. Calman, *Linear Programming and Cash Management/Cash ALPHA*, Cambridge, MIT Press, 1968.

4. "Cash Management: The New Art of Wringing More Profit From Corporate Funds," *Business Week*, March 13, 1978, pp. 62-68.

5. F.F. Ciochetto, H.S. Swanson, J.R. Lee, and R.E.D. Woolsey, "The Lock Box Problem and Some Startling But True Computational Results For Large Scale Systems," Working Paper presented at the 41st National Meeting of the Operations Research Society of America, New Orleans, April 26-28, 1972.

6. Gerard Cornuejols, Marshall L. Fisher, and George L. Nemhauser, "Location of Bank Accounts to Optimize Float: An Analytic Study of Exact and Approximate Algorithms," *Management Science* (April 1977), pp. 789-810.

7. L.B. Ellwein, "Fixed Charge Location-Allocation Problems with Capacity and Configuration Constraints," Technical Report No. 70-2, Department of Industrial Engineering, Stanford University, August 1970.

8. A.M. Geoffrion and R.E. Marsten, "Integer Programming Algorithms: A Framework and State-of-the-Art Survey," *Management Science* (May 1972), pp. 465-91.

9. Lawrence J. Gitman, Keith D. Forrester, and John R. Forrester, "Maximizing Cash Disbursement Float," *Financial Management* (Summer 1976), pp. 15-24.

10. "How Business Lives Beyond Its Means," *Business Week*, November 15, 1969, pp. 72*ff.*

11. Robert L. Kramer, "Analysis of Lock-box Locations," *Bankers Monthly Magazine*, May 15, 1966, pp. 36-40.

12. Alan Kraus, Christian Janssen, and Alan K. McAdams, "The Lock-box Location Problem," *Journal of Bank Research* (Autumn 1970), pp. 51-58.

13. Ferdinand K. Levy, "An Application of Heuristic Problem Solving to Accounts Receivable Management," *Management Science* (February 1966), pp. B236-244.

14. Alan K. McAdams, "Critique of: A Lock-box Model," *Management Science* (October 1968), pp. 888-90.

15. S.F. Maier and J.H. Vander Weide, "The Lock-Box Location Problem: A Practical Reformulation," *Journal of Bank Research* (Summer 1974), pp. 92-95.

16. S.F. Maier and J.H. Vander Weide, "A Unified Location Model for Cash Disbursements and Lock-Box Collections," *Journal of Bank Research* (Summer 1976), pp. 166-72.

17. "Making Millions by Stretching the Float," *Business Week*, November 23, 1974, pp. 89-90.

18. R.M. Nauss, "An Improved Algorithm for the Capacitated Facility Location Problem," forthcoming in *Operational Research Quarterly.*

19. R.M. Nauss and R.E. Markland, "Real World Experience with an Optimal Lock Box Location Algorithm," Working Paper presented at TIMS/ORSA Joint National Meeting, San Francisco, May 1977.

20. Gerald A. Pogue, Russell B. Faucett, and Ralph N. Bussard, "Cash Management: A Systems Approach," *Industrial Management Review* (Winter 1970), pp. 55-73.

21. G. Sa, "Branch-and-Bound and Approximate Solutions to the Capacitated Plant-Location Problem," *Operations Research* (November-December 1969), pp. 1005-16.

22. R.J. Shanker and A.A. Zoltners, "The Corporate Payments Problem," *Journal of Bank Research* (Spring 1972), pp. 47-53.

23. R.J. Shanker and A.A. Zoltners, "An Extension of the Lock Box Location Problem," *Journal of Bank Research* (Winter 1972), p. 62.

24. James McN. Stancill, "A Decision Rule Model for the Establishment of a Lock-box," *Management Science* (October 1968), pp. 884-87.

25. William J. Tallent, "Cash Management: A Case Study," *Management Accounting* (July 1974), pp. 20-24.

An Assessment of Marketable Securities Management Practices

Lawrence J. Gitman and Mark D. Goodwin

The management of a firm's marketable security portfolio is an important aspect of financial management. Decisions relative to the quantity, timing, and types of marketable securities purchased can significantly impact the risk and return of the firm. As an aid to decision makers who must make cash-marketable security decisions, a large body of academic research has been developed. Keynes in *The General Theory of Employment, Interest, and Money* [10, pp. 170-174] isolated three basic motives—transactions, precautionary, and speculative—for maintaining liquid balances. Subsequently a variety of authors such as Baumol [2], Tobin [15], Archer [1], Miller and Orr [11], and Weitzman [17] addressed the cash-marketable security problem. Their work has provided various techniques for determining when and in what amount cash should be invested, and vice versa.

Although a variety of marketable security management techniques are described in the academic literature, not a great deal is known about the actual practices employed by the financial manager. Since the publication of the findings of Jacobs [9], who in 1957 surveyed the investment practices and trends of 209 of the largest nonfinancial corporations, only a limited amount of information has been gathered relative to marketable security management practices. The purpose of this paper is to assess the "state of the art" in the real-world of short-term investment of excess funds. The paper addresses itself to a number of important aspects of the marketable security management process in order to assess and relate actual practice to the key theories, concepts, and techniques discussed in the financial literature. The main area investigated is marketable security investment procedures and preferences, although at the outset cash forecasting is discussed since it significantly impacts the marketable security investment activity.

The findings reported throughout the remainder of this paper are based upon over 150 responses received in August of 1977 from 300 questionnaires sent to firms falling in the range of 201 to 631 on the Fortune 1000 listing [6, 14]. This range was used because it was believed to provide excellent variation in the size of companies surveyed. It was also believed that a sample of large firms would provide indications of the level of sophistication in marketable security management achieved by the nation's leading firms. The largest firm in the sample had sales in 1976 of approximately $1.1 billion, while sales of the smallest were $221 million. Because of the nonstatistical nature of the sample as well as the non-response bias, generalization of the survey results to the universe of business firms cannot be made.

CASH FORECASTING

Forecasting cash requirements accurately can have a direct effect on the efficiency of marketable security management[1]. The results of a cash forecast will determine both the type and maturity of marketable security invest-

---

[1] See Gitman [8, pp. 105-111], Van Horne [16, pp. 61-68], or Weston and Brigham [18, pp. 151-159] for detailed discussions of the use, preparation, and interpretation of cash forecasts.

Source: Reprinted with permission of the publisher and authors from *The Journal of Financial Research*, Vol. II, No. 2, Fall 1979.

ments. The overall yield from these investments will depend upon the firm's ability to successfully coordinate the maturity structures of marketable securities with forecasted cash needs. The increasing availability of both deterministic and probabilistic computer-based models is believed to have improved the accuracy of forecasting short-term cash levels and allowed for a more frequent review of the firm's short-term cash position.

Cash Forecasting Techniques

If increased innovation in the area of cash forecasting exists, it is expected that the improved accuracy should decrease the risk of insolvency that accompanies a strategy of minimizing cash balances to avoid the opportunity cost of holding cash. It should also follow that a large percentage of total cash could be declared surplus and available for short-term investment as a result of improved forecasts since less cash would have to be held for precautionary reasons. This situation could result in more dollars being invested in marketable securities or a general reduction in the level of cash and marketable securities.[2] When asked what method they used to forecast short-run cash balances, 117 of the 148 respondents (79 percent) indicated the use of manual as opposed to computer-based models. When asked how accurate they felt their forecasts were, the majority of respondents (97 of 147, or 66 percent) indicated confidence levels of less than or equal to 85 percent. Given the dominance of the manual forecasting method, the level of confidence reflected may not be especially surprising. This finding seems to confirm that of Reed [13, p. 41] whose study of the excess cash of 39 Fortune 500 firms found that of the firms surveyed about 37 percent of their average book balances were in excess of the liquidity needs of the company.[3] These findings seem a bit surprising when one considers the potential savings that might be achieved through the application of a more sophisticated forecasting technique. The responses given may indicate that possibly the firms surveyed do not fully understand probabilistic types of forecasting models. This conclusion seems consistent with those of Petty and Bowlin [12] who found in a sample of approximately 200 firms that of the 49.3 percent that indicated use of statistically-based techniques, 22.4 percent used them when making working capital-related decisions.

Monitoring and Controlling Cash Flows

In spite of the dominant use of manual cash forecasting techniques it appears that the respondent firms closely monitored their cash balances. When asked how frequently they assess their cash position, 140 of 148 respondents (95 percent) indicated they made the assessment daily. Daily assessment of course may be necessary if an accurate forecast is to be made using manual methods. As indicated earlier, the accuracy of cash forecasts has a direct impact on the maturity structure of marketable securities. Respondents overwhelmingly indicated (142 of 148, or 96 percent) that they attempted to coordinate the forecasted cash needs and the maturity structure of marketable securities. In a followup question respondents were asked to indicate which securities offered the best opportunity for aligning forecasted cash needs and maturities. As

---

[2] A reduction in the general level of cash and marketable securities would be anticipated in the event that a long-term excess of funds existed. In such a case those funds which are not needed for precautionary or transactions purposes could be used for fixed asset investment or debt reduction.

[3] In Reed's survey the "liquidity needs" included a compensating balance requirement. His finding that firms tend to maintain cash balances in excess of compensating balances was recently confirmed by Campbell and Brendsel [3] whose empirical findings suggest that "the compensating balance constraint is not binding."

shown in Table 1, commercial paper was felt to be best, while repurchase agreements were the second most dominant response, followed by certificates of deposit. These results are not surprising since each of these securities offer tailored maturities.

Table 1 Marketable Securities Providing the Greatest Opportunities to Align Maturities with Projected Cash Needs

Security	Number of Responses	Percent of Total Responses
Commercial Paper	83	35.9
Repurchase Agreements	48	20.8
Certificates of Deposit	45	19.5
Treasury Bills	22	9.5
Time Deposits	11	4.8
Banker's Acceptances	7	3.0
Eurodollars	5	2.2
Other Securities	10	4.3
Total Responses	231	100.0

In summary it appears that of the firms surveyed most use manual cash forecasting techniques in which they have a level of confidence of 85 percent or less. The firms tend to monitor their cash balances on a daily basis and attempt to coordinate the forecasted cash needs and the maturity structure of marketable securities. They feel that the best opportunity for matching needs and maturities is provided by commercial paper followed by repurchase agreements, and certificates of deposit, respectively.

MARKETABLE SECURITY INVESTMENT PROCEDURES AND PREFERENCES

Generally, firms are believed to purchase marketable securities in order to earn income on temporarily idle funds. Commonly used marketable securities, which include treasury bills, federal agency issues, banker's acceptances, commercial paper, repurchase agreements, negotiable certificates of deposit, federal funds, foreign short-term securities, eurodollar securities, and money market funds, are appealing to corporate treasurers due to their high liquidity and ease of purchase. Because of the diversity of marketable securities, a firm can purchase them with maturities of almost any length of time (from one day to one year). Because of the flexibility provided by the wide range of security types and maturities, basic theory would suggest that the firm align maturity structures of marketable securities acquired with its known cash needs. Such a strategy should provide maximum returns since excess cash is allowed to earn for the maximum period of time. Of course, the more uncertainty that exists concerning future cash needs, the more excess cash required in order to provide for these unexpected needs. This condition may reduce the potential returns from excess cash. In a study of cash management practices by Gitman, Moses, and White [7] it was found that 60.6 percent of the respondents (100 out of 300 of Fortune's top 1,000) held cash and marketable security balances for transaction purposes; another 27.3 percent held balances for safety; while the remaining respondents held balances for both speculation and to meet compensating balance requirements. Although this question was not explicitly addressed by this study, the data which follows tends to suggest that the respondent firms behave in a fashion similar to that found in the study described above. The possibility also exists that in order to meet unexpected needs a marketable security might have to be sold prior to maturity; such action might result in some type of price concession.

Marketable Security Holding Period Frequency

In an article by Dallenbach [5, p. 608] he indicated that an unpublished study by Collins [4] of 20 medium- and large-size West Coast firms tended to suggest that firms generally hold marketable securities to maturity. Such a finding suggests that firms may in fact closely match maturities and needs. When asked if they normally held marketable securities to maturity, 131 of 148 respondents (89 percent) to our survey responded affirmatively. It appears from this response that firms are relatively successful in their attempts to match maturities of marketable securities with forecasted cash needs since most of the time they appear able to hold the marketable security until maturity.[4] In a follow-up question, respondents were asked to indicate the frequency with which they held marketable securities relative to four possible holding periods. Their responses as well as the average response for each holding period are given in Table 2. It should be observed that based upon the average ranking the most frequent holding period appears to be between one week and one month (i.e., the lowest average rank). This response tends to support the belief that marketable securities are held primarily to meet transactions demand since many large disbursements, such as payroll, have cycles within this holding period. Holding periods of less than one week or greater than three months appear to be less frequent. From Table 2 it can be concluded that the respondent firms generally hold marketable securities for short periods of time (i.e., three months or less).[5]

Marketable Security Selection Criteria

As a basis for examining perceptions and preferences relative to the various marketable securities, respondents were asked to rank certain selection criteria. Table 3 presents responses to this question. An examination of the average responses makes it quite clear that the dominant characteristic (of those given) in the marketable security selection process is risk (i.e., the lowest average rank). Liquidity and time to maturity are the next most important characteristics. Price stability and status appear to be least important. Another response given to this question was the yield on the marketable security. This finding tends to support the findings of Collins' [4] study which found risk, liquidity, and yield in that order to be the most important marketable security investment criteria. These findings are also supported by those of Gitman, Moses, and White [7] who found market price stability and marketability to be

---

[4] Of course this result may be attributable to the fact that respondents primarily hold marketable securities in order to meet transactions demand, while they hold idle cash balances in order to satisfy their precautionary demands.

[5] It is interesting to note that in his 1957 study, Jacobs [9, p. 343] found for a sample of 209 large nonfinancial firms that more than 75 percent of their portfolios matured within six months, 15 percent matured within six months to one year, and the remaining 10 percent had maturities beyond one year.

Table 2 Marketable Security Holding Period Frequency

| Rank* | Holding Period | | | |
	Less Than One Week	One Week to One Month	One to Three Months	Over Three Months
1	45	46	46	10
2	13	45	20	8
3	18	15	43	16
4	19	6	—	55
Avg. Rank**	2.10	1.83	2.00	3.30

* 1 = Most Frequent, 2 = Next Most Frequent, ... , 4 = Least Frequent.
** The average rank is calculated by dividing the sum of the products of each rank and the number of corresponding responses by the total number of responses.

most important with maturity and yield of least importance. In their study, the high importance given to market price stability is attributed to the absence of a risk choice. It is believed that given the absence of such a choice, respondents reflected the importance of risk in choosing market price stability since it is a reasonable surrogate measure of risk. Table 3 coupled with the findings of others tends to suggest the importance of risk in the marketable security selection process.

Table 3 Importance of Various Characteristics In Marketable Security Selection

| Rank* | Characteristics | | | | |
	Liquidity	Time To Maturity	Status	Price Stability	Risk
1	15	12	2	6	114
2	64	35	6	18	19
3	42	52	5	28	7
4	19	31	26	39	1
5	2	7	58	28	5
Avg. Rank**	2.50	2.90	4.36	3.55	1.38

* 1 = Most Important, 2 = Next Most Important, ... , 5 = Least Important.
** The average rank is calculated using the technique described in the note to Table 2.

Marketable Security Risk Perceptions

To assess the respondents' perception of risk relative to the available marketable securities they were asked to rank a list of commonly purchased marketable securities according to their risk. Table 4 summarizes their responses for the first seven rankings. An analysis of the average rankings clearly indicates that treasury securities are viewed as least risky (i.e., the lowest average rank) with federal agency issues ranked second least risky. In terms of commonly discussed marketable securities it can be seen that the government-based issues (treasury securities and federal agency issues) are least risky while bank (negotiable C.D.s), corporate (commercial paper), and foreign securities are considered most risky.

Table 4   Marketable Security Risk Rankings

Risk Rank**	Marketable Security	Rank*							Avg. Rank***
		1	2	3	4	5	6	7	
1	Treasury Securities	131	4	0	1	0	1	0	1.09
2	Federal Agency Issues	43	65	11	2	3	0	1	1.89
3	Federal Funds	31	13	21	1	3	3	6	2.55
4	Repurchase Agreements	21	36	21	16	8	6	9	3.07
5	Money Market Funds	4	14	5	1	2	3	3	3.13
6	Banker's Acceptances	8	33	23	23	12	12	4	3.43
7	Negotiable C.D.s	10	35	12	28	26	11	2	3.53
8	Commercial Paper	8	32	9	13	19	23	18	4.18
9	Foreign S-T Securities	1	6	6	2	2	2	8	4.33

* 1 = Least Risky, 2 = Next Least Risky, ... , 7 = Most Risky.

** Based upon the average rank shown in the final column of this table. The securities are listed from lowest to highest risk.

*** The average rank is calculated using the technique described in the note to Table 2.

Marketable Security Preferences

Given the risk perceptions described above, the respondents were asked to rank the same group of securities with respect to their preference for use. Table 5 summarizes their responses for the first seven rankings. The results seem to indicate that commercial paper, negotiable C.D.'s, and repurchase agreements are the most preferred instruments, while foreign short-term securities and money market funds are least preferred. The preference for commercial paper and repurchase agreements over treasury bills indicated by respondents is reinforced by the results of the Gitman, Moses, and White (GMW) study [7] cited earlier. When asked to indicate the types of marketable securities they purchase, GMW's study found commercial paper, repurchase agreements, treasury bills, and negotiable C.D.'s to be ranked 1 through 4 respectively. The results of this study seem to be generally in line with their findings.[6]

---

[6] In contrast, Jacobs in his 1957 study [9, p. 344] reported that 75 percent of the total holdings of the 209 respondent firms were invested in U.S. Government securities. It seems quite clear that a significant shift in investment preferences has taken place since Jacobs' study.

Table 5 Marketable Security Utilization Preference Rankings

Preference Rank**	Marketable Security	Rank*							Avg. Rank***
		1	2	3	4	5	6	7	
1	Commercial Paper	57	19	21	11	7	6	2	2.33
2	Negotiable C.D.'s	18	39	28	21	7	3	0	2.73
3	Repurchase Agreements	26	29	23	25	12	4	2	2.90
4	Treasury Securities	23	19	17	16	13	8	2	3.09
5	Federal Funds	1	2	1	0	1	0	1	3.33
6	Banker's Acceptances	8	12	21	19	18	8	1	3.63
7	Federal Agency Issues	1	15	12	9	8	11	1	3.79
8	Foreign S-T Securities	2	1	2	2	2	3	1	4.08
9	Money Market Funds	0	2	0	2	0	0	2	4.33

* 1 = Most Preferred, 2 = Next Most Preferred, ... , 7 = Least Preferred.

** Based upon the average rank shown in the final column of this table. The securities are listed from highest to lowest preference.

*** The average rank is calculated using the technique described in the note to Table 2.

Comparison of Risk and Choice of Marketable Security

It is interesting to compare the findings given in Tables 3, 4, and 5. In Table 3 the respondents indicated that the most important characteristic in the marketable security selection process is risk. In Table 4, they ranked (on average) the risk of commercial paper eighth out of nine, and the risk of negotiable C.D.'s seventh out of nine. When asked which marketable securities they prefer to utilize, respondents indicated commercial paper and negotiable C.D.s to be their first two choices. It appears from these findings that respondents may not consider the risk differences between the various marketable securities to be significant. In light of such feelings they select marketable securities offering the highest yield for an acceptable level of risk which they believe is provided by all types of marketable securities. Given the respondents' stated concern for risk and their stated preference for commercial paper, we must conclude that they must place highest emphasis on yield in light of their apparent ability to live with the marginally differing risks of marketable securities. This conclusion tends to agree with that of Jacobs [9, p. 352], who concluded that "corporate investors more and more believe that the existing differential in yields between Treasury and non-Treasury Securities is not warranted by differences in risk and liquidity."

This apparent yield preference is also supported by responses to a question concerning "money market funds." When asked if their firm invested in money market funds, 135 out of 146 respondents (92 percent) answered negatively. Since these funds are safe, low-yielding instruments due to their diversification coupled with professional management and administrative costs, the responses are not surprising.

Marketable Security Management Procedures

In order to assess certain procedural as well as behavioral factors relating to the management of marketable securities, a few additional questions were asked. In response to a question concerning the existence of internal policy limitations relative to the amount or proportion of the firm's short-term investment placed in a given marketable security, 94 out of 146 respondents

(64 percent) indicated that their firm had no such internal limitations. This response agrees with the trend described in Jacobs' 1957 study [9, p. 352]. Although Jacobs found that many firms were restricted to government security investments, he concluded that such restrictions were being relaxed and more non-Treasury investments would be permitted in the future.

When asked whether any office space, salaries or computer programs could be entirely eliminated if the company eased its short-term investment activities, 130 out of 146 respondents (89 percent) indicated that such would not be the case. This information seems to suggest that the short-term investing activity was not a mainline activity, but rather appears to be treated as only one aspect of the overall cash management process. A similar conclusion was drawn by Jacobs [9, p. 348] who noted that "a large portion of corporate portfolios is managed as a part-time activity of a corporate officer with many additional important duties."

The Impact of Interest on Demand Deposits

A final question asked the respondents concerned the impact that the initiation of interest payments on demand deposits might have on their short-term investment of cash. Of the 149 responses to this question, 78 percent felt that such a change would have little or no effect, 20 percent felt it would cause a significant change, and approximately 2 percent believed it would result in a radical change. This result suggests that the firms recognize that as a result of the current acceptance of compensating balances as compensation for loans and services, they are currently being implicitly rewarded for their demand deposits. The payment of interest on these balances can therefore be viewed as an *explicit* payment that in effect will replace the implicit compensation currently being received for demand deposit balances. It appears that merely changing the form of payment for balances is recognized by most respondents (*i.e.*, 116 of 149, or 78 percent) not to represent a change in the basic economics of their banking relationship.

SUMMARY AND CONCLUSIONS

This paper has assessed the "state of the art" in the real world of corporate investing. Based upon 150 responses to a questionnaire sent to a sample of 300 of Fortune's 1000 largest firms, new insights relative to the cash forecasting and marketable security management practices of large corporations have been gained. It appears from the survey that most firms: use manual cash forecasting techniques; monitor their cash balances on a daily basis; attempt to coordinate forecasted cash needs with the maturity structure of marketable securities; and prefer commercial paper, certificates of deposit, and repurchase agreements, respectively. The firms tend to hold marketable securities to maturity; the most frequent holding period is between one week and one month.

Although the respondents indicated risk to be the most important consideration in the selection process, a comparison of their risk rankings with their preference rankings indicated that of the traditionally cited marketable securities, they prefer those they deem most risky (*i.e.*, commercial paper, negotiable C.D.'s, *etc.*). Most respondents indicated that they had no internal limitations placed on their marketable security investment activities. When asked if the initiation of interest payments on demand deposits would impact their marketable security management activities, most individuals responded negatively.

In conclusion, it appears from the firms surveyed that most handled their marketable security activities in a fashion consistent with the basic principles presented in the academic literature. The area in which they appear to have greatest opportunity for improvement is in the use of sophisticated cash forecasting methods. Comparing the findings reported with those of Jacobs' 1957 study [9] of the same issue, it is quite clear that the trend in S-T investing is away from government securities due to a general feeling of risk indifference, as well as the relaxation of restrictions placed upon the firm's marketable security investment activity. With the continuing development of more sophisticated cash forecasting methods, the initiation of new banking services, the development of new short-term investment vehicles, and changes in our system of payment from the use of checks to real-time transfer systems, it is likely that the next 20 years will result in even more significant changes in the marketable security management activities of large firms.

REFERENCES

1. Stephen H. Archer, "A Model for the Determination of Firm Cash Balances," *Journal of Financial and Quantitative Analysis*, March 1966, pp. 1-11.

2. William J. Baumol, "The Transactions Demand for Cash: An Inventory Theoretic Approach," *Quarterly Journal of Economics* 65 (November 1952), 545-556.

3. Tim Campbell, and Leland Brendsel, "The Impact of Compensating Balance Requirements on the Cash Balances of Manufacturing Corporations: An Empirical Study," *Journal of Finance*, 32 (March 1977), 31-40.

4. M.F. Collins, Title not known, Unpublished M.B.A. Research paper, University of Washington, 1970.

5. Hans G. Dallenbach, "Are Cash Management Optimization Models Worthwhile?" *Journal of Financial and Quantitative Analysis*, 9 (September 1974), 601-626.

6. "The Fortune Directory of the 500 Largest U.S. Industrial Corporations," *Fortune* (May 1977), pp. 366-385.

7. Lawrence J. Gitman, Edward A. Moses, and I. Thomas White, "An Assessment of Corporate Cash Management Practices," *Financial Management*, 8 (Spring 1979), 32-41.

8. Lawrence J. Gitman, *Principles of Managerial Finance*, 2nd ed., (New York: Harper and Row, 1979).

9. Donald P. Jacobs, "The Marketable Security Portfolios of Non-financial Corporations: Investment Practices and Trends," *Journal of Finance*, 15 (September 1960), 341-352.

10. John Maynard Keynes, *The General Theory of Employment, Interest and Money*, (New York: Harcourt, Brace and Jovanovich, 1936).

11. Merton H. Miller and Daniel Orr, "A Model of the Demand for Money by Firms," *Quarterly Journal of Economics*, 80 (August 1966), 413-435.

12. J. William Petty and Oswald D. Bowlin, "The Financial Manager and Quantitative Decision Models," *Financial Management*, 5 (Winter 1976), 32-41.

13. Ward L. Reed, Jr., "Profits from Better Cash Management," *Financial Executive*, 40 (May 1972), 40-56.

14. "The Second 500 Largest Industrial Corporations," *Fortune*, June 1977, pp. 206-225.

15. James Tobin, "The Interest Elasticity of the Transactions Demand for Cash," *Review of Economics and Statistics*, 37 (August 1956), 241-247.

16. James C. Van Horne, *Fundamentals of Financial Management*, 4th ed. (Englewood Cliffs: Prentice-Hall, 1977).

17. Martin Weitzman, "A Model of the Demand for Money by Firms: Comment," *Quarterly Journal of Economics*, 82 (March 1968), 161-164.

18. J. Fred Weston and Eugene F. Brigham, *Essentials of Managerial Finance*, 5th ed., (Hinsdale, Ill: The Dryden Press, 1979).

Managing Interest Expense with Futures Contracts

Robert E. Walgren

Would it be unusual if a corporate funding manager's job performance was judged by an ability to control interest expenses? It certainly would be, yet results-oriented performance reviews are the province of just about every other department in a firm except financial management. This accountability can be applied in some financial areas as well.

The traditional view of managing business costs has been to consider financing requirements independently from other expenditures. Such a tradition was a product of very low interest rates and minimum leverage. The concept of "borrowing money to be in business" did not assume borrowing costs to be an integral part of business costs, and because borrowing was only a temporary condition, it was separated from business costs.

Traditionally, managing costs has included only expenses for raw materials, labor, production, and distribution. The method that managers use to control these expenses includes regular and careful performance reviews of people who have been granted the authority and responsibility for keeping operations running smoothly and for continually improving productivity. The simple test is actual versus planned expenses for the division. However, the manager can further break down expense categories and line personnel performance. This could yield a measurement such as cost per unit, a basic test of productivity.

Lower-level managers involved in this process are usually expected to make decisions on such routine issues as making up work schedules, ordering materials, and controlling quality. Middle-level managers supervise the lower managers and deal with nonroutine issues which may affect not only their own but other related divisions as well. In turn, senior managers work with middle managers to deal with company-wide concerns including shareholder relations and overall policy issues.

In most financial management structures, the chief financial officer (CFO) establishes financial policy and deals with broad, company-wide financial issues. He is responsible for tactical decisions, short- and long-term funding, and controllership and accounting as well as administrative duties, such as personnel benefits and pension funds. The treasurer usually is responsible for actual funding strategy decisions, such as timing of long-term placements, and for foreign exchange activities. The assistant treasurer, in charge of short-term funding, interacts with the controller for budget processes and manages short-term borrowing activities by issuing commercial paper, securing bank funding, and maintaining and developing good relationships with strong banks.

The funding activities of the assistant treasurer involve working with cash budgets and understanding potential borrowing needs. When these needs arise, the response is to borrow funds from prearranged lines of credit. When needs diminish, lines are paid back to minimize interest expense. In this respect, the assistant treasurer merely reacts to production requirements, and cannot be judged on how many days are outstanding or how much was drawn down. Under this structure, financial management is not being judged on how

Source: Reprinted with permission of the publisher and author from the December 1982 issue of *Financial Executive,* published by Financial Executives Institute, Morristown, N.J.

much interest is paid, although this cost has risen tremendously in recent years. Management of short-term interest cost is delegated by the CFO as a tactical decision to the treasurer, and by the treasurer as a strategic decision to the assistant.

The assistant treasurer is measured by the use of the cheapest funding source available. Following this principle, he should borrow commercial paper and bankers' acceptances before borrowing at prime rate. In an environment in which interest costs may fluctuate by several hundred basis points over a few months, this kind of relative measurement can be grossly inadequate. First, it has no relationship to expense budget projections, and, second, while it may show that overall interest expense averaged below the prime rate, it can mask the fact that interest cost is very high.

The reason interest cost has become so significant lies not only in the rate itself but also in the volume of credit. Equity market limitations in the last decade have prompted corporate growth to be funded in the debt market. Thus, debt to worth ratios ballooned well above old benchmarks. Furthermore, high interest rates and weakness in long-term markets forced borrowers to stay short and float with the market.

A strong need has arisen for the corporate treasury to be responsible for developing new ways to manage costs so that interest expense can be budgeted realistically, and the performance of the assistant treasurer can be measured in concrete rather than relative terms. These objectives should be established as corporate policy, and responsibilities must be delegated before any progress can be expected. It also is important that authority flows with responsibility once strategies have been established.

A financial futures contracts hedging program is one way of managing interest rate costs. Hedging certainly is not a traditional responsibility of assistant treasurers, although it does involve management of short-term interest rate risk. Furthermore, hedging can be a reliable and effective way of locking in interest rates for a year or more, and it can be treated as an accounting effect on interest expense.

Hedging allows budgeting interest expenses as an absolute cost rather than as a general forecast, which could be totally unrealistic. It also provides a managed program of locking in some or all of a company's floating rate debt, which can be adjusted according to interest rate expectations.

In establishing a hedge, a company simply is recognizing an existing interest rate risk, such as a prime rate borrowing or commercial paper issuance, and taking on an opposing risk. This is a risk that will be beneficial to the borrower if interest rates fall. Thus, the interest rate risk is neutralized. If rates rise, a company could pay more interest expense, while it accrued a positive interest position in futures contracts. Conversely, if rates fall, a company could pay less in interest expense, and, as long as a futures position is in place, it would accrue a negative interest position.

For a borrower, one method of this hedging program is selling 90-day U.S. Treasury Bills in $1 million contracts, which would settle on specific dates several months ahead. For example, one contract could be sold for 12.50 percent, or a price of $87.50 as the dealers trade it. If rates rise on U.S. Treasury Bills to 13.00 percent and the price falls to $87.00, a contract could be bought to close out a position and take a gain of .50 basis points. If a similar rate rise were to occur in the company's $1 million borrowing position, the increase interest expense is offset by the .50 basis points futures gain. In this instance, the gain is on a 90-day instrument of $1 million, and each .01 basis point is worth $25.00. Thus, the borrowing for 90 days is hedged with one contract, and a borrowing for 180 days is hedged with two contracts.

The full hedge program would be effective with any exposure of short-term credits greater than $10 million, either in commercial paper, London Interbank Offered Rate borrowings, bankers acceptance, or prime rate loans. Such a financial risk could be hedged for a year, and an average locked-in rate could be predicted for the overall period within a narrow range. This would involve selling the total number of 90-day contracts required at the beginning of the year and gradually buying back a pro-ratio share of contracts at regular intervals. The important benefit of this program is budgeting ability. If the purchase schedule is managed properly, the forecasted rate should be realized, because rate movements on one side of the hedge are offset by opposing positions.

A hedging program also offers an opportunity to unlock the forecasted rate. All that is required is for the remaining purchase program to be accomplished immediately. Any further movement in rates from that time would be an unhedged financial exposure.

CONCLUSION

Interest rate hedging, new to financial managers, is slowly being accepted as a solution to volatile interest rates. It is not an easy concept to grasp at first, especially for anyone who has never hedged commodities, raw materials, or foreign exchange, where the principles are easily transposed.

Hedging also gives financial managers the tools to meet budgeted costs, just as other division managers are expected to do. This allows financial managers to be measured on planned versus actual performance in the implementation of short-term funding programs.

Bibliography

Bibliography

Brigham, Eugene F. *Financial Management: Theory and Practice.* 3rd ed. Hinsdale, Ill: The Dryden Press, 1982.

Cook, Timothy Q., ed. *Instruments of the Money Market.* 4th ed. Federal Reserve Bank of Richmond, 1977.

Hornonoff, R., and Mullins, P.W., Jr. *Cash Management.* Lexington, Mass.: Lexington Books, 1975.

Lordan, James F. *The Banking Side of Corporate Cash Management.* New Brunswick, N.J.: Rutgers University Press, 1971.

Mehta, D.R. *Working Capital Management.* Englewood Cliffs, N.J.: Prentice Hall, 1974.

Milling, B.E. *Cash Flow Problem Solver.* Radnor, Penn.: Chilton Book Company, 1981.

Orr, Daniel. *Cash Management and the Demand for Money.* New York: Praeger Publishers, 1971.

Smith, Keith V. *Guide to Working Capital Management.* New York: McGraw-Hill Book Company, 1979.

Van Horne, James C. *Financial Management Policy.* 5th ed. Englewood Cliffs, N.J.: Prentice Hall, 1980.